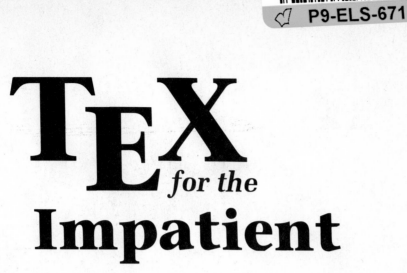

TeX *for the*
Impatient

TeX *for the* Impatient

Paul W. Abrahams

with

Karl Berry

Kathryn A. Hargreaves

Illustrated by Kathryn A. Hargreaves

 ADDISON-WESLEY PUBLISHING COMPANY

Reading, Massachusetts ■ Menlo Park, California ■ New York
Don Mills, Ontario ■ Wokingham, England ■ Amsterdam ■ Bonn
Sydney ■ Singapore ■ Tokyo ■ Madrid ■ San Juan

'TEX' is a trademark of the American Mathematical Society.
'METAFONT' is a trademark of Addison-Wesley Publishing Company.

The character of the impatient rabbit was inspired by John Tenniel's illustrations for *Alice's Adventures in Wonderland* and *Through the Looking Glass*, by Lewis Carroll. The illustration for the chapter "Using TEX" is based partly on an illustration in *Alice*, and partly on a Tenniel illustration in *The Tenniel Illustrations to the "Alice" books*, by Michael Hancher. Finally, the one for the chapter "Using this book" is based on a photograph in an article by W. Sheldon Bivin and Edward H. Timmons, in *The Biology of the Laboratory Rabbit*, S.H. Weisbroth, R.E. Flatt, and A.C. Kraus, editors, Academic Press, 1974, with the publisher's and authors' permissions.

Library of Congress Cataloging-in-Publication Data

```
Abrahams, Paul W.
     TeX for the impatient / Paul W. Abrahams,
  Kathryn A. Hargreaves, Karl Berry.
          p.    cm.
     Includes bibliographical references.
     ISBN 0-201-51375-7
     1. TeX (computer system). 2. Computerized typesetting.
3. Mathematics printing. I. Hargreaves, Kathryn A.
II. Berry, Karl. III. Title.
Z253.4.T47A27   1990
686.2'2544--dc20                                90-35533
                                                    CIP
```

ABCDEFGHIJ-HA-943210

For Jodi.
—P.W.A.

In memory of my father,
who had faith in me.
—K.A.H.

For Dan.
—K.B.

Preface

Donald Knuth's TeX, a computerized typesetting system, provides nearly everything needed for high-quality typesetting of mathematical notations as well as of ordinary text. It is particularly notable for its flexibility, its superb hyphenation, and its ability to choose aesthetically satisfying line breaks. Because of its extraordinary capabilities, TeX has become the leading typesetting system for mathematics, science, and engineering and has been adopted as a standard by the American Mathematical Society. A companion program, METAFONT, can construct arbitrary letterforms including, in particular, any symbols that might be needed in mathematics. Both TeX and METAFONT are widely available within the scientific and engineering community and have been implemented on a variety of computers. TeX isn't perfect—it lacks integrated support for graphics, and some effects such as revision bars are very difficult to produce—but these drawbacks are far outweighed by its advantages.

TeX for the Impatient is intended to serve scientists, mathematicians, and technical typists for whom TeX is a useful tool rather than a primary interest, as well as computer people who have a strong interest in TeX for its own sake. We also intend it to serve both newcomers to TeX and those who are already familiar with TeX. We assume that our readers are comfortable working with computers and that they want to get the information they need as quickly as possible. Our aim is to provide that information clearly, concisely, and accessibly.

This book therefore provides a bright searchlight, a stout walking-stick, and detailed maps for exploring and using TeX. It will enable you to master TeX at a rapid pace through inquiry and experiment, but it will not lead you by the hand through the entire TeX system. Our approach is to provide you with a handbook for TeX that makes it easy for you to retrieve whatever information you need. We explain both the full repertoire of TeX commands and the concepts that underlie them. You won't have to waste your time plowing through material that you neither need nor want.

In the early sections we also provide you with enough orientation so that you can get started if you haven't used TeX before. We assume that you have access to a TEX implementation and that you know how to use a text editor, but we don't assume much else about your background. Because this book is organized for ready reference, you'll continue to find it useful as you become more familiar with TEX. If you prefer to start with a carefully guided tour, we recommend that you first read Knuth's *The TEXbook* (see page 18 for a citation), passing over the "dangerous bend" sections, and then return to this book for additional information and for reference as you start to use TEX. (The dangerous bend sections of *The TEXbook* cover advanced topics.)

The structure of TEX is really quite simple: a TEX input document consists of ordinary text interspersed with commands that give TEX further instructions on how to typeset your document. Things like math formulas contain many such commands, while expository text contains relatively few of them.

The time-consuming part of learning TEX is learning the commands and the concepts underlying their descriptions. Thus we've devoted most of the book to defining and explaining the commands and the concepts. We've also provided examples showing TEX typeset output and the corresponding input, hints on solving common problems, information about error messages, and so forth. We've supplied extensive cross-references by page number and a complete index.

We've arranged the descriptions of the commands so that you can look them up either by function or alphabetically. The functional arrangement is what you need when you know what you want to do but you don't know what command might do it for you. The alphabetical arrangement is what you need when you know the name of a command but you don't know exactly what it does.

We must caution you that we haven't tried to provide a complete definition of TEX. For that you'll need *The TEXbook*, which is the original source of information on TEX. *The TEXbook* also contains a lot of information about the fine points of using TEX, particularly on the subject of composing math formulas. We recommend it highly.

In 1989 Knuth made a major revision to TEX in order to adapt it to 8-bit character sets, needed to support typesetting for languages other than English. The description of TEX in this book incorporates that revision (see p. 18).

You may be using a specialized form of TEX such as LATEX or $\mathcal{A}\mathcal{M}\mathcal{S}$-TEX (see p. 18). Although these specialized forms are self-contained, you may still want to use some of the facilities of TEX itself now and then in order to gain the finer control that only TEX can provide. This book can help you to learn what you need to know about those facilities without having to learn about a lot of other things that you aren't interested in.

Two of us (K.A.H. and K.B.) were generously supported by the University of Massachusetts at Boston during the preparation of this book. In particular, Rick Martin kept the machines running, and Robert A. Morris and Betty O'Neil made the machines available. Paul English of Interleaf helped us produce proofs for a cover design.

We wish to thank the reviewers of our book: Richard Furuta of the University of Maryland, John Gourlay of Arbortext, Inc., Jill Carter Knuth, and Richard Rubinstein of the Digital Equipment Corporation. We took to heart their perceptive and unsparing criticisms of the original manuscript, and the book has benefitted greatly from their insights.

We are particularly grateful to our editor, Peter Gordon of Addison-Wesley. This book was really his idea, and throughout its development he has been a source of encouragement and valuable advice. We thank his assistant at Addison-Wesley, Helen Goldstein, for her help in so many ways, and Loren Stevens of Addison-Wesley for her skill and energy in shepherding this book through the production process. Were it not for our copyeditor, Janice Byer, a number of small but irritating errors would have remained in this book. We appreciate her sensitivity and taste in correcting what needed to be corrected while leaving what did not need to be corrected alone. Finally, we wish to thank Jim Byrnes of Prometheus Inc. for making this collaboration possible by introducing us to each other.

Deerfield, Massachusetts   P. W. A.
Manomet, Massachusetts   K. A. H., K. B.

Brief contents

Contents

Read this first

If you're new to TeX:

- Read Sections 1–2 first.
- Look at the examples in Section 3 for things that resemble what you want to do. Look up any related commands in "Capsule summary of commands", Section 13. Use the page references there to find the more complete descriptions of those commands and others that are similar.
- Look up unfamiliar words in "Concepts", Section 4, using the list on the back cover of the book to find the explanation quickly.
- Experiment and explore.

If you're already familiar with TeX, or if you're editing or otherwise modifying a TeX document that someone else has created:

- For a quick reminder of what a command does, look in Section 13, "Capsule summary of commands". It's alphabetized and has page references for more complete descriptions of the commands.
- Use the functional groupings of command descriptions to find those related to a particular command that you already know, or to find a command that serves a particular purpose.
- Use Section 4, "Concepts", to get an explanation of any concept that you don't understand, or need to understand more precisely, or have forgotten. Use the list on the inside back cover of the book to find a concept quickly.

1 Using this book

This book is a do-it-yourself guide and handbook for TeX. Here in this section we tell you how to use the book to maximum advantage.

We recommend that you first either read or skim in sequence Sections 1 through 3, which tell you what you need to know in order to get started using TeX. If you've already had experience using TeX, it will still be helpful to know what kinds of information are in these sections of the book. Sections 4–10, which occupy most of the rest of the book, are designed to be accessed randomly. Nevertheless, if you're the kind of person who likes to read reference manuals, you'll find that it *is* possible to proceed sequentially if you're willing to take a lot of detours at first.

In Section 2, "Using TeX", we explain how to produce a TeX document from a TeX input file. We also describe the conventions for preparing that input file, explain a little about how TeX works, and tell you about additional resources that are available. Reading this section will help you understand the examples in the next section.

Section 3, "Examples", contains a sequence of examples that illustrate the use of TeX. Each example consists of a page of output together with the input that we used to create it. These examples will orient you and help you locate the more detailed material that you'll need as you go. By seeing which commands are used in the input, you'll know where to look for more detailed information on how to achieve the effects shown in the output. The examples can also serve as models for simple documents, although we must caution you that because we've tried to pack a variety of TeX commands into a small number of pages, the examples are not necessarily illustrations of good or complete document design.

As you read the explanation of a command, you may encounter some unfamiliar technical terms. In Section 4, "Concepts", we define and explain these terms. We also discuss other topics that aren't covered elsewhere in the book. The inside back cover of the book contains a list of all the concepts and the pages where they are described. We suggest that you make a copy of this list and keep it nearby so that you'll be able to identify and look up an unfamiliar concept immediately.

TeX's commands are its primary vocabulary, and the largest part of this book is devoted to explaining them. In Sections 5 through 9 we describe the commands. You'll find general information about the command descriptions on page 3. The command descriptions are arranged functionally, rather like a thesaurus, so if you know what you want to do but you don't know which command does it for you, you can use the table of contents to guide you to the right group of commands. Commands that we think are both particularly useful and easy to understand are indicated with a pointing hand (☞).

Section 13, "Capsule summary of commands", is a specialized index that complements the more complete descriptions in Sections 5–9. It lists TeX's commands alphabetically, with a brief explanation of each command and a reference to the page where it is described more completely. The capsule summary will help you when you just want a quick reminder of what a command does.

TeX is a complex program that occasionally works its will in mysterious ways. In Section 10, "Tips and techniques", we provide advice on solving a variety of specific problems that you may encounter from time to time. And if you're stumped by TeX's error messages, you'll find succor in Section 11, "Making sense of error messages".

The gray tabs on the side of the book will help you locate parts of the book quickly. They divide the book into the following major parts:

(1) general explanations and examples

(2) concepts

(3) descriptions of commands (five shorter tabs)

(4) advice, error messages, and the `eplain.tex` macros

(5) capsule summary of commands

(6) index

Syntactic conventions

In any book about preparing input for a computer, it's necessary to indicate clearly the literal characters that should be typed and to distinguish those characters from the explanatory text. We use the Computer Modern typewriter font for `literal input like this`, and also for the names of TeX commands. When there's any possibility of confusion, we enclose TeX input in single quotation marks, '`like this`'. However, we occasionally use parentheses when we're indicating single characters such as ('`'`) (you can see why).

For the sake of your eyes we usually just put spaces where you should put spaces. In some places where we need to emphasize the space, however, we use a '␣' character to indicate it. Naturally enough, this character is called a *visible space*.

Descriptions of the commands

Sections 5–9 contain a description of what nearly every TeX command does. Both the primitive commands and those of plain TeX are covered. The primitive commands are those built into the TeX computer program, while the plain TeX commands are defined in a standard file of auxiliary definitions (see p. 88). The only commands we've omitted are those that are used purely locally in the definition of plain TeX (Appendix B of *The TeXbook*). The commands are organized as follows:

- "Commands for composing paragraphs", Section 5, deal with characters, words, lines, and entire paragraphs.
- "Commands for composing pages", Section 6, deal with pages, their components, and the output routine.
- "Commands for horizontal and vertical modes", Section 7, have corresponding or identical forms for both horizontal modes (paragraphs and hboxes) and vertical modes (pages and vboxes). These commands provide boxes, spaces, rules, leaders, and alignments.
- "Commands for composing math formulas", Section 8, provide capabilities for constructing math formulas.
- "Commands for general operations", Section 9, provide TeX's programming features and everything else that doesn't fit into any of the other sections.

You should think of these categories as being suggestive rather than rigorous, because the commands don't really fit neatly into these (or any other) categories.

Within each section, the descriptions of the commands are organized by function. When several commands are closely related, they are described as a group; otherwise, each command has its own explanation. The description of each command includes one or more examples and the output produced by each example when examples are appropriate (for some commands they aren't). When you are looking at a subsection containing functionally related commands, be sure to check the end of a subsection for a "see also" item that refers you to related commands that are described elsewhere.

Some commands are closely related to certain concepts. For instance, the `\halign` and `\valign` commands are related to "alignment", the `\def` command is related to "macro", and the `\hbox` and `\vbox` commands are related to "box". In these cases we've usually given a bare-bones description of the commands themselves and explained the underlying ideas in the concept.

The examples associated with the commands have been typeset with `\parindent`, the paragraph indentation, set to zero so that paragraphs are normally unindented. This convention makes the examples easier to read. In those examples where the paragraph indentation is essential, we've set it explicitly to a nonzero value.

The pointing hand in front of a command or a group of commands indicates that we judged this command or group of commands to be particularly useful and easy to understand.

Many commands expect arguments of one kind or another (p. 11). The arguments of a command give TEX additional information that it needs in order to carry out the command. Each argument is indicated by an italicized term in angle brackets that indicates what kind of argument it is:

⟨*argument*⟩   a single token or some text enclosed in braces
⟨*charcode*⟩   an integer between 0 and 255
⟨*dimen*⟩   a dimension, i.e., a length
⟨*glue*⟩   glue (with optional stretch and shrink)
⟨*number*⟩   an optionally signed integer (whole number)
⟨*register*⟩   a register number between 0 and 255

All of these terms are explained in more detail in Section 4. In addition, we sometimes use terms such as ⟨*token list*⟩ that are either self-explanatory or explained in the description of the command. Some commands have special formats that require either braces or particular words. These are set in the same bold font that we use for the command headings.

Some commands are parameters (p. 12) or table entries. This is indicated in the command's listing. You can either use a parameter as an argument or assign a value to it. The same holds for table entries. We use the term "parameter" to refer to entities such as `\pageno` that are actually registers but behave just like parameters.

2 Using TEX

Turning input into ink

■ Programs and files you need

In order to produce a TEX document, you'll need to run the TEX program and several related programs as well. You'll also need supporting files for TEX and possibly for these other programs. In this book we can tell you about TEX, but we can't tell you about the other programs and the supporting files except in very general terms because they depend on your local TEX environment. The people who provide you with TEX should be able to supply you with what we call *local information*. The local information tells you how to start up TEX, how to use the related programs, and how to gain access to the supporting files.

Input to TEX consists of a file of ordinary text that you can prepare with a text editor. A TEX input file, unlike an input file for a typical word processor, doesn't ordinarily contain any invisible control characters. Everything that TEX sees is visible to you too if you look at a listing of the file.

Your input file may turn out to be little more than a skeleton that calls for other input files. TEX users often organize large documents such as books this way. You can use the \input command (p. 247) to embed one input file within another. In particular, you can use \input to incorporate files containing *macro definitions*—auxiliary definitions that enhance TEX's capabilities. If any macro files are available at your TEX installation, the local information about TEX should tell you how to get

at the macro files and what they can do for you. The standard form of
TEX, the one described in this book, incorporates a collection of macros
and other definitions known as plain TEX (p. 88).

When TEX processes your document, it produces a file called the `.dvi`
file. The abbreviation "`dvi`" stands for "device independent". The abbreviation was chosen because the information in the `.dvi` file is independent
of the device that you use to print or display your document.

To print your document or view it with a *previewer*, you need to process
the `.dvi` file with a *device driver* program. (A previewer is a program that
enables you to see on a screen some approximation of what the typeset
output will look like.) Different output devices usually require different
device drivers. After running the device driver, you may also need to
transfer the output of the device driver to the printer or other output
device. The local information about TEX should tell you how to get the
correct device driver and use it.

Since TEX has no built-in knowledge of particular fonts, it uses *font files*
to obtain information about the fonts used in your document. The font
files should also be part of your local TEX environment. Each font normally requires two files: one containing the dimensions of the characters
in the font (the *metrics file*) and one containing the shapes of the characters (the *shape file*). Magnified versions of a font share the metrics file
but have different shape files. Metrics files are sometimes referred to as
`.tfm` files, and the different varieties of shape files are sometimes referred
to as `.pk` files, `.pxl` files, and `.gf` files. These names correspond to the
names of the files that TEX and its companion programs use. For example, `cmr10.tfm` is the metrics file for the `cmr10` font (10-point Computer
Modern Roman).

TEX itself uses only the metrics file, since it doesn't care what the
characters look like but only how much space they occupy. The device
driver ordinarily uses the shape file, since it's responsible for creating the
printed image of each typeset character. Some device drivers need to
use the metrics file as well. Some device drivers can utilize fonts that are
resident in a printer and don't need shape files for those fonts.

■ *Running TEX*

You can run TEX on an input file `screed.tex` by typing something like '`run tex`' or just '`tex`' (check your local information). TEX will respond with something like:

```
This is TeX, Version 3.0 (preloaded format=plain 90.4.23)
**
```

The "preloaded format" here refers to a predigested form of the plain TEX macros that come with TEX. You can now type '`screed`' to get TEX to process your file. When it's done, you'll see something like:

```
(screed.tex [1] [2] [3] )
Output written on screed.dvi (3 pages, 400 bytes).
Transcript written on screed.log.
```

displayed on your terminal, or printed in the record of your run if you're not working at a terminal. Most of this output is self-explanatory. The numbers in brackets are page numbers that TEX displays when it ships out each page of your document to the `.dvi` file. TEX will usually assume an extension '`.tex`' to an input file name if the input file name you gave doesn't have an extension. For some forms of TEX you may be able to invoke TEX directly for an input file by typing:

```
tex screed
```

or something like this.

Instead of providing your TEX input from a file, you can type it directly at your terminal. To do so, type '`\relax`' instead of '`screed`' at the '`**`' prompt. TEX will now prompt you with a '`*`' for each line of input and interpret each line of input as it sees it. To terminate the input, type a command such as '`\bye`' that tells TEX you're done. Direct input is sometimes a handy way of experimenting with TEX.

When your input file contains other embedded input files, the displayed information indicates when TEX begins and ends processing each embedded file. TEX displays a left parenthesis and the file name when it starts working on a file and displays the corresponding right parenthesis when it's done with the file. If you get any error messages in the displayed output, you can match them with a file by looking for the most recent unclosed left parenthesis.

For a more complete explanation of how to run TEX, see Chapter 6 of *The TEXbook* and your local information.

Preparing an input file

In this section we explain some of the conventions that you must follow in preparing input for TEX. Some of the information given here also appears in the examples in Section 3 of this book.

■ Commands and control sequences

Input to TEX consists of a sequence of commands that tell TEX how to typeset your document. Most characters act as commands of a particularly simple kind: "typeset me". The letter 'a', for instance, is a command to typeset an 'a'. But there's another kind of command—a *control sequence*—that gives TEX a more elaborate instruction. A control sequence ordinarily starts with a backslash (\), though you can change that convention if you need to. For instance, the input:

```
She plunged a dagger (\dag) into the villain's heart.
```

contains the control sequence \dag; it produces the typeset output:

She plunged a dagger (†) into the villain's heart.

Everything in this example except for the \dag and the spaces acts like a "typeset me" command. We'll explain more about spaces on page 12.

There are two kinds of control sequences: *control words* and *control symbols*:

- A control word consists of a backslash followed by one or more letters, e.g., '\dag'. The first character that isn't a letter marks the end of the control word.
- A control symbol consists of a backslash followed by a single character that isn't a letter, e.g., '\$'. The character can be a space or even the end of a line (which is a perfectly legitimate character).

A control word (but not a control symbol) absorbs any spaces or ends of line that follow it. If you don't want to lose a space after a control word, follow the control sequence with a control space (\␣) or with '{}'. Thus either:

```
The wonders of \TeX\␣shall never cease!
```

or:

```
The wonders of \TeX{} shall never cease!
```

produces:

The wonders of TEX shall never cease!

rather than:

The wonders of TEXshall never cease!

which is what you'd get if you left out the '\␣' or the '{}'.

Don't run a control word together with the text that follows it—TEX won't know where the control word ends. For instance, the \c control sequence places a cedilla accent on the character that follows it. The French word *garçon* must be typed as 'gar\c␣con', not 'gar\ccon'; if you write the latter, TEX will complain about an undefined control sequence \ccon.

A control symbol, on the other hand, doesn't absorb anything that follows it. Thus you must type '\$13.56' as '\\$13.56', not '\\$␣13.56'; the latter form would produce '\$ 13.56'. However, those accenting commands that are named by control symbols are defined in such a way that they produce the effect of absorbing a following space. Thus, for example, you can type the French word *déshabiller* either as 'd\'eshabiller' or as 'd\'␣eshabiller'.

Every control sequence is also a command, but not the other way around. For instance, the letter 'N' is a command, but it isn't a control sequence. In this book we ordinarily use "command" rather than "control sequence" when either term would do. We use "control sequence" when we want to emphasize aspects of TEX syntax that don't apply to commands in general.

■ *Arguments*

Some commands need to be followed by one or more *arguments* that help to determine what the command does. For instance, the \vskip command, which tells TEX to skip down (or up) the page, expects an argument specifying how much space to skip. To skip down two inches, you would type '\vskip 2in', where 2in is the argument of \vskip.

Different commands expect different kinds of arguments. Many commands expect dimensions, such as the 2in in the example above. Some commands, particularly those defined by macros, expect arguments that are either a single character or some text enclosed in braces. Yet others require that their arguments be enclosed in braces, i.e., they don't accept single-character arguments. The description of each command in this book tells you what kinds of arguments, if any, the command expects. In some cases, required braces define a group (see p. 15).

■ *Parameters*

Some commands are parameters (p. 87). You can use a parameter in either of two ways:

(1) You can use the value of a parameter as an argument to another command. For example, the command `\vskip\parskip` causes a vertical skip by the value of the `\parskip` (paragraph skip) glue parameter.

(2) You can change the value of the parameter by assigning something to it. For example, the assignment `\hbadness=200` causes the value of the `\hbadness` number parameter to be 200.

We also use the term "parameter" to refer to entities such as `\pageno` that are actually registers but behave just like parameters.

Some commands are names of tables. These commands are used like parameters, except that they require an additional argument that specifies a particular entry in the table. For example, `\catcode` names a table of category codes (p. 53). Thus the command `\catcode'~=13` sets the category code of the '~' character to 13.

■ *Spaces*

You can freely use extra spaces in your input. Under nearly all circumstances TEX treats several spaces in a row as being equivalent to a single space. For instance, it doesn't matter whether you put one space or two spaces after a period in your input. Whichever you do, TEX performs its end-of-sentence maneuvers and leaves the appropriate (in most cases) amount of space after the period. TEX also treats the end of an input line as equivalent to a space. Thus you can end your input lines wherever it's convenient—TEX makes input lines into paragraphs in the same way no matter where the line breaks are in your input.

A blank line in your input marks the end of a paragraph. Several blank lines are equivalent to a single one.

TEX ignores input spaces within math formulas (see below). Thus you can include or omit spaces anywhere within a math formula—TEX doesn't care. Even within a math formula, however, you must not run a control word together with a following letter.

If you are defining your own macros, you need to be particularly careful about where you put and ends of line in their definitions. It's all too easy to define a macro that produces an unwanted space in addition to whatever else it's supposed to produce. We discuss this problem elsewhere since it's somewhat technical; see page 270.

A space or its equivalent between two words in your input doesn't simply turn into a space character in your output. A few of these input spaces turn into ends of lines in the output, since input lines generally don't correspond to output lines. The others turn into spaces of variable width called "glue" (p. 66), which has a natural size (the size it "wants to be") but can stretch or shrink. When TEX is typesetting a paragraph that is supposed to have an even right margin (the usual case), it adjusts the widths of the glue in each line to get the lines to end at the margin. (The last line of a paragraph is an exception, since it isn't ordinarily required to end at the right margin.)

You can prevent an input space from turning into an end of line by using a tie (~). For example, you wouldn't want TEX to put a line break between the 'Fig.' and '8' of 'Fig. 8'. By typing 'Fig.~8' you can prevent such a line break.

■ Comments

You can include comments in your TEX input. When TEX sees a comment it just passes over it, so what's in a comment doesn't affect your typeset document in any way. Comments are useful for providing extra information about what's in your input file. For example:

```
% ========= Start of Section 'Hedgehog' =========
```

A comment starts with a percent sign (%) and extends to the end of the input line. TEX ignores not just the comment but the end of the line as well, so comments have another very important use: connecting two lines so that the end of line between them is invisible to TEX and doesn't generate an output space or an end of line. For instance, if you type:

```
A fool with a spread%
sheet is still a fool.
```

you'll get:

A fool with a spreadsheet is still a fool.

■ Punctuation

TEX normally adds some extra space after what it thinks is a punctuation mark at the end of a sentence, namely, '.', '?', or '!' followed by an input space. TEX doesn't add the extra space if the punctuation mark follows a capital letter, though, because it assumes the capital letter to be an initial in someone's name. You can force the extra space where it wouldn't otherwise occur by typing something like:

```
A computer from IBM\null?
```

The `\null` doesn't produce any output, but it does prevent TEX from associating the capital 'M' with the question mark. On the other hand, you can cancel the extra space where it doesn't belong by typing a control space after the punctuation mark, e.g.:

```
Proc.\␣Royal Acad.\␣of Twits
```

so that you'll get:

Proc. Royal Acad. of Twits

rather than:

Proc. Royal Acad. of Twits

Some people prefer not to leave more space after punctuation at the end of a sentence. You can get this effect with the `\frenchspacing` command (p. 106). `\frenchspacing` is often recommended for bibliographies.

For single quotation marks, you should use the left and right single quotes (' and ') on your keyboard. For left and right double quotation marks, use two left single quotes or two right single quotes ('' or '') rather than the double quote (") on your keyboard. The keyboard double quote will in fact give you a right double quotation mark in many fonts, but the two right single quotes are the preferred TEX style. For example:

```
There is no 'q' in this sentence.
''Talk, child,'' said the Unicorn.
She said, ''He said 'Enough!'\thinspace''.
```

These three lines yield:

> There is no 'q' in this sentence.
> "Talk, child," said the Unicorn.
> She said, "He said 'Enough!'".

The `\thinspace` in the third input line prevents the single quotation mark from coming too close to the double quotation marks. Without it, you'd just see three equally spaced quotation marks in a row.

TEX has three kinds of dashes:

- Short ones (hyphens) like this (-). You get them by typing '-'.
- Medium ones (en-dashes) like this (–). You get them by typing '--'.
- Long ones (em-dashes) like this (—). You get them by typing '---'.

Typically you'd use hyphens to indicate compound words like "will-o'-the-wisp", en-dashes to indicate page ranges such as "pages 81–87", and em-dashes to indicate a break in continuity—like this.

■ *Special characters*

Certain characters have special meaning to TeX, so you shouldn't use them in ordinary text. They are:

```
$  #  &  %  _  ^  ~  {  }  \
```

In order to produce them in your typeset document, you need to use circumlocutions. For the first five, you should instead type:

```
\$  \#  \&  \%  \_
```

For the others, you need something more elaborate:

```
\^{␣}   \~{␣}   $\{$   $\}$   $\backslash$
```

■ *Groups*

A *group* consists of material enclosed in matching left and right braces ({ and }). By placing a command within a group, you can limit its effects to the material within the group. For instance, the \bf command tells TeX to set something in **boldface** type. If you were to put \bf into your input and do nothing else to counteract it, everything in your document following the \bf would be set in boldface. By enclosing \bf in a group, you limit its effect to the group. For example, if you type:

```
We have {\bf a few boldface words} in this sentence.
```

you'll get:

We have **a few boldface words** in this sentence.

You can also use a group to limit the effect of an assignment to one of TeX's parameters. These parameters contain values that affect how TeX typesets your document. For example, the value of the \parindent parameter specifies the indentation at the beginning of a paragraph. The assignment \parindent = 15pt sets the indentation to 15 printer's points. By placing this assignment at the beginning of a group containing a few paragraphs, you can change the indentation of just those paragraphs. If you don't enclose the assignment in a group, the changed indentation will apply to the rest of the document (or up to the next assignment to \parindent, if there's a later one).

Not all pairs of braces indicate a group. In particular, the braces associated with an argument for which the braces are *not* required don't indicate a group—they just serve to delimit the argument. Of those commands that do require braces for their arguments, some treat the braces as defining a group and the others interpret the argument in some special way that depends on the command.[1]

■ *Math formulas*

A math formula can appear in text (*text math*) or set off on a line by itself with extra vertical space around it (*display math*). You enclose a text formula in single dollar signs (**$**) and a displayed formula in double dollar signs (**$$**). For example:

```
If $a<b$, then the relation $$e^a < e^b$$ holds.
```

This input produces:

If $a < b$, then the relation

$$e^a < e^b$$

holds.

Section 8 describes the commands that are useful in math formulas.

How TEX works

In order to use TEX effectively, it helps to have some idea of how TEX goes about its activity of transmuting input into output. You can imagine TEX as a kind of organism with "eyes", "mouth", "gullet", "stomach", and "intestines". Each part of the organism transforms its input in some way and passes the transformed input to the next stage.

The eyes transform an input file into a sequence of characters. The mouth transforms the sequence of characters into a sequence of *tokens*, where each token is either a single character or a control sequence. The gullet expands the tokens into a sequence of *primitive commands*, which are also tokens. The stomach carries out the operations specified by the primitive commands, producing a sequence of pages. Finally, the intestines transform each page into the form required for the `.dvi` file and send it there. These actions are described in more detail in Section 4 under "anatomy of TEX" (p. 46).

---

[1] More precisely, for primitive commands either the braces define a group or they enclose tokens that aren't processed in TEX's stomach. For `\halign` and `\valign` the group has a trivial effect because everything within the braces either doesn't reach the stomach (because it's in the template) or is enclosed in a further inner group.

The real typesetting goes on in the stomach. The commands instruct
TeX to typeset such-and-such a character in such-and-such a font, to
insert an interword space, to end a paragraph, and so on. Starting with
individual typeset characters and other simple typographic elements, TeX
builds up a page as a nest of boxes within boxes within boxes (see "box",
p. 51). Each typeset character occupies a box, and so does an entire
page. A box can contain not just smaller boxes but also *glue* (p. 66)
and a few other things. The glue produces space between the smaller
boxes. An important property of glue is that it can stretch and shrink;
thus TeX can make a box larger or smaller by stretching or shrinking
the glue within it.

Roughly speaking, a line is a box containing a sequence of character
boxes, and a page is a box containing a sequence of line boxes. There's
glue between the words of a line and between the lines of a page. TeX
stretches or shrinks the glue on each line so as to make the right margin
of the page come out even and the glue on each page so as to make the
bottom margins of different pages be equal. Other kinds of typographical elements can also appear in a line or in a page, but we won't go
into them here.

As part of the process of assembling pages, TeX needs to break paragraphs into lines and lines into pages. The stomach first sees a paragraph
as one long line, in effect. It inserts *line breaks* in order to transform the
paragraph into a sequence of lines of the right length, performing a rather
elaborate analysis in order to choose the set of breaks that makes the
paragraph look best (see "line break", p. 74). The stomach carries out a
similar but simpler process in order to transform a sequence of lines into
a page. Essentially the stomach accumulates lines until no more lines can
fit on the page. It then chooses a single place to break the page, putting
the lines before the break on the current page and saving the lines after
the break for the next page (see "page break", p. 85).

When TeX is assembling an entity from a list of items (boxes, glue,
etc.), it is in one of six *modes* (p. 81). The kind of entity it is assembling
defines the mode that it is in. There are two ordinary modes: ordinary
horizontal mode for assembling paragraphs (before they are broken into
lines) and ordinary vertical mode for assembling pages. There are two
restricted modes: restricted horizontal mode for appending items horizontally to form a horizontal box and internal vertical mode for appending items vertically to form a vertical box (other than a page). Finally,
there are two math modes: text math mode for assembling math formulas
within a paragraph and display math mode for assembling math formulas
that are displayed on lines by themselves (see "Math formulas", p. 16).

New TEX versus old TEX

In 1989 Knuth made a major revision to TEX in order to adapt it to the character sets needed to support typesetting for foreign languages. The revision included a few minor extra features that could be added without disturbing anything else. This book describes "new TEX". If you're still using an older version of TEX (version 2.991 or earlier), you'll want to know what features of new TEX you can't use. The following features aren't available in the older versions:

- `\badness` (p. 170)
- `\emergencystretch` (p. 124)
- `\errorcontextlines` (p. 262)
- `\holdinginserts` (p. 149)
- `\language`, `\setlanguage`, and `\newlanguage` (pp. 128, 244)
- `\lefthyphenmin` and `\righthyphenmin` (p. 128)
- `\noboundary` (p. 101)
- `\topglue` (p. 156)
- The `^^`xy notation for hexadecimal digits (p. 55)

We recommend that you obtain new TEX if you can.

Resources

A number of resources are available to help you in using TEX. *The TEXbook* is the definitive source of information on TEX:

Knuth, Donald E., *The TEXbook*. Reading, Mass.: Addison-Wesley, 1984.

Be sure to get the seventeenth printing (January 1990) or later; the earlier printings don't cover the features of new TEX.

LATEX is a very popular collection of commands designed to simplify the use of TEX. It is described in:

Lamport, Leslie, *The LATEX Document Preparation System*. Reading, Mass.: Addison-Wesley, 1986.

AMS-TEX is the collection of commands adopted by the American Mathematical Society as a standard for submitting mathematical manuscripts electronically. It is described in:

Spivak, Michael D., *The Joy of TEX*. Providence, R.I.: American Mathematical Society, 1986.

You can join the TEX Users Group (TUG), which publishes a newsletter called *TUGBoat*. TUG is an excellent source not only for information about TEX but also for collections of macros, including $\mathcal{A}\mathcal{M}\mathcal{S}$-TEX. Its address is:

TEX Users Group
c/o American Mathematical Society
P.O. Box 9506
Providence, RI 02940
U.S.A.

Finally, you can obtain copies of the `eplain.tex` macros described in Section 12 as well as the macros used in typesetting this book. They are available through the Internet network by anonymous `ftp` from the following hosts:

```
labrea.stanford.edu [36.8.0.47]
ics.uci.edu [128.195.1.1]
june.cs.washington.edu [128.95.1.4]
```

The electronic version includes additional macros that format input for the BIBTEX computer program, written by Oren Patashnik at Stanford University, and print the output from that program. If you find bugs in the macros, or think of improvements, you can send electronic mail to Karl at `karl@cs.umb.edu`.

The macros are also available for US $10.00 on $5\,1/4''$ or $3\,1/2''$ PC-format diskettes from:

Paul Abrahams
214 River Road
Deerfield, MA 01342
Email: `Abrahams%Wayne-MTS@um.cc.umich.edu`

These addresses are correct as of June 1990; please be aware that they may change after that, particularly the electronic addresses.

3 | Examples

This section of the book contains a set of examples to help get you started and to show you how to do various things with TeX. Each example has TeX output on the left-hand page and the TeX input that led to that output on the right-hand page. You can use these examples both as forms to imitate and as a way of finding the TeX commands that you need in order to achieve a particular effect. However, these examples can illustrate only a few of the about 900 TeX commands.

Some of the examples are self-descriptive—that is, they discuss the very features of TeX that they are illustrating. These discussions are necessarily sketchy because there isn't room in the examples for all the information you'd need. The capsule summary of commands (Section 13) and the index will help you locate the complete explanation of every TeX feature shown in the examples.

Because we've designed the examples to illustrate many things at once, some examples contain a great variety of typographical effects. These examples generally are *not* good models of typographical practice. For instance, Example 8 has some of its equation numbers on the left and some on the right. You'd never want to do that in a real publication.

Each example except for the first one starts with a macro (see p. 75) named `\xmpheader`. We've used `\xmpheader` in order to conserve space in the input, since without it each example would have several lines of material you'd already seen. `\xmpheader` produces the title of an example and the extra space that goes with it. You can see in the first example what `\xmpheader` does, so you can imitate it if you wish. Except for `\xmpheader`, every command that we use in these examples is defined in plain TeX.

Example 1: *Entering simple text*

It's easy to prepare ordinary text for TeX since TeX usually doesn't care about how you break up your input into lines. It treats the end of a line of text like a space.† If you don't want a space there, put a percent sign (the comment character) at the end of the line. TeX ignores spaces at the start of a line, and treats more than one space as equivalent to a single space, even after a period. You indicate a new paragraph by skipping a line (or more than one line).

When TeX sees a period followed by a space (or the end of the line, which is equivalent), it ordinarily assumes you've ended a sentence and inserts a little extra space after the period. It treats question marks and exclamation points the same way.

But TeX's rules for handling periods sometimes need fine tuning. TeX assumes that a capital letter before a period doesn't end the sentence, so you have to do something a little different if, say, you're writing about DNA. It's a good idea to tie words together in references such as "see Fig. 8" and in names such as V. I. Lenin and in ... so that TeX will never split them in an awkward place between two lines. (The three dots indicate an ellipsis.)

You should put quotations in pairs of left and right single "quotes" so that you get the correct left and right double quotation marks. "For adjacent single and double quotation marks, insert a 'thinspace'". You can get en-dashes–like so, and em-dashes—like so.

---

† TeX treats a tab like a space too, as we point out in this *footnote*.

```
% TeX ignores anything on a line after a %
% The next two lines define fonts for the title
\font\xmplbx = cmbx10 scaled \magstephalf
\font\xmplbxti = cmbxti10 scaled \magstephalf
% Now here's the title.
\leftline{\xmplbx Example 1:\quad\xmplbxti Entering simple text}
\vglue .5\baselineskip % skip an extra half line
It's easy to prepare ordinary text for \TeX\ since
\TeX\ usually doesn't care about how you break up your input into
lines. It treats the end of a line of text like a space.%
\footnote \dag{\TeX\ treats a tab like a space too, as we point
out in this {\it footnote}.}  If you don't want a space there,
put a per%
cent sign (the comment character) at the end of the line.
   \TeX\ ignores spaces at the start of a line, and treats more
than         one       space as equivalent to a single space,
even after a period.      You indicate a new paragraph by
skipping a line (or more than one line).


When \TeX\ sees a period followed by a space (or the end of the
line, which is equivalent), it ordinarily assumes you've ended a
sentence and inserts a little extra space after the period.  It
treats question marks and exclamation points the same way.

   But \TeX's rules for handling periods sometimes need fine
tuning. \TeX\ assumes that a capital letter before a period
doesn't end the sentence, so you have to do something a little
different if, say, you're writing about DNA\null.
% The \null prevents TeX from perceiving the capital 'A'
% as being next to the period.
It's a good idea to tie words together in references such as
''see Fig.~8'' and in names such as V.~I\null. Lenin and in
$\ldots$ so that \TeX\ will never split them in an awkward place
between two lines.  (The three dots indicate an ellipsis.)

You should put quotations in pairs of left and right
single ''quotes'' so that you get the correct left and right
double quotation marks.  ''For adjacent single and double
quotation marks, insert a 'thinspace'\thinspace''. You can
get en-dashes--like so, and em-dashes---like so.

\bye % end the document
```

Example 2: *Indentation*

Now let's see how to control indentation. If an ordinary word processor can do it, so surely can TeX. Note that this paragraph isn't indented.

Usually you'll either want to indent paragraphs or to leave extra space between them. Since we haven't changed anything yet, this paragraph is indented.

Let's do these two paragraphs a different way, with no indentation and six printer's points of extra space between paragraphs.

So here's another paragraph that we're typesetting without indentation. If we didn't put space between these paragraphs, you would have a hard time knowing where one ends and the next begins.

It's also possible to indent both sides of entire paragraphs. The next three paragraphs illustrate this:

> "We've indented this paragraph on both sides by the paragraph indentation. This is often a good way to set long quotations.
>
> "You can do multiple paragraphs this way if you choose. This is the second paragraph that's singly indented."
>
> > You can even make paragraphs doubly narrow if that's what you need. This is an example of a doubly narrowed paragraph.

In this paragraph we're back to the normal margins, as you can see for yourself. We'll let it run on a little longer so that the margins are clearly visible.

> Now we'll indent the left margin by half an inch and leave the right margin at its usual position.

Finally, we'll indent the right margin by half an inch and leave the left margin at its usual position.

```
\xmpheader 2/{Indentation}% see p. 21
\noindent Now let's see how to control indentation.  If an
ordinary word processor can do it, so surely can \TeX. Note
that this paragraph isn't indented.

Usually you'll either want to indent paragraphs or to leave
extra space between them.  Since we haven't changed anything
yet, this paragraph is indented.

{\parindent = 0pt \parskip = 6pt
% The left brace starts a group containing the unindented text.
Let's do these two paragraphs a different way,
with no indentation and six printer's points of extra space
between paragraphs.

So here's another paragraph that we're typesetting without
indentation.  If we didn't put space between these paragraphs,
you would have a hard time knowing where one ends
and the next begins.
\par % The paragraph *must* be ended within the group.
}% The right brace ends the group containing unindented text.

It's also possible to indent both sides of entire paragraphs.
The next three paragraphs illustrate this:
\smallskip % Provide a little extra space here.
% Skips like this and \vskip below end a paragraph.
{\narrower
``We've indented this paragraph on both sides by the paragraph
indentation.  This is often a good way to set long quotations.

``You can do multiple paragraphs this way if you choose.  This
is the second paragraph that's singly indented.''\par}

{\narrower \narrower You can even make paragraphs doubly narrow
if that's what you need.  This is an example of a doubly
narrowed paragraph.\par}
\vskip 1pc % Skip down one pica for visual separation.
In this paragraph we're back to the normal margins, as you can
see for yourself.  We'll let it run on a little longer so that
the margins are clearly visible.

{\leftskip .5in Now we'll indent the left margin by half
an inch and leave the right margin at its usual position.\par}
{\rightskip .5in Finally, we'll indent the right margin by half
an inch and leave the left margin at its usual position.\par}
\bye % end the document
```

Example 3: *Fonts and special characters*

Here are a few words in an italic font, **a few words in a boldface font,** *and a* **mixture** *of the two, with two* roman words *inserted.* Where an italic font is followed by a nonitalic font, we've inserted an "italic correction" (\/) to make the spacing look right. Here's a smaller word—but the standard TEX fonts won't give you anything smaller than this.

If you need any of the ten characters:

$$ \$ \quad \& \quad \# \quad \_ \quad \% \quad \verb|^| \quad \verb|~| \quad \{ \quad \} \quad \backslash $$

you'll need to write them a special way. Look at the facing page to see how to do it.

TEX has the accents and letters that you'll need for French words such as *rôle* and *élève,* for German words such as *Schuß,* and for words in several other languages as well. You'll find a complete list of TEX's accents and foreign letters on page 100 and page 97.

You can also get Greek letters such as "α" and "Ω" for use in math, card suits such as "$\spadesuit$" and "$\diamondsuit$", music symbols such as "$\sharp$" and "$\flat$", and many other special symbols that you'll find listed on page 188. TEX will only accept these sorts of special symbols in its "math mode", so you'll need to enclose them within '$' characters.

```
\xmpheader 3/{Fonts and special characters}% see p. 21
\chardef \\ = '\\ % Let \\ denote a backslash.
{\it Here are a few words in an italic font}, {\bf a
few words in a boldface font}, {\it and a\/ {\bf mixture}
of the two, with two\/ {\rm roman words} inserted}.
Where an italic font is followed by a nonitalic font, we've
inserted an ''italic correction'' ({\tt \\/}) to make the
spacing look right.
Here's a {\sevenrm smaller} word---but the standard \TeX\
fonts won't give you anything smaller than {\fiverm this}.

If you need any of the ten characters:
\medskip
\centerline{\$ \quad \& \quad \# \quad \_ \quad \% \quad
   \char '\^ \quad \char '\~ \quad $\{$ \quad
   $\}$ \quad $\backslash$}
% The \quad inserts an em space between characters.
\medskip
\noindent  you'll need to write them a special way.  Look at
the facing page to see how to do it.

\TeX\ has the accents and letters that you'll need
for French words such as {\it r\^ ole\/} and  {\it \'
el\' eve\/}, for German words such as {\it Schu\ss\/},
and for words in several other languages as well.
You'll find a complete list of \TeX's accents and foreign
letters on page 100 and page 97.

You can also get Greek letters such as ''$\alpha$'' and
''$\Omega$'' for use in math, card suits such as
''$\spadesuit$'' and ''$\diamondsuit$'', music symbols
such as ''$\sharp$'' and ''$\flat$'', and many other special
symbols that you'll find listed on page 188.
\TeX\ will only accept these sorts of special symbols in its
''math mode'', so you'll need to enclose them
within '{\tt \$}' characters.
\bye % end the document
```

Example 4:   *Interline spacing*

Once in a while you may want to print a document with extra space between the lines. For instance, bills before Congress are printed this way so that the legislators can mark them up. For the same reason, book publishers usually insist that manuscripts be double-spaced. Double spacing is rarely appropriate for finished documents, however.

A baseline is an imaginary line that acts like the lines on a pad of ruled paper. You can control the interline spacing—what printers call "leading"—by setting the amount of space between baselines. Take a look at the input to see how to do it. You could use the same method for 1 1/2 spacing as well, using `1.5` instead of `2`. (You can also write $1\frac{1}{2}$ a nicer way.)

For this example we've also increased the paragraph indentation and skipped an extra line between paragraphs.

```
\xmpheader 4/{Interline spacing}% see p. 21
\baselineskip = 2\baselineskip % double spacing
\parskip = \baselineskip % Skip a line between paragraphs.
\parindent = 3em % Increase indentation of paragraphs.

% The following macro definition gives us nice inline
% fractions.  You'll find it in our eplain macros.
\def\frac#1/#2{\leavevmode
   \kern.1em \raise .5ex \hbox{\the\scriptfont0 #1}%
   \kern-.1em $/$%
   \kern-.15em \lower .25ex \hbox{\the\scriptfont0 #2}%
}%
```

Once in a while you may want to print a document with extra
space between the lines. For instance, bills before Congress
are printed this way so that the legislators can mark them up.
For the same reason, book publishers usually insist that
manuscripts be double-spaced. Double spacing is rarely
appropriate for finished documents, however.

A baseline is an imaginary line that acts like the lines
on a pad of ruled paper.   You can control the interline
spacing---what printers call ``leading''---%
by setting the amount of space between baselines. Take a
look at the input to see how to do it. You could use
the same method for $1\;1/2$ spacing as well, using {\tt 1.5}
instead of {\tt 2}. (You can also write $1\frac 1/2$
a nicer way.)
% Here we've used the macro definition given above.

For this example we've also increased the paragraph indentation
and skipped an extra line between paragraphs.

```
\bye % end the document
```

Example 5: *Spacing, rules, and boxes*

Here's an example of a "description list". In practice you'd be better off using a macro to avoid the repetitive constructs and to make sure that the subhead widths are wide enough:

Queen of Hearts   An ill-tempered woman, prone to saying "Off with his head!" at the slightest provocation.

Cheshire Cat   A cat with an enormous smile that Alice found in a tree.

Mock Turtle   A lachrymose creature, quite a storyteller, who was a companion to the Gryphon. Reputedly the principal ingredient of Mock Turtle Soup.

Here's an example of some words in a ruled box, just as Lewis Carroll wrote them:

> Who would not give all else for twop ennyworth only of Beautiful Soup?

* * * * * * * * * * * * * * * *

Here we've gotten the effect of a revision bar on the material in this paragraph. The revision bar might indicate a change.

```
\xmpheader 5/{Spacing, rules, and boxes}% see p. 21
Here's an example of a ''description list''.  In practice you'd
be better off using a macro to avoid the repetitive constructs
and to make sure that the subhead widths are wide enough:
\bigskip
% Call the indentation for descriptions \descindent
% and set it to 8 picas.
\newdimen\descindent \descindent = 8pc
% Indent paragraphs by \descindent.
% Skip an additional half line between paragraphs.
{\noindent \leftskip = \descindent  \parskip = .5\baselineskip
% Move the description to the left of the paragraph.
\llap{\hbox to \descindent{\bf Queen of Hearts\hfil}}%
An ill-tempered woman, prone to saying ''Off with his
head!''\ at the slightest provocation.\par
\noindent\llap{\hbox to \descindent{\bf Cheshire Cat\hfil}}%
A cat with an enormous smile that Alice found
in a tree.\par
\noindent\llap{\hbox to \descindent{\bf Mock Turtle\hfil}}%
A lachrymose creature, quite a  storyteller, who was a
companion to the Gryphon.  Reputedly the principal ingredient
of Mock Turtle Soup.
\par}
\bigskip\hrule\bigskip % A line with vertical space around it.
Here's an example of some words in a ruled box, just as
Lewis Carroll wrote them:
\bigskip
% Put 8pt of space between the text and the surrounding rules.
\hbox{\vrule\vbox{\hrule
   \hbox spread 8pt{\hfil\vbox spread 8pt{\vfil
      \hbox{Who would not give all else for twop}%
      \hbox{ennyworth only of Beautiful Soup?}%
   \vfil}\hfil}
\hrule}\vrule}%

\bigskip\line{\hfil\hbox to 3in{\leaders\hbox{ * }\hfil}\hfil}
\bigskip

\line{\hskip -4pt\vrule\hfil\vbox{
Here we've gotten the effect of a revision bar on the material
in this paragraph.  The revision bar might indicate a change.}}
\bye % end the document
```

Example 6: *Odds and ends*

TEX knows how to hyphenate words, but it isn't infallible. If you are discussing the chemical *5*-[p-(Flourosulfonyl)benzoyl]-l,N^6-ethenoadenosine and TEX complains to you about an "overfull hbox", try inserting some "discretionary hyphens". The notation '\-' tells TEX about a discretionary hyphen, that is, one that it might not have inserted otherwise.

You can typeset text unjustified, i.e., with an uneven right margin. In the old days, before word processors were common, typewritten documents were unjustified because there was no convenient alternative. Some people prefer text to be unjustified so that the spacing between words can be uniform. Most books are set with justified margins, but not all.

Assertion 27. *There is an easy way to typeset the headings of assertions, lemmas, theorems, etc.*

Here's an example of how to typeset an itemized list two levels deep. If you need more levels, you'll have to program it yourself, alas.

1. This is the first item.
2. This is the second item. It consists of two paragraphs. We've indented the second paragraph so that you can easily see where it starts.

   The second paragraph has three subitems underneath it.
   (a) This is the first subitem.
   (b) This is the second subitem.
   (c) This is the third subitem.
- This is a strange-looking item because it's completely different from the others.

Here's a left-justified line.⇐

⇒Here's a right-justified line.

⇒Here's a centered line.⇐

```
\xmpheader 6/{Odds and ends}% see p. 21
\chardef \\ = `\\ % Let \\ denote a backslash.
\footline{\hfil{\tenit - \folio -}\hfil}
% \footline provides a footer line.
% Here it's a centered, italicized page number.
\TeX\ knows how to hyphenate words, but  it isn't infallible.
If you are discussing the chemical
${\it 5}$-[p-(Flouro\-sul\-fonyl)ben\-zoyl]-1,%
$N^6$-ethe\-no\-adeno\-sine
and \TeX\ complains to you about an ``overfull hbox'', try
inserting some ``discretionary hyphens''. The notation
`{\tt \\-}' tells \TeX\ about a  dis\-cre\-tion\-ary hyphen,
that is, one that it might not have inserted otherwise.
\medskip
{\raggedright  You can typeset text unjustified, i.e., with
an uneven right margin. In the old days, before word
processors were common, typewritten documents were
unjustified because there was no convenient alternative.
Some people  prefer text to be  unjustified so that the
spacing between words can be uniform.  Most books are set
with justified margins, but not all. \par}

\proclaim Assertion 27. There is an easy way to typeset
the headings of assertions, lemmas, theorems, etc.

Here's an example of how to typeset an itemized list two
levels deep.  If you need more levels, you'll have to
program it yourself, alas.
\smallskip
\item {1.} This is the first item.
\item {2.} This is the second item.  It consists of two
paragraphs.  We've indented the second paragraph so that
you can easily see where it starts.

\item{} \indent The second paragraph has three subitems
underneath it.
\itemitem {(a)} This is the first subitem.
\itemitem {(b)} This is the second subitem.
\itemitem {(c)} This is the third subitem.
\item {$\bullet$} This is a strange-looking item because it's
completely different from the others.
\smallskip
\leftline{Here's a left-justified line.$\Leftarrow$}
\rightline{$\Rightarrow$Here's a right-justified line.}
\centerline{$\Rightarrow$Here's a centered line.$\Leftarrow$}
% Don't try to use these commands within a paragraph.
\bye % end the document
```

Example 7:   *Using fonts from other sources*

You aren't restricted to using the Computer Modern fonts that come with TEX. Other fonts are available from many sources, and you may prefer them. For instance, we've set this page in 10-point Palatino Roman. Palatino was designed by Hermann Zapf, considered to be one of the greatest type designers of the twentieth century. This page will give you some idea of what it looks like.

Fonts can be provided either as outlines or as bitmaps. An outline font describes the shapes of the characters, while a bitmap font specifies each pixel (dot) that makes up each character. A font outline can be used to generate many different sizes of the same font. The Metafont program that's associated with TEX provides a particularly powerful way of generating bitmap fonts, but it's not the only way.

The fact that a single outline can generate a great range of point sizes for a font tempts many vendors of digital typefaces to provide just one set of outlines for a typeface such as Palatino Roman. This may be a sensible economic decision, but it is an aesthetic sacrifice. Fonts cannot be scaled up and down linearly without loss of quality. Larger sizes of letters should not, in general, have the same proportions as smaller sizes; they just don't look right. For example, a font that's linearly scaled down will tend to have too little space between strokes, and its x-height will be too small.

A type designer can compensate for these changes by providing different outlines for different point sizes, but it's necessary to go to the expense of designing these different outlines. One of the great advantages of Metafont is that it's possible to parameterize the descriptions of characters in a font. Metafont can then maintain the typographical quality of characters over a range of point sizes by adjusting the character shapes accordingly.

```
\xmpheader 7/{Using fonts from other sources}% see p. 21
\font\tenrm = bs0023 % Bitstream Zapf Calligraphic
% Define a macro for invoking Palatino.
\def\pal{\let\rm = \tenrm \baselineskip=12.5pt \rm}
\pal % Use Palatino from now on.
```

You aren't restricted to using the Computer Modern fonts that
come with \TeX. Other fonts are available from many sources,
and you may prefer them. For instance, we've set this page
in 10-point Palatino Roman. Palatino was designed by
Hermann Zapf, considered to be one of the greatest type
designers of the twentieth century. This page will
give you some idea of what it looks like.

Fonts can be provided either as outlines or as bitmaps. An
outline font describes the shapes of the characters, while a
bitmap font specifies each pixel (dot) that makes up each
character. A font outline can be used to generate many
different sizes of the same font. The Metafont program
that's associated with \TeX\ provides a particularly
powerful way of generating bitmap fonts, but it's not the
only way.

The fact that a single outline can generate a great range of
point sizes for a font tempts many vendors of digital
typefaces to provide just one set of outlines for a typeface
such as Palatino Roman. This may be a sensible economic
decision, but it is an aesthetic sacrifice. Fonts cannot be
scaled up and down linearly without loss of quality.
Larger sizes of letters should not, in general, have the
same proportions as smaller sizes; they just don't look
right. For example, a font that's linearly scaled down will
tend to have too little space between strokes, and its
x-height will be too~small. % tie added to avoid widow word

A type designer can compensate for these changes by
providing different outlines for different point sizes, but
it's necessary to go to the expense of designing these
different outlines. One of the great advantages of Metafont
is that it's possible to parameterize the descriptions of
characters in a font. Metafont can then maintain the
typographical quality of characters over a range of point
sizes by adjusting the character shapes accordingly.
\bye % end the document

Example 8: *A ruled table*

Some Choice Edible Mushrooms

Botanical Name	Common Name	Identifying Characteristics
Pleurotus ostreatus	Oyster mushroom	Grows in shelflike clusters on stumps or logs, pink-gray oyster-shaped caps, stem short or absent.
Lactarius hygrophoroides	Milky hygroph	Butterscotch-brown cap and stem, copious white latex, often on ground in woods near streams.
Morchella esculenta	White morel	Conical cap with black pits and white ridges; no gills. Often found near old apple trees and dying elms in the spring.
Boletus edulus	King bolete	Reddish-brown to tan cap with yellow pores (white when young), bulbous stem, often near conifers, birch, or aspen.

```
\xmpheader 8/{A ruled table}% see p. 21
\bigskip
\offinterlineskip % So the vertical rules are connected.
% \tablerule constructs a thin rule across the table.
\def\tablerule{\noalign{\hrule}}
% \tableskip creates 9pt of space between entries.
\def\tableskip{\omit&height 9pt&&&\omit\cr}
% & separates templates for each column. TeX substitutes
% the text of the entries for #. We must have a strut
% present in every row of the table; otherwise, the boxes
% won't butt together properly, and the rules won't join.
\halign{\tabskip = .7em plus 1em  % glue between columns
% Use \vtop for short multiline entries in the first column.
% Typeset the lines ragged right, without hyphenation.
    \vtop{\hsize=6pc\pretolerance = 10000\hbadness = 10000
        \normalbaselines\noindent\it#\strut}%
  &\vrule #&#\hfil &\vrule #% the rules and middle column
% Use \vtop to get whole paragraphs in the last column.
  &\vtop{\hsize=11pc \parindent=0pt \normalbaselineskip=12pt
      \normalbaselines \rightskip=3pt plus2em #}\cr
% The table rows begin here.
\noalign{\hrule height2pt depth2pt \vskip3pt}
  % The header row spans all the columns.
  \multispan5\bf Some Choice Edible Mushrooms\hfil\strut\cr
\noalign{\vskip3pt} \tablerule
  \omit&height 3pt&\omit&&\omit\cr
  \bf Botanical&&\bf Common&&\omit \bf Identifying \hfil\cr
\noalign{\vskip -2pt}% close up lines of heading
  \bf Name&&\bf Name &&\omit \bf Characteristics \hfil\cr
\tableskip Pleurotus ostreatus&&Oyster mushroom&&
  Grows in shelf\kern 1pt like clusters on stumps or logs,
  % without the kern, the 'f' and 'l' would be too close
  pink-gray oyster-shaped caps, stem short or absent.\cr
\tableskip Lactarius hygrophoroides&&Milky hygroph&&
  Butterscotch-brown cap and stem, copious white latex,
  often on ground in woods near streams.\cr
\tableskip Morchella esculenta&&White morel&&Conical cap
  with black pits and white ridges; no gills. Often found
  near old apple trees and dying elms in the spring.\cr
\tableskip Boletus edulus&&King bolete&&Reddish-brown to
  tan cap with yellow pores (white when young),
  bulbous stem, often near conifers, birch, or~aspen.\cr
\tableskip \tablerule \noalign{\vskip 2pt} \tablerule
}\bye
```

Example 9: *Typesetting mathematics*

For a spherical triangle with sides a, b, and c, and opposite angles α, β, and γ, we have:

$$\cos \alpha = -\cos \beta \cos \gamma + \sin \beta \sin \gamma \cos \alpha \quad \text{(Law of Cosines)}$$

and:

$$\tan \frac{\alpha}{2} = \sqrt{\frac{-\cos \sigma \cdot \cos(\sigma - \alpha)}{\cos(\sigma - \beta) \cdot \cos(\sigma - \gamma)}}, \quad \text{where } \sigma = \tfrac{1}{2}(a + b + c)$$

We also have:

$$\sin x = \frac{e^{ix} - e^{-ix}}{2i}$$

and:

$$\int_0^\infty \frac{\sin ax \sin bx}{x^2} \, dx = \frac{\pi a}{2}, \quad \text{if } a < b$$

The number of combinations $_nC_r$ of n things taken r at a time is:

$$C(n, r) = {_nC_r} = \binom{n}{r} = \frac{n(n - 1) \cdots (n - r + 1)}{r(r - 1) \cdots (1)} = \frac{n!}{r!(n - r)!}$$

The value of the determinant D of order n:

$$D = \begin{vmatrix} a_{11} & a_{12} & \cdots & a_{1n} \\ a_{21} & a_{22} & \cdots & a_{2n} \\ \vdots & \vdots & \ddots & \vdots \\ a_{n1} & a_{n2} & \cdots & a_{nn} \end{vmatrix}$$

is defined as the sum of $n!$ terms:

$$\sum (\pm) \, a_{1i} a_{2j} \ldots a_{nk}$$

where i, j, $\ldots$, k take on all possible values between 1 and n, and the sign of the product is $+$ if the sequence i, j, $\ldots$, k is an even permutation and $-$ otherwise. Moreover:

$$Q(\xi) = \lambda_1 y_1^2 \sum_{i=2}^{n} \sum_{j=2}^{n} y_i b_{ij} y_j, \qquad B = \|b_{ij}\| = B'$$

```
\xmpheader 9/{Typesetting mathematics}% see p. 21
For a spherical triangle with sides $a$, $b$, and $c$, and
opposite angles $\alpha$, $\beta$, and $\gamma$, we have:
$$\cos \alpha = -\cos \beta \cos \gamma +
  \sin \beta \sin \gamma \cos \alpha \quad
  \hbox{(Law of Cosines)}$$
and:
$$\tan {\alpha \over 2} = \sqrt{
  {- \cos \sigma \cdot \cos(\sigma - \alpha)} \over
  {\cos (\sigma - \beta) \cdot \cos (\sigma - \gamma)}},\quad
  \hbox{where $\sigma = {1 \over 2}(a+b+c)$}$$
We also have:$$\sin x = {{e^{ix}-e^{-ix}}\over 2i}$$
and:
$$\int _0 ^\infty {{\sin ax \sin bx}\over{x^2}}\,dx
% The \, above produces a thin space
  = {\pi a\over 2}, \quad \hbox{if $a < b$}$$

\noindent The number of combinations ${}_nC_r$ of $n$
things taken $r$ at a time is:
$$C(n,r) = {}_nC_r = {n \choose r} =
  {{n(n-1) \cdots (n-r+1)} \over {r(r-1) \cdots (1)}} =
  {{n!}\over {r!(n-r)!}}$$

\noindent
The value of the determinant $D$ of order $n$:
$$D = \left|\matrix{a_{11}&a_{12}&\ldots&a_{1n}\cr
  a_{21}&a_{22}&\ldots&a_{2n}\cr
  \vdots&\vdots&\ddots&\vdots\cr
  a_{n1}&a_{n2}&\ldots&a_{nn}\cr}\right| $$
is defined as the sum of $n!$ terms:
$$\sum\>(\pm)\>a_{1i}a_{2j} \ldots a_{nk}$$
% The \> above produces a medium space.
where $i$, $j$, \dots,~$k$\/ take on all possible values
between $1$ and $n$, and the sign of the product is
$+$ if the sequence $i$, $j$, \dots,~$k$\/ is an
even permutation and $-$ otherwise.  Moreover:
$$Q(\xi) = \lambda_1 y_1^2 \sum_{i=2}^n \sum_{j=2}^n y_i
b_{ij} y_j,\qquad B = \Vert b_{ij} \Vert = B'$$
\bye
```

Example 10:   *More mathematics*

The absolute value of X, $|x|$, is defined by:

$$|x| = \begin{cases} x, & \text{if } x \geq 0; \\ -x, & \text{otherwise.} \end{cases}$$

Now for some numbered equations. It is the case that for $k \geq 0$:

$$x^{k^2} = \overbrace{x\,x\,\cdots\,x}^{2k \text{ times}} \tag{1}$$

Here's an example that shows some spacing controls, with a number on the left:

$$(2a) \qquad\qquad\qquad [u][v][w]\,[x]\ [y]\ [z]$$

The amount of space between the items in brackets gradually increases from left to right. (We've made the space between the first two items be *less* than the natural space.) It is sometimes the case that

$$(2b) \qquad\qquad\qquad u_1' + tu_2'' = u_2' + tu_1''$$
$$(2c) \qquad\qquad\qquad \hat{\imath} \neq \hat{\jmath}$$
$$\vec{a} \approx \vec{b}$$

The result is of order $O(n \log \log n)$. Thus

$$\sum_{i=1}^{n} x_i = x_1 + x_2 + \cdots + x_n = \mathrm{Sum}(x_1, x_2, \ldots, x_n). \tag{3}$$

and

$$dx\,dy = r\,dr\,d\theta. \tag{4}$$

The set of all q such that $q \leq 0$ is written as:

$$\{\, q \mid q \leq 0 \,\}$$

Thus

$$\forall x \exists y\ P(x, y) \Rightarrow \exists x \exists y\ P(x, y)$$

where

$$P(x, y) \stackrel{\text{def}}{\equiv} \text{any predicate in } x \text{ and } y.$$

```
\xmpheader 10/{More mathematics}% see p. 21
The absolute value of $X$, $|x|$, is defined by:
$$|x| = \cases{x, &if $x\ge 0$;\cr
-x,&otherwise.\cr}$$
Now for some numbered equations.
It is the case that for $k \ge 0$:
$$x^{k^2}=\overbrace{x\>x\>\cdots\> x}^{2k\ \rm times}
    \eqno (1)$$

Here's an example that shows some spacing controls, with
a number on the left:
$$[u]\!\[v][w]\,[x]\>[y]\;[z]\leqno(2a)$$
The amount of space between the items in brackets
gradually increases from left to right.  (We've made
the space between the first two items be {\it less\/}
than the natural space.)
It is sometimes the case that $$\leqalignno{
u'_1 + tu''_2 &= u'_2 + tu''_1&(2b)\cr
\hat\imath &\ne \hat \jmath&(2c)\cr
\vec {\vphantom{b}a}&\approx \vec b\cr}$$
% The \vphantom is an invisible rule as tall as a 'b'.
The result is of order $O(n \log\log n)$.  Thus
$$\sum_{i=1}^n x_i = x_1+x_2+\cdots+x_n
= {\rm Sum}(x_1,x_2,\ldots,x_n). \eqno(3)$$
and
$$dx\,\dy = r\,dr\,d\theta\!.\eqno(4)$$
The set of all $q$ such that $q\le0$ is written as:
$$\{\,q\mid q\le0\, \}$$
Thus
$$\forall x\exists y\;P(x,y)\Rightarrow
\exists x\exists y\;P(x,y)$$
where
$$P(x,y) \buildrel \rm def \over \equiv
\hbox{\rm any predicate in $x$ and $y$} . $$
\bye
```

4 Concepts

This part of the book contains definitions and explanations of the concepts that we use in describing TeX. The concepts include both technical terms that we use in explaining the commands and important topics that don't fit elsewhere in the book.

The concepts are arranged alphabetically. The inside back cover of the book contains a complete list of concepts and the pages on which they are explained. We suggest that you make a copy of the inside back cover and keep it nearby so that you'll be able to identify and look up an unfamiliar concept immediately. As far as possible, we've kept our terminology consistent with that of *The TeXbook*.

active character.   An *active character* is a character that has a definition, e.g., a macro definition, associated with it. You can think of an active character as a special kind of control sequence. When TeX encounters an active character, it executes the definition associated with the character. If TeX encounters an active character that does not have an associated definition, it will complain about an undefined control sequence.

An active character has a category code of 13 (the value of \active). To define an active character, you should first use the \catcode command (p. 251) to make it active and then provide the definition of the character, using a command such as \def, \let, or \chardef. The definition of an active character has the same form as the definition of a control sequence. If you try to define the macro for an active character before you make the character active, TeX will complain about a missing control sequence.

For example, the tilde character (~) is defined as an active character in plain TeX. It produces a space between two words but links those words so that TEX will not turn the space into a line break. Plain TEX defines '~' by the commands:

```
\catcode '~ = \active \def~{\penalty10000\ }
```

(The \penalty inhibits a line break and the '\ ' inserts a space.)

alignment.   An *alignment* is a construct for aligning material, such as a table, in columns or rows. To form an alignment you need to (a) describe the layout of the columns or rows and (b) tell TEX what material goes into the columns or rows. A tabbing alignment or a horizontal alignment is organized as a sequence of rows; a vertical alignment is organized as a sequence of columns. We first describe tabbing and horizontal alignments and then more briefly describe vertical alignments.

Tabbing alignments are defined by plain TEX. They are simpler but less flexible than horizontal alignments. Tabbing and horizontal alignments differ principally in how you describe their layouts.

To construct a tabbing alignment you first issue a \settabs command (p. 176) that specifies how TEX should divide the available horizontal space into columns. Then you provide a sequence of rows for the table. Each row consists of a \+ control sequence (p. 176) followed by a list of "entries", i.e., row/column intersections. Adjacent entries in a row are separated by an ampersand (&). The end of a row is indicated by \cr after its last entry. If a row has fewer entries than there are columns in the alignment, TEX effectively fills out the row with blank entries.

As long as it's preceded by a \settabs command, you can put a row of a tabbing alignment anywhere in your document. In particular, you can put other things between the rows of a tabbing alignment or describe several tabbing alignments with a single \settabs. Here's an example of a tabbing alignment:

```
{\hsize = 1.7 in \settabs 2 \columns
\+cattle&herd\cr
\+fish&school\cr
\+lions&pride\cr}
```

The \settabs 2 \columns command in this example (p. 176) tells TEX to produce two equally wide columns. The line length is 1.7 inches. The typeset alignment looks like this:

cattle   herd
fish   school
lions   pride

There's another form of tabbing alignment in which you specify the column widths with a template. The column widths in the template determine the column widths in the rest of the alignment:

```
{\settabs\+cattle\quad&school\cr
```

```
\+cattle&herd\cr
\+fish&school\cr
\+lions&pride\cr}
```

Here's the result:

cattle	herd
fish	school
lions	pride

Horizontal alignments are constructed with `\halign` (p. 178). TEX adjusts the column widths of a horizontal alignment according to what is in the columns. When TEX encounters the `\halign` command that begins a horizontal alignment, it first examines all the rows of the alignment to see how wide the entries are. It then sets each column width to accommodate the widest entry in that column.

A horizontal alignment governed by `\halign` consists of a "preamble" that indicates the row layout followed by the rows themselves.

- The preamble consists of a sequence of templates, one for each column. The template for a column specifies how the text for that column should be typeset. Each template must include a single `#` character to indicate where TEX should substitute the text of an entry into the template. The templates are separated by ampersands (`&`), and the end of the preamble is indicated by `\cr`. By providing an appropriate template you can obtain effects such as centering a column, left or right justifying a column, or setting a column in a particular font.

- The rows have the same form as in a tabbing alignment, except that you omit the `\+` at the beginning of each row. As before, entries are separated by `&` and the end of the row is indicated by `\cr`. TEX treats each entry as a group, so any font-setting command or other assignment in a column template is in effect only for the entries in that column.

The preamble and the rows must all be enclosed in the braces that follow `\halign`. Each `\halign` alignment must include its own preamble.

For example, the horizontal alignment:

```
\tabskip=2pc
\halign{\hfil#\hfil &\hfil#\hfil &\hfil#\hfil \cr
  &&\it Table\cr
\noalign{\kern -2pt}
  \it Creature&\it Victual&\it Position\cr
\noalign{\kern 2pt}
  Alice&crumpet&left\cr
  Dormouse&muffin&middle\cr
  Hatter&tea&right\cr}
```

produces the result:

		Table
Creature	*Victual*	*Position*
Alice	crumpet	left
Dormouse	muffin	middle
Hatter	tea	right

The \tabskip (p. 184) in this example tells TeX to insert 2pc of glue between the columns. The \noalign (p. 183) commands tell TeX to insert vertical mode material between two rows. In this example we've used \noalign to produce some extra space between the title rows and the data rows, and also to bring "Table" and "Position" closer together. (You can also use \noalign before the first row or after the last row.)

You can construct a vertical alignment with the \valign command (p. 179). A vertical alignment is organized as a series of columns rather than as a series of rows. A vertical alignment follows the same rules as a horizontal alignment except that the roles of rows and columns are interchanged. For example, the vertical alignment:

```
{\hsize=0.6in \parindent=0pt
\valign{#\strut&#\strut&#\strut\cr
  one&two&three\cr
  four&five&six\cr
  seven&eight&nine\cr
  ten&eleven\cr}}
```

yields:

one	four	seven	ten
two	five	eight	eleven
three	six	nine	

The \strut commands (p. 167) in the template are necessary to get the entries in each row to line up properly, i.e., to have a common baseline, and to keep the distance between baselines uniform.

anatomy of TeX.   *The TeXbook* describes the way that TeX processes its input in terms of TeX's "digestive tract"—its "eyes", "mouth", "gullet", "stomach", and "intestines". Knowing how this processing works can be helpful when you're trying to understand subtle aspects of TeX's behavior as it's digesting a document.

- Using its "eyes", TeX reads characters from input files and passes them to its mouth. Since an input file can contain \input commands (p. 247), TeX can in effect "shift its gaze" from one file to another.
- Using its "mouth", TeX assembles the characters into tokens and passes them to its gullet. Each token is either a control sequence or a single character. A control sequence always starts with an escape

character. Note that spaces and ends-of-line are characters in their own right, although TeX compresses a sequence of input spaces into a single space token. See pages 46–47 of *The TeXbook* for the rules by which TeX assembles characters into tokens.

- Using its "gullet", TeX expands any macros, conditionals, and similar constructs that it finds (see pages 212–216 of *The TeXbook*) and passes the resulting sequence of tokens to TeX's stomach. Expanding one token may yield other tokens that in turn need to be expanded. TeX carries out this expansion from left to right unless the order is modified by a command such as `\expandafter` (p. 233). In other words, TeX's gullet always expands the leftmost unexpanded token that it has not yet sent to TeX's stomach.

- Using its "stomach", TeX processes the tokens in groups. Each group contains a primitive command followed by its arguments, if any. Most of the commands are of the "typeset this character" variety, so their groups consist of just one token. Obeying the instructions given by the commands, TeX's stomach assembles larger and larger units, starting with characters and ending with pages, and passes the pages to TeX's intestines. TeX's stomach handles the tasks of line breaking—i.e., breaking each paragraph into a sequence of lines— and of page breaking—i.e., breaking a continuous sequence of lines and other vertical mode material into pages.

- Using its "intestines", TeX transforms the pages produced by its stomach into a form intended for processing by other programs. It then sends the transformed output to the `.dvi` file.

Most of the time you can think of the processes that take place in TeX's eyes, mouth, gullet, stomach, and intestines as happening one after the other. But the truth of the matter is that commands executed in TeX's stomach can influence the earlier stages of digestion. For instance, when TeX's stomach encounters the `\input` command (p. 247), its eyes start reading from a different file; when TeX's stomach encounters a `\catcode` command (p. 251) specifying a category code for a character c, the interpretation of c by TeX's mouth is affected. And when TeX's stomach encounters a macro definition, the expansions carried out in TeX's gullet are affected.

You can understand how the processes interact by imagining that each process eagerly gobbles up the output of its predecessor as soon as it becomes available. For instance, once TeX's stomach has seen the last character of the filename in an `\input` command, TeX's gaze immediately shifts to the first character of the specified input file.

argument. An *argument* contains text that is passed to a command. The arguments of a command complete the description of what the command is supposed to do. The command can either be a primitive command or a macro.

Each primitive command has its own convention about the form of its arguments. For instance, the sequence of tokens:

```
\hskip 3pc plus 1em
```

consists of the command '\hskip' and the arguments '3pc plus 1em'. But if you were to write:

```
\count11 3pc plus 1em
```

you'd get an entirely different effect. TeX would treat '\count11' as a command with argument '3', followed by the ordinary text tokens 'pc plus 1em' (because count registers expect a number to be assigned to them)—probably not what you intended. The effect of the command, by the way, would be to assign 3 to count register 11 (see the discussion of \count, p. 242).

Macros, on the other hand, all follow the same convention for their arguments. Each argument passed to a macro corresponds to a parameter in the definition of that macro. A macro parameter is either "delimited" or "undelimited". The macro definition determines the number and nature of the macro parameters and therefore the number and nature of the macro arguments.

The difference between a delimited argument and an undelimited argument lies in the way that TeX decides where the argument ends.

- A delimited argument consists of the tokens from the start of the argument up to, but not including, the particular sequence of tokens that serves as the delimiter for that argument. The delimiter is specified in the macro definition. Thus you supply a delimited argument to a macro by writing the argument itself followed by the delimiter. A delimited argument can be empty, i.e., have no text at all in it. Any braces in a delimited argument must be paired properly, i.e., every left brace must have a corresponding right brace and vice versa.

- An undelimited argument consists of a single token or a sequence of tokens enclosed in braces, like this: '{Here is {the} text.}'. Despite appearances, the outer braces don't form a group—TeX uses them only to determine what the argument is. Any inner braces, such as the ones around 'the', must be paired properly. If you make a mistake and put in too many right braces, TeX will complain about an unexpected right brace. TeX will also complain if you put in too many left braces, but you'll probably get *that* complaint long after the place where you intended to end the argument (see p. 275).

See "macro" (p. 75) for more information about parameters and arguments. You'll find the precise rules pertaining to delimited and undelimited arguments in pages 203–204 of *The TEXbook*.

ASCII. ASCII is the abbreviation of "American Standard Code for Information Interchange". There are 256 ASCII characters, each with its own code number, but the meanings of only the first 128 have been standardized. You can find these meanings in an ASCII "code table" such as the one on page 367 of *The TEXbook*. Characters 32–126 are "printable characters", such as letters, numbers, and punctuation marks. The remaining characters are "control characters" that are typically used (in the computer industry, not in TEX) to control input/output and data communications devices. For instance, ASCII code 84 corresponds to the letter 'T', while ASCII code 12 corresponds to the "form feed" function (interpreted by most printers as "start a new page"). Although the ASCII standard specifies meanings for the control characters, many manufacturers of equipment such as modems and printers have used the control characters for purposes other than the standard ones.

The meaning of a character in TEX is usually consistent with its meaning in standard ASCII, and fonts that contain ASCII printable characters usually have those characters in the same positions as their ASCII counterparts. But some fonts, notably those used for math, replace the ASCII printable characters by other characters unrelated to the ASCII characters. For instance, the Computer Modern math font `cmsy10` has the math symbol '$\forall$' in place of the ASCII digit '8'.

assignment. An *assignment* is a construct that tells TEX to assign a value to a register, to one of its internal parameters, to an entry in one of its internal tables, or to a control sequence. Some examples of assignments are:

```
\tolerance = 2000
\advance\count12 by 17
\lineskip = 4pt plus 2pt
\everycr = {\hskip 3pt \relax}
\catcode\'@ = 11
\let\graf = \par
\font\myfont = cmbx12
```

The first assignment indicates that TEX should assign the numeric value 2000 to the numeric parameter `\tolerance`, i.e., make the value of `\tolerance` be 2000. The other assignments are similar. The '=' and the spaces are optional, so you could also write the first assignment more tersely as:

```
\tolerance2000
```

See pages 276–277 of *The TEXbook* for the detailed syntax of assignments.

badness. The *badness* of a line is a measure of how far the interword spaces in the line deviate from their natural values, i.e., the values specified in the fonts used in the line. The greater the deviation, the greater the badness. Similarly, the badness of a page is a measure of how far the spaces between the boxes that make up the page deviate from their ideal values. (Ordinarily, most of these boxes are single lines of paragraphs.)

More precisely, the badness is a measure of how much the glue associated with these spaces needs to stretch or shrink to fill the line or page exactly. TEX computes the badness as approximately 100 times the cube of the ratio by which it must stretch or shrink the glue in order to compose a line or a page of the required size. For example, stretching the glue by twice its stated stretch yields a ratio of 2 and a badness of 800; stretching it by half its stated stretch yields a ratio of .5 and a badness of 13. TEX treats a badness greater than 10000 as equal to 10000.

TEX uses the badness of a line when it's breaking a paragraph into lines (see "line break", p. 74). It uses this information in two stages:

(1) When TEX is choosing line breaks, it will eventually accept lines whose badness is less than or equal to the value of \tolerance (p. 123). If TEX cannot avoid setting a line whose badness exceeds this value, it will set it as an underfull or overfull hbox. TEX will set an overfull or underfull hbox only as a last resort, i.e., only if there's no other way to break the paragraph into lines.

(2) Assuming that all lines are tolerably bad, TEX uses the badness of lines in order to evaluate the different ways of breaking the paragraph into lines. During this evaluation it associates "demerits" with each potential line. The badness increases the number of demerits. TEX then breaks the paragraph into lines in a way that minimizes the total demerits for the paragraph. Most often TEX arranges the paragraph in a way that minimizes the badness of the worst line. See pages 97–98 of *The TEXbook* for the details of how TEX breaks a paragraph into lines.

TEX's procedure for assembling a sequence of lines and other vertical mode material into pages is similar to its procedure for line breaking. However, assembling pages is not as complicated because TEX only considers one page at a time when it looks for page breaks. Thus the only decision it must make is where to end the current page. In contrast, when TEX is choosing line breaks it considers several of them simultaneously. (Most word processors choose line breaks one at a time, and thus don't do as good a job at it as TEX does.) See pages 111–113 of *The TEXbook* for the details of how TEX chooses its page breaks.

baseline.   The *baseline* of a box is an imaginary line that runs across the box. When TeX is assembling the boxes of a horizontal list into a larger box, it lines up the boxes in the list so that their baselines coincide. As an analogy, think of writing on a pad of ruled paper. Each letter that you write has an implicit baseline. In order to line up the letters horizontally, you place them on the pad so that their baselines agree with the light guidelines that are printed on the pad.

A box can and often does extend below its baseline. For instance, the letter 'g' extends below the baseline of its box because it has a descender (the bottom loop of the 'g').

box.   A *box* is a rectangle of material to be typeset. A single character is a box by itself, and an entire page is also a box. TeX forms a page as a nest of boxes within boxes within boxes. The outermost box is the page itself, the innermost boxes are mostly single characters, and single lines are boxes that are somewhere in the middle.

TeX carries out most of its box-building activities implicitly as it constructs paragraphs and pages. You can construct boxes explicitly using a number of TeX commands, notably \hbox (p. 160), \vbox (p. 161), and \vtop (p. 161). The \hbox command constructs a box by appending smaller boxes horizontally from left to right; it operates on a horizontal list and yields an hbox (horizontal box). The \vbox and \vtop commands construct a box by appending smaller boxes vertically from top to bottom; they operate on a vertical list and yield a vbox (vertical box). These horizontal and vertical lists can include not just smaller boxes but several other kinds of entities as well, e.g., glue and kerns.

A box has height, depth, and width, like this:

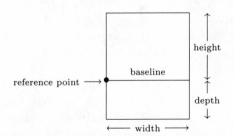

The baseline is like one of the light guidelines on a pad of ruled paper. The boxes for letters such as 'g' extend below the baseline; the boxes for letters such as 'h' don't. The height of a box is the distance that the box extends above its baseline, while its depth is the distance that it extends below its baseline. The reference point of a box is the place where its baseline intersects its left edge.

TeX builds an hbox H from a horizontal list by assuming a reference point for H and then appending the items in the list to H one by one from left to right. Each box in the list is placed so that its baseline coincides with the baseline of H, i.e., the component boxes are lined up horizontally.[1] The height of H is the height of the tallest box in the list, and the depth of H is the depth of the deepest box in the list. The width of H is the sum of the widths of all the items in the list. If any of these items are glue and TEX needs to stretch or shrink the glue, the width of H will be larger or smaller accordingly. See page 77 of *The TEXbook* for the details.

Similarly, TEX builds a vbox V from a vertical list by assuming a temporary reference point for V and then appending the items in the list to V one by one from top to bottom. Each box in the list is placed so that its reference point is lined up vertically with the reference point of V.[2] As each box other than the first one is added to V, TEX puts interline glue just above it. (This interline glue has no analogue for hboxes.) The width of V is the width of the widest box in the list, and the vertical extent (height plus depth) of V is the sum of the vertical extents of all the items in the list.

The difference between \vbox and \vtop is in how they partition the vertical extent of V into a height and a depth. Choosing the reference point of V determines that partition.

- For \vbox, TEX places the reference point on a horizontal line with the reference point of the last component box or rule of V, except that if the last box (or rule) is followed by glue or a kern, TEX places the reference point at the very bottom of V.[3]

- For \vtop, TEX places the reference point on a horizontal line with the reference point of the first component box or rule of V, except that if the first box (or rule) is preceded by glue or a kern, TEX places the reference point at the very top of V.

Roughly speaking, then, \vbox puts the reference point near the bottom of the vbox and \vtop puts it near the top. When you want to align a row of vboxes so that their tops line up horizontally, you should usually use \vtop rather than \vbox. See pages 78 and 80–81 of *The TEXbook* for the details of how TEX builds vboxes.

You have quite a lot of freedom in constructing boxes. The typeset material in a box can extend beyond the boundaries of the box as it does for some letters (mostly italic or slanted ones). The component boxes of a larger box can overlap. A box can have negative width, depth, or height, though boxes like that are not often needed.

You can save a box in a box register and retrieve it later. Before using a box register, you should reserve it and give it a name with the

---

[1] If a box is moved up or down with \raise or \lower, TEX uses its reference point before the move when placing it.

[2] If a box is moved left or right with \moveleft or \moveright, TEX uses its reference point before the move when placing it.

[3] The depth is limited by the parameter \boxmaxdepth (p. 163).

`\newbox` command (p. 244). See "register" (p. 89) for more information about box registers.

category code.   The *category code* of a character determines that character's role in TEX. For instance, TEX assigns a certain role to letters, another to space characters, and so forth. TEX attaches a code to each character that it reads. When TEX reads the letter 'r', for example, it ordinarily attaches the category code 11 (letter) to it. For simple TEX applications you won't need to worry about category codes, but they become important when you are trying to achieve special effects.

Category codes apply only to characters that TEX reads from input files. Once a character has gotten past TEX's gullet (see "anatomy of TEX", p. 46) and been interpreted, its category code no longer matters. A character that you produce with the `\char` command (p. 99) does not have a category code because `\char` is an instruction to TEX to produce a certain character in a certain font. For instance, the ASCII code for '\' (the usual escape character) is 92. If you type '\char92 grok', it is *not* equivalent to `\grok`. Instead it tells TEX to typeset '*c*grok', where *c* is the character in position 92 of the code table for the current font.

You can use the `\catcode` command (p. 251) to reassign the category code of any character. By changing category codes you can change the roles of various characters. For instance, if you type '`\catcode`'`\@ = 11`', the category code of the at sign (`@`) will be set to "letter". You then can use '`@`' in the name of a control sequence.

Here is a list of the category codes as they're defined in plain TEX (see p. 55 for an explanation of the `^^` notation), together with the characters in each category:

Code	*Meaning*	
0	Escape character	\
1	Beginning of group	{
2	End of group	}
3	Math shift	$
4	Alignment tab	&
5	End of line	`^^M` ≡ ASCII ⟨return⟩
6	Macro parameter	#
7	Superscript	^ and `^^K`
8	Subscript	_ and `^^A`
9	Ignored character	`^^@` ≡ ASCII ⟨null⟩
10	Space	␣ and `^^I` ≡ ASCII ⟨horizontal tab⟩
11	Letter	A ... Z and a ... z
12	Other character	(everything not listed above or below)
13	Active character	~ and `^^L` ≡ ASCII ⟨form feed⟩
14	Comment character	%
15	Invalid character	`^^?` ≡ ASCII ⟨delete⟩

Except for categories 11–13, all the characters in a particular category produce the same effect. For instance, suppose that you type:

```
\catcode`\[ = 1 \catcode`\] = 2
```

Then the left and right bracket characters become beginning-of-group and end-of-group characters equivalent to the left and right brace characters. With these definitions '[a b]' is a valid group, and so are '[a b}' and '{a b]'.

The characters in categories 11 (letter) and 12 (other character) act as commands that mean "produce a box containing this character typeset in the current font". The only distinction between letters and "other" characters is that letters can appear in control words but "other" characters can't.

A character in category 13 (active) acts like a control sequence all by itself. TeX complains if it encounters an active character that doesn't have a definition associated with it.

If TeX encounters an invalid character (category 15) in your input, it will complain about it.

The '^^K' and '^^A' characters have been included in categories 8 (subscript) and 9 (superscript), even though these meanings don't follow the standard ASCII interpretation. That's because some keyboards, notably some at Stanford University where TeX originated, have down arrow and up arrow keys that generate these characters.

There's a subtle point about the way TeX assigns category codes that can trip you up if you're not aware of it. TeX sometimes needs to look at a character twice as it does its initial scan: first to find the end of some preceding construct, e.g., a control sequence, and later to turn that character into a token. TeX doesn't assign the category code until its *second* look at the character. For example:

```
\def\foo{\catcode`\$ = 11 }% Make $ be a letter.
\foo$ % Produces a `$'.
\foo$ % Undefined control sequence `foo$'.
```

This bit of TeX code produces '$' in the typeset output. When TeX first sees the '$' on the second line, it's looking for the end of a control sequence name. Since the '$' isn't yet a letter, it marks the end of '\foo'. Next, TeX expands the '\foo' macro and changes the category code of '$' to 11 (letter). Then TeX reads the '$' "for real". Since '$' is now a letter, TeX produces a box containing the '$' character in the current font. When TeX sees the third line, it treats '$' as a letter and thus considers it to be part of the control sequence name. As a result it complains about an undefined control sequence \foo$.

TeX behaves this way even when the terminating character is an end of line. For example, suppose that the macro \fum activates the end-of-line character. Then if \fum appears on a line ℓ by itself, TeX will first interpret the end of line of ℓ as the end of the \fum control sequence and then will *reinterpret* the end of line of ℓ as an active character.

character. TeX works with *characters* in two contexts: as input characters, which it reads, and as output characters, which it typesets. TeX transforms most input characters into the output characters that depict them. For example, it normally transforms the input letter 'h' into the letter 'h' typeset in the current font. That is not the case, however, for an input character such as '$' that has a special meaning.

TeX gets its input characters by reading them from input files (or from your terminal) and by expanding macros. These are the *only* ways that TeX can acquire an input character. Each input character has a code number corresponding to its position in the ASCII code table. For instance, the letter 'T' has ASCII code 84.

When TeX reads a character, it attaches a category code to it. The category code affects how TeX interprets the character once it has been read in. TeX determines (and remembers) the category codes of the characters in a macro when it reads the macro's definition. As TeX reads characters with its eyes (see "anatomy of TeX", p. 46) it does some "filtering", such as condensing sequences of spaces to a single space. See pages 46–48 of *The TeXbook* for the details of this filtering.

The ASCII "control characters" have codes 0–31 and 127–255. They either don't show up or cause strange behavior on most terminals if you try to display them. Nonetheless they are sometimes needed in TeX input, so TeX has a special notation for them. If you type '^^c', where c is any character, you get the character whose ASCII code is either 64 greater or 64 less than c's ASCII code. The largest acceptable code value using this notation is 127, so the notation is unambiguous. Three particularly common instances of this notation are '^^M' (the ASCII ⟨return⟩ character), '^^J' (the ASCII ⟨line feed⟩ character) and '^^I' (the ASCII ⟨horizontal tab⟩ character).

TeX also has another notation for indicating ASCII code values that works for all character codes from 0 to 255. If you type '^^xy', where x and y are any of the hexadecimal digits '0123456789abcdef', you get the single character with the specified code. (Lower case letters are required here.) TeX opts for the "hexadecimal digits" interpretation whenever it has a choice, so you must not follow a character like '^^a' with a lowercase hexadecimal digit—if you do, you'll get the wrong interpretation. If you need to use this notation you'll find it handy to have a table of ASCII codes.

An output character is a character to be typeset. A command for producing an output character has the meaning "Produce a box containing character number n from the current font", where n is determined by the command. TeX produces your typeset document by combining such boxes with other typographical elements and arranging them on the page.

An input character whose category code is 11 (letter) or 12 (other) acts as a command to produce the corresponding output character. In addition you can get TeX to produce character n by issuing the command '\char n' (p. 99), where n is a number between 0 and 255. The commands 'h', \char'h, and \char104 all have the same effect. (104 is the ASCII code for 'h'.)

class.   The *class* of a character specifies that character's role in math formulas. The class of a character is encoded in its mathcode. For example, the equals sign '=' is in class 3 (Relation). TeX uses its knowledge of character classes to decide how much space to put between different components of a math formula. For example, here's a math formula shown first as TeX normally prints it and then with the class of each character randomly changed:

$$a + (b - a) = a \qquad a+ (b-a)=a$$

See page 218 of this book or page 154 of *The TeXbook* for a list of the classes and their meanings.

command.   A *command* instructs TeX to carry out a certain action. Every token that reaches TeX's stomach (see "anatomy of TeX", p. 46) acts as a command, except for those that are parts of arguments to other commands (see below). A command can be invoked by a control sequence, by an active character, or by an ordinary character. It might seem odd that TeX treats an ordinary character as a command, but in fact that's what it does: when TeX sees an ordinary character it constructs a box containing that character typeset in the current font.

A command can have arguments. The arguments of a command are single tokens or groups of tokens that complete the description of what the command is supposed to do. For example, the command '\vskip 1in' tells TeX to skip 1 inch vertically. It has an argument '1in', which consists of three tokens. The description of what \vskip is supposed to do would be incomplete without specifying how far it is supposed to skip. The tokens in the arguments to a command are not themselves considered to be commands.

Some examples of different kinds of TeX commands are:

- Ordinary characters, such as 'W', which instructs TeX to produce a box containing a typeset 'W'
- Font-setting commands, such as \bf, which begins boldface type
- Accents, such as \`, which produces a grave accent as in 'è'
- Special symbols and ligatures, such as \P (¶) and \ae (æ)
- Parameters, such as \parskip, the amount of glue that TeX puts between paragraphs
- Math symbols, such as \alpha (α) and \in ($\in$)
- Math operators, such as \over, which produces a fraction

conditional test. A *conditional test* is a command that tests whether or not a certain condition is true and causes TeX either to expand or to skip some text, depending on the outcome. The general form of a conditional test is either:

   \if$\alpha$⟨*true text*⟩\else⟨*false text*⟩\fi

or:

   \if$\alpha$⟨*true text*⟩\fi

where α specifies the particular test. For example, \ifvmode tests the condition that TeX is currently in a vertical mode. If the condition is true, TeX expands ⟨*true text*⟩. If the condition is false, TeX expands ⟨*false text*⟩ (if it's present). Conditional tests are interpreted in TeX's gullet (see "anatomy of TeX", p. 46), so any expandable tokens in the interpreted text are expanded after the test has been resolved. The various conditional tests are explained in "Conditional tests" (p. 235).

control sequence. A *control sequence* is a name for a TeX command. A control sequence always starts with an escape character, usually a backslash (\). A control sequence takes one of two forms:

- A control word is a control sequence consisting of an escape character followed by one or more letters. The control word ends when TeX sees a nonletter. For instance, when TeX reads '\hfill␣,␣the', it sees six tokens: the control sequence '\hfill', comma, space, 't', 'h', 'e'. The space after '\hfill' ends the control sequence and is absorbed by TeX when it scans the control sequence. (For the text '\hfill,␣the', on the other hand, the comma both ends the control sequence and counts as a character in its own right.)

- A control symbol is a control sequence consisting of an escape character followed by any character other than a letter—even a space or an end of line. A control symbol is self-delimited, i.e., TeX knows where it ends without having to look at what character comes after it. The character after a control symbol is never absorbed by the control symbol.

See page 12 for more information about spaces after control sequences.

   TeX provides a great many predefined control sequences. The primitive control sequences are built into the TeX computer program and thus are available in all forms of TeX. Other predefined control sequences are provided by plain TeX, the form of TeX described in this book.

   You can augment the predefined control sequences with ones of your own, using commands such as \def and \let to define them. Section 12 of this book contains a collection of control sequence definitions that you may find useful. In addition, your computing facility may be able to provide a collection of locally developed TeX macros.

control symbol. A *control symbol* is a control sequence that consists of an escape character followed by any character other than a letter—even a space or end of line.

control word. A *control word* is a control sequence that consists of an escape character followed by one or more letters.[4] TeX ignores any spaces or ends-of-line that follow a control word, except to note that they end the control word.

decimal constant. See "number" (p. 82).

delimiter. A *delimiter* is a character that is intended to be used as a visible boundary of a math formula. The essential property of a delimiter is that TeX can adjust its size according to the vertical size (height plus depth) of the subformula. However, TeX performs the adjustment only if the delimiter appears in a "delimiter context", namely, as an argument to one of the commands `\left`, `\right`, `\overwithdelims`, `\atopwith-delims`, or `\abovewithdelims` (see pp. 201, 204). The delimiter contexts also include any argument to a macro that uses the argument in a delimiter context.

For example, the left and right parentheses are delimiters. If you use parentheses in a delimiter context around a formula, TeX makes the parentheses big enough to enclose the box that contains the formula (as long as the fonts you're using have big enough parentheses). For example:

```
$$ \left( a \over b \right) $$
```

yields:

$$\left(\frac{a}{b}\right)$$

Here TeX has made the parentheses big enough to accommodate the fraction. But if you write, instead:

```
$$({a \over b})$$
```

you'll get:

$$(\frac{a}{b})$$

Since the parentheses aren't in a delimiter context, they are *not* enlarged.

Delimiters come in pairs: an opening delimiter at the left of the subformula and a closing delimiter at its right. You can explicitly choose a larger height for a delimiter with the commands `\bigl`, `\bigr`, and their relatives (p. 211).[5] For instance, in order to get the displayed formula:

$$\bigl(f(x) - x\bigr)\bigl(f(y) - y\bigr)$$

---

[4] A "letter" here has the strict meaning of a character with category code 11.

[5] Plain TeX defines the various `\big` commands by using `\left` and `\right` to provide a delimiter context. It sets the size by constructing an empty formula with the desired height.

in which the outer parentheses are a little bigger than the inner ones, you should write:

```
$$\bigl( f(x) - x \bigr) \bigl( f(y) - y \bigr)$$
```

The 22 plain TeX delimiters, shown at their normal size, are:

$$( ) [ ] \{ \} \lfloor \rfloor \lceil \rceil \langle \rangle / \backslash \mid \| \uparrow \downarrow \Updownarrow \Uparrow \Downarrow \updownarrow$$

Here they are at the largest size provided explicitly by plain TeX (the \Biggl, \Biggr, etc., versions):

$$\Biggl(\Biggr) \Biggl[\Biggr] \Biggl\{ \Biggr\} \Biggl\lfloor \Biggr\rfloor \Biggl\lceil \Biggr\rceil \Biggl\langle \Biggr\rangle \Big/ \Big\backslash \Biggl\| \Biggl| \Biggl\downarrow \Biggl\updownarrow \Biggl\uparrow \Biggl\Updownarrow \Biggl\Downarrow$$

The delimiters (except for '(', ')', and '/') are among the symbols listed on pages 191–192. They are listed in one place on page 146 of *The TeXbook*.

A delimiter can belong to any class. For a delimiter that you enlarge with \bigl, \bigr, etc., the class is determined by the command: "opener" for l-commands, "closer" for r-commands, "relation" for m-commands, and "ordinary symbol" for g-commands, e.g., \Big.

You can obtain a delimiter in two different ways:

(1) You can make a character be a delimiter by assigning it a nonnegative delimiter code (see below) with the \delcode command (p. 251). Thereafter the character acts as a delimiter whenever you use it in a delimiter context.[6]

(2) You can produce a delimiter explicitly with the \delimiter command (p. 204), in analogy to the way that you can produce an ordinary character with the \char command or a math character with the \mathchar command. The \delimiter command uses the same delimiter codes that are used in a \delcode table entry, but with an extra digit in front to indicate a class. It's rare to use \delimiter outside of a macro definition.

A delimiter code tells TeX how to search for an appropriate output character to represent a delimiter. The rules for this search are rather complicated (see pages 156 and 442 of *The TeXbook*). A complete understanding of these rules requires knowing about the organization of font metrics files, a topic that is not just beyond the scope of this book but beyond the scope of *The TeXbook* as well.

In essence the search works like this. The delimiter code specifies a "small" output character and a "large" output character by providing a font position and a font family for each (see p. 251). Using this information, TeX can find (or construct) larger and larger versions of the delimiter. TeX first tries different sizes (from small to large) of the

---

[6] It's possible to use a character with a nonnegative delimiter code in a context where it isn't a delimiter. In this case TeX doesn't perform the search; instead it just uses the character in the ordinary way (see page 156 of *The TeXbook*).

"small" character in the "small" font and then different sizes (also from small to large) of the "large" character in the "large" font, seeking one whose height plus depth is sufficiently large. If none of the characters it finds are large enough, it uses the largest one that it finds. It's possible that the small character, the large character, or both have been left unspecified (indicated by a zero in the appropriate part of the delimiter code). If only one character has been specified, TeX uses that one. If neither has been specified, it replaces the delimiter by a space of width `\nulldelimiterspace`.

demerits. TeX uses demerits as a measure of how undesirable a line is when it's breaking a paragraph into lines (see "line break", p. 74). The demerits of a line are affected both by the badness of the line and by penalties associated with the line. TeX's goal in choosing a particular arrangement of lines is to minimize the total demerits for the paragraph, which it computes by adding up the demerits for the individual lines. See pages 97–98 of *The TeXbook* for the details of how TeX breaks a paragraph into lines. TeX does not use demerits when it's choosing page breaks; instead, it uses a similar measure known as the "cost" of a particular page break.

depth. The *depth* of a box is the distance that the box extends below its baseline.

dimension. A *dimension* specifies a distance, that is, a linear measure of space. You use dimensions to specify sizes of things, such as the length of a line. Printers in English-speaking countries traditionally measure distance in points and picas, while printers in continental Europe traditionally measure distance in didôt points and ciceros. You can use these units or others, such as inches, that may be more familiar to you. The font-independent units of measure that TeX understands are:

pt	point (72.27 points = 1 inch)
pc	pica (1 pica = 12 points)
bp	big point (72 big points = 1 inch)
in	inch
cm	centimeter (2.54 centimeters = 1 inch)
mm	millimeter (10 millimeters = 1 centimeter)
dd	didôt point (1157 didôt points = 1238 points)
cc	cicero (1 cicero = 12 didôt points)
sp	scaled point (65536 scaled points = 1 point)

Two additional units of measure are associated with every font: 'ex', a vertical measure usually about the height of the letter 'x' in the font, and 'em', a horizontal measure usually equal to the point size of the font and about the width of the letter 'M' in the font. Finally, TeX provides three "infinite" units of measure: 'fil', 'fill', and 'filll', in increasing order of strength.

A dimension is written as a factor, i.e, a multiplier, followed by a unit of measure. The factor can be either a whole number or a decimal constant containing a decimal point or decimal comma. The factor can be preceded by a plus or minus sign, so a dimension can be positive or negative. The unit of measure must be there, even if the number is zero. Spaces between the number and the unit of measure are permitted but not required. You'll find a precise definition of a dimension on page 270 of *The TEXbook*. Here are some examples of dimensions:

```
5.9in     0pt     -2,5 pc     2fil
```

The last of these represents a first-order infinite distance.

An infinite distance outweighs any finite distance or any weaker infinite distance. If you add `10in` to `.001fil`, you get `.001fil`; if you add `2fil` to `-1fill` you get `-1fill`; and so forth. TEX accepts infinite distances only when you are specifying the stretch and shrink of glue.

TEX multiplies all dimensions in your document by a magnification factor $f/1000$, where f is the value of the `\mag` parameter. Since the default value of `\mag` is 1000, the normal case is that your document is typeset just as specified. You can specify a dimension as it will be measured in the final document independent of magnification by putting 'true' in front of the unit. For instance, '`\kern 8 true pt`' produces a kern of 8 points whatever the magnification.

display math. The term *display math* refers to a math formula that TEX places on a line by itself with extra space above and below so as to set it off from the surrounding text. A display math formula is enclosed by '`$$`'s. TEX reads display math in display math mode.

escape character. An *escape character* introduces a control sequence. The escape character in plain TEX is the backslash (\). You can change the escape character from c_1 to c_2 by reassigning the category codes of c_1 and c_2 with the `\catcode` command (p. 251). You can also define additional escape characters similarly. If you want to typeset material containing literal escape characters, you must either (a) define a control sequence that stands for the printed escape character or (b) temporarily disable the escape character by changing its category code, using the method shown on page 277. The definition:

```
\def\\{$\backslash$}
```

is one way of creating a control sequence that stands for '\' (a backslash typeset in a math font).

You can use the `\escapechar` parameter (p. 226) to specify how the escape character is represented in synthesized control sequences, e.g., those created by `\string` and `\message`.

family. A *family* is a group of three related fonts used when TEX is in math mode. Outside of math mode, families have no effect. The three fonts in a family are used for normal symbols (text size), subscripts and superscripts (script size), and sub-subscripts, super-superscripts, etc. (scriptscript size). For example, the numeral '2' set in these three fonts would give you '2', '₂', and '₂' (in plain TEX). Ordinarily you would set up the three fonts in a family as different point sizes of the same typeface, but nothing prevents you from using different typefaces for the three fonts as well or using the same font twice in a family.

TEX provides for up to sixteen families, numbered 0–15. For example, family 0 in plain TEX consists of 10-point roman for text, 7-point roman for script, and 5-point roman for scriptscript. Plain TEX also defines family 1 to consist of math italic fonts and reserves families 2 and 3 for special symbols and math extensions respectively.[7] If you need to define a family for yourself, you should use the `\newfam` command (p. 244) to get the number of a family that isn't in use, and the `\textfont`, `\scriptfont`, and `\scriptscriptfont` commands (p. 210) to assign fonts to that family.

file. A *file* is a stream of information that TEX interprets or creates. Files are managed by the operating system that supervises your TEX run. TEX deals with files in four different contexts:

(1) A "source file" is one that TEX reads with its "eyes" (see "anatomy of TEX", p. 46) and interprets according to its ordinary rules. Your primary input file—the one you specify after '`**`' or on the command line when you invoke TEX—is a source file, and so is any file that you call for with an `\input` command (p. 247).

(2) A "result file" is one that contains the results of running TEX. A TEX run creates two result files: the `.dvi` file and the log file. The `.dvi` file contains the information needed to print your document; the log file contains a record of what happened during the run, including any error messages that TEX generated. If your primary source file is named `screed.tex`, your `.dvi` file and log file will be named `screed.dvi` and `screed.log`.[8]

(3) To read from a file with the `\read` command (p. 248) you need to associate the file with an input stream. You can have up to 16 input streams active at once, numbered 0–15. The `\read` command reads a single line and makes it the value of a designated control sequence, so reading with `\read` is very different from reading with `\input` (which brings in an entire file). TEX takes any input stream number

---

[7] Families 2 and 3 are special in that their font metric files must include parameters for math spacing.

[8] This is the usual convention, but particular implementations of TEX are free to change it.

not between 0 and 15 to refer to the terminal, so '\read16', say, reads the next line that you type at the terminal.

(4) To write to a file with the \write command (p. 249) you need to associate the file with an output stream. You can have up to 16 output streams active at once, numbered 0–15. Input and output streams are independent. Anything sent to an output stream with a negative number goes to the log file; anything sent to an output stream with a number greater than 15 goes both to the log file and to the terminal. Thus '\write16', say, writes a line on the terminal and also sends that line to the log file.

You must open a stream file before you can use it. An input stream file is opened with an \openin command (p. 247) and an output stream file is opened with an \openout command (p. 249). For tidiness you should close a stream file when you're done with it, although TeX will do that at the end of the run if you don't. The two commands for closing a stream file are \closein (p. 248) and \closeout (p. 249). An advantage of closing a stream when you're done with it is that you can then reuse the stream for a different file. Doing this can be essential when you're reading a long sequence of files.

Although you can assign numbers yourself to input and output streams, it's better to do it with the \newread and \newwrite (p. 244) commands. You can have more than one stream associated with a particular file, but you'll get (probably undiagnosed) garbage unless all of the streams are input streams. Associating more than one stream with an input file can be useful when you want to use the same input file for two different purposes.

TeX ordinarily defers the actions of opening, writing to, or closing an output stream until it ships out a page with \shipout (see page 227 of *The TeXbook* for the details). This behavior applies even to messages written to the terminal with \write. But you can get TeX to perform an action on an output stream immediately by preceding the action command with \immediate (p. 250). For example:

```
\immediate\write16{Do not pass GO! Do not collect $200!}
```

file name. A *file name* names a file that is known to the operating system that in turn supervises your TeX run. The syntax of a file name does *not* follow the usual rules of TeX syntax, and in fact it is different in different implementations of TeX. In particular, most TeX implementations consider a file name to be terminated by a blank or an end of line. Thus TeX is likely to misinterpret '{\input chapter2}' by taking the right brace as part of the file name. As a general rule, you should follow a file name by a blank or the end of the line as in '{\input chapter2␣}'.

font. A *font* in TEX is a collection of up to 256 output characters, usually having the same typeface design, style (roman, italic, bold, condensed, etc.), and point size.[9] The Computer Modern fonts that generally come with TEX have only 128 characters. The colophon on the last page of this book describes the typefaces that we used to set this book.

For instance, here is the alphabet in the Palatino Roman 10 point font:

ABCDEFGHIJKLMNOPQRSTUVWXYZ
abcdefghijklmnopqrstuvwxyz

And here it is in the Computer Modern Bold Extended 12 point font:

ABCDEFGHIJKLMNOPQRSTUVWXYZ
abcdefghijklmnopqrstuvwxyz

The characters in a font are numbered. The numbering usually agrees with the ASCII numbering for those characters that exist in the ASCII character set. The code table for each font indicates what the character with code n looks like in that font. Some fonts, such as the ones used for mathematical symbols, have no letters at all in them. You can produce a box containing the character numbered n, typeset in the current font, by writing '`\char` n' (p. 99).

In order to use a font in your document, you must first name it with a control sequence and load it. Thereafter you can select it by typing that control sequence whenever you want to use it. Plain TEX provides a number of fonts that are already named and loaded.

You name and load a font as a single operation, using a command such as '`\font\twelvebf=cmbx12`'. Here '`\twelvebf`' is the control sequence that you use to name the font and '`cmbx12`' identifies the font metrics file `cmbx12.tfm` in your computer's file system. You then can start to use the font by typing '`\twelvebf`'. After that, the font will be in effect until either (a) you select another font or (b) you terminate the group, if any, in which you started the font. For example, the input:

```
{\twelvebf white rabbits like carrots}
```

will cause the `cmbx12` font to be in effect just for the text '`white rabbits like carrots`'.

You can use TEX with fonts other than Computer Modern (look at the example on page 34 and at the page headers). The files for such fonts need to be installed in your computer's file system in a place where TEX can find them. TEX and its companion programs generally need two files for each font: one to give its metrics (`cmbx12.tfm`, for example) and another to give the shape of the characters (`cmbx12.pk`, for example). TEX itself uses only the metrics file. Another program, the device driver, converts

---

[9] Plain TEX uses a special font for constructing math symbols in which the characters have different sizes. Other special fonts are often useful for applications such as typesetting logos.

the `.dvi` file produced by TeX to a form that your printer or other output device can handle. The driver uses the shape file (if it exists).

The font metrics file contains the information that TeX needs in order to allocate space for each typeset character. Thus it includes the size of each character, the ligatures and kerns that pertain to sequences of adjacent characters, and so on. What the metrics file *doesn't* include is any information about the shapes of the characters in the font.

The shape (pixel) file may be in any of several formats. The extension part of the name (the part after the dot) tells the driver which format the shape file is in. For example, `cmbx12.pk` might be the shape file for font `cmbx12` in packed format, while `cmbx12.gf` might be the shape file for font `cmbx12` in generic font format. A shape file may not be needed for a font that's resident in your output device.

footer. A *footer* is material that TeX puts at the bottom of every page, below the text of that page. The default footer in plain TeX is a centered page number. Ordinarily a footer consists of a single line, which you can set by assigning a token list to `\footline` (p. 143). See page 274 for a method of producing multiline footers.

format file. A *format file* is a file that contains an image of TeX's memory in a form in which it can be reloaded quickly. A format file can be created with the `\dump` command (p. 263). The image contains a complete record of the definitions (of fonts, macros, etc.) that were present when the dump took place. By using `virtex`, a special "virgin" form of TeX, you can then reload the format file at high speed and continue in the same state that TeX was in at the time of the dump. The advantage of a format file over an ordinary input file containing the same information is that TeX can load it much faster.

Format files can only be created by `initex`, another special form of TeX intended just for that purpose. Neither `virtex` nor `initex` has any facilities other than the primitives built into the TeX program itself.

A preloaded form of TeX is one that has a format file already loaded and is ready to accept user input. The form of TeX that's called `tex` often has the plain TeX definitions preloaded. (Plain TeX is ordinarily available in two other forms as well: as a format file and as a TeX source file. In some environments, `tex` is equivalent to calling `virtex` and then loading `plain`.) Creating preloaded forms of TeX requires a special program; it cannot be done using only the facilities of TeX itself.

global. A *global* definition is effective until the end of the document or until it is overridden by another definition, even when it occurs within a group. Thus a global definition is unaffected by group boundaries. You can make any definition global by prefixing it with the `\global` command (p. 228) unless `\globaldefs` (p. 228) is negative.

There's a special way of making a macro definition global. Normally you define a macro using either the `\def` command or the `\edef` command (p. 230). If you use `\gdef` or `\xdef` instead of `\def` and `\edef` respectively, the macro definition will be global. That is, '`\gdef`' is equivalent to '`\global\def`' and '`\xdef`' is equivalent to '`\global\edef`'.

glue.   *Glue* is blank space that can stretch or shrink. Glue gives TEX the flexibility that it needs in order to produce handsome documents. Glue comes in two flavors: horizontal glue and vertical glue. Horizontal glue occurs within horizontal lists, while vertical glue occurs within vertical lists. You can produce a glue item either implicitly, e.g., with an interword space, or explicitly, e.g., with the `\hskip` command. TEX itself produces many glue items as it typesets your document. We'll just describe horizontal glue—vertical glue is analogous.

When TEX assembles a list of boxes and glue into a larger unit, it adjusts the size of the glue to meet the space requirements of the larger unit. For instance, TEX ensures that the right margin of a page is uniform by adjusting the horizontal glue within lines. Similarly, it ensures that different pages have the same bottom margin by adjusting the glue between blocks of text such as paragraphs and math displays (where the change is least likely to be conspicuous).

A glue item has a natural space—the size it "wants to be". Glue also has two other attributes: its stretch and its shrink. You can produce a specific amount of horizontal glue with the `\hskip` command (p. 155). The command `\hskip 6pt plus 2pt minus 3pt` produces a horizontal glue item whose natural size is 6 points, whose stretch is 2 points, and whose shrink is 3 points. Similarly, you can produce a specific amount of vertical glue with the `\vskip` command (p. 155).

The best way to understand what stretch and shrink are about is to see an example of glue at work. Suppose you're constructing an hbox from three boxes and two glue items, as in this picture:

box	*glue*	*box*	*glue*	*box*
width 4	size 6 / stretch 4 / shrink 1 / width 6	width 5	size 10 / stretch 8 / shrink 3 / width 10	width 4

←—————————————— width 29 ——————————————→

The units of measurement here could be points, millimeters, or anything else. If the hbox is allowed to assume its natural width, then each glue item in the box also assumes its natural width. The total width of the hbox is then the sum of the widths of its parts, namely, 29 units.

Next, suppose that the hbox is required to be wider than 29 units, say 35 units. This could happen, for example, if the hbox is required to occupy an entire line and the line width is 35 units. Since the boxes can't change their width, TEX produces the necessary extra space by making the glue items wider. The picture now looks like this:

box	*glue*	*box*	*glue*	*box*
	size 6 stretch 4 shrink 2		size 10 stretch 8 shrink 6	
width 4	width 8	width 5	width 14	width 4

←——————————————— width 35 ———————————————→

The glue items don't become wider equally; they became wider in proportion to their stretch. Since the second glue item has twice as much stretch as the first one, it gets wider by four units while the first glue item gets wider by only two units. Glue can be stretched as far as necessary, although TEX is somewhat reluctant to stretch it beyond the amount of stretch given in its definition.

Finally, suppose that the hbox is required to be narrower than 29 units, say 25 units. In this case TEX makes the glue items narrower. The picture looks like this:

box	*glue*	*box*	*glue*	*box*
	size 6 stretch 4 shrink 2		size 10 stretch 8 shrink 6	
width 4	width 5	width 5	width 7	width 4

←————————— width 25 —————————→

The glue items become narrower in proportion to their shrink. The first glue item becomes narrower by one unit, while the second glue item becomes narrower by three units. Glue cannot shrink by a distance less than the amount of shrink given in its definition even though the distance it can stretch is unlimited. In this important sense the shrink and the stretch behave differently.

A good rule of thumb for glue is to set the natural size to the amount of space that looks best, the stretch to the largest amount of space that TEX can add before the document starts to look bad, and the shrink to the largest amount of space that TEX can take away before the document starts to look bad. You may need to set the values by experiment.

You can produce glue that is infinitely stretchable by specifying its stretch in units of 'fil', 'fill', or 'filll'. Glue measured in 'fill' is infinitely more stretchable than glue measured in 'fil', and glue measured in 'filll' is infinitely more stretchable than glue measured in 'fill'. You should rarely have any need for 'filll' glue. Glue whose stretch is 2fil has twice as much stretch as glue whose stretch is `1fil`, and similarly for the other kinds of infinitely stretchable glue.

When TeX is apportioning extra space among glue items, the infinitely stretchable ones, if there are any, get all of it. Infinitely stretchable glue is particularly useful for setting text flush left, flush right, or centered:

- To set text flush left, put infinitely stretchable horizontal glue to the right of it. That glue will consume all the extra space that's available on the line. You can use the `\leftline` command (p. 108) or the `\raggedright` command (p. 116) to do this.
- To set text flush right, put infinitely stretchable horizontal glue to the left of it. As before, that glue will consume all the extra space on the line. You can use the `\rightline` command (p. 108) to do this.
- To set centered text, put identical infinitely stretchable horizontal glue items on both sides of it. These two glue items will divide all the extra space on the line equally between them. You can use the `\centerline` command (p. 108) to do this.

You can also specify infinitely shrinkable glue in a similar way. Infinitely shrinkable glue can act as negative space. Note that `fil`, etc., can be used only to specify the stretch and shrink of glue—they can't be used to specify its natural size.

group. A _group_ is a part of your manuscript that TeX treats as a unit. You indicate a group by enclosing it in the braces '{' and '}' (or any other characters with the appropriate category codes).

The most important property of a group is that any nonglobal definition or assignment that you make inside a group disappears when the group ends. For instance, if you write:

```
Please don't pour {\it any} more tea into my hat.
```

the `\it` control sequence causes TeX to set the word 'any' in italic type but does not affect the rest of the text. As another example, if you use the `\hsize` parameter (p. 114) to change the line length within a group, the line length reverts to its previous value once TeX has gotten past the group.

Groups are also useful as a way of controlling spacing. For instance, if you write:

```
\TeX for the Impatient and the Outpatient too.
```

you'll get:

TeXfor the Impatient and the Outpatient too.

since the control sequence `\TeX` (which produces the TeX logo) absorbs the following space. What you probably want is:

TeX for the Impatient and the Outpatient too.

One way to get it is to enclose '`\TeX`' in a group:

`{\TeX} for the Impatient and the Outpatient too.`

The right brace prevents the control sequence from absorbing the space.

hbox.   An *hbox* (horizontal box) is a box that TeX constructs by placing
the items of a horizontal list one after another, left to right. An hbox,
taken as a unit, is neither inherently horizontal nor inherently vertical,
i.e., it can appear as an item of either a horizontal list or a vertical list.
You can construct an hbox with the `\hbox` command (p. 160).

header.   A *header* is material that TeX puts at the top of every page,
above the text of that page. The header for a simple report might consist
of the title on the left side of the page and the text "Page *n*" on the right
side of the page. Ordinarily a header consists of a single line, which you
can set by assigning a token list to `\headline` (p. 143). The default plain
TeX header is blank. It's possible to produce multiline headers too; see
page 274 for how to do it.

height.   The *height* of a box is the distance that the box extends above
its baseline.

horizontal list.   A *horizontal list* is a list of items that TeX has produced
while it is in one of its horizontal modes, i.e., assembling either a paragraph or an hbox. See "horizontal mode" below.

horizontal mode.   When TeX is assembling a paragraph or an hbox, it is
in one of two *horizontal modes*: ordinary horizontal mode for assembling
paragraphs and restricted horizontal mode for assembling hboxes. Whenever TeX is in a horizontal mode its stomach (see "anatomy of TeX", p. 46)
is constructing a horizontal list of items (boxes, glue, penalties, etc.). TeX
typesets the items in the list one after another, left to right.

   A horizontal list can't contain any items produced by inherently vertical
commands, e.g., `\vskip`.

  - If TeX is assembling a horizontal list in ordinary horizontal mode and
    encounters an inherently vertical command, TeX ends the paragraph
    and enters vertical mode.
  - If TeX is assembling a horizontal list in restricted horizontal mode
    and encounters an inherently vertical command, it complains.

   Two commands that you might at first think are inherently horizontal
are in fact inherently vertical: `\halign` (p. 178) and `\hrule` (p. 172). See
page 286 of *The TeXbook* for a list of the inherently vertical commands.

   You should be aware of a subtle but important property of restricted
horizontal mode: *you can't enter restricted horizontal mode when you're in*

ordinary horizontal mode. What this means in practice is that when TEX is assembling an hbox it won't handle paragraph-like text, i.e., text for which it does line breaking. You can get around this restriction by enclosing the paragraph-like text in a vbox within the hbox. The same method works if you want to put, say, a horizontal alignment inside an hbox.

hyphenation. TEX automatically hyphenates words as it is processing your document. TEX is not eager to insert hyphens, preferring instead to find good line breaks by adjusting the spacing between words and moving words from one line to another. TEX is clever enough to understand hyphens that are already in words.

You can control TEX's hyphenation in several ways:

- You can tell TEX to allow a hyphen in a particular place by inserting a discretionary hyphen with the \- command (p. 126).
- You can tell TEX how to hyphenate particular words throughout your document with the \hyphenation command (p. 127).
- You can enclose a word in an hbox, thus preventing TEX from hyphenating it.
- You can set the value of penalties such as \hyphenpenalty (p. 125).

If a word contains an explicit or discretionary hyphen, TEX will never break it elsewhere.

input stream.   See "file" (p. 62).

insertion.   An *insertion* is a vertical list containing material to be inserted into a page when TEX has finished building that page.[10] Examples of such insertions are footnotes and figures. The plain TEX commands for creating insertions are \footnote, \topinsert, \midinsert, and \pageinsert, as well as the primitive \insert command itself (pp. 145–148). TEX's mechanism for handling insertions is rather complicated; see pages 122–125 of *The TEXbook* for the details.

interline glue.   *Interline glue* is the glue that TEX inserts in front of every box in a vertical list except for the first one. The interline glue is ordinarily specified so as to maintain a constant distance between the baselines of the boxes. Its value is jointly determined by the \baselineskip, \lineskip, and \lineskiplimit parameters (p. 133).

---

[10] TEX itself doesn't insert the material—it just makes the material available to the output routine, which is then responsible for transferring it to the composed page. The only immediate effect of the \insert command (p. 147) is to change TEX's page break calculations so that it will leave room on the page for the inserted material. Later, when TEX actually breaks the page, it divides the inserted material into two groups: the material that fits on the current page and the material that doesn't. The material that fits on the page is placed into box registers, one per insertion, and the material that doesn't fit is carried over to the next page. This procedure allows TEX to do such things as distributing parts of a long footnote over several consecutive pages.

item. The term *item* is often used to refer to a component of a horizontal, vertical, or math list, i.e., a list of items that TeX is building while it is in a horizontal, vertical, or math mode.

justified text. *Justified text* is text that has been typeset so that both margins are even. Unjustified text, on the other hand, has been typeset with "ragged" margins on one or both sides. Documents typed on old-fashioned typewriters almost always have ragged right margins. Although documents produced by TeX are justified by default, you can if you wish produce documents (or sequences of lines) that have ragged right—or ragged left—margins. You can also get TeX to center a sequence of lines, thus making both margins ragged. You can use the `\leftskip`, `\rightskip`, and `\raggedright` commands (pp. 115, 116) for these purposes.

When TeX is producing justified text, it usually needs to stretch or shrink the glue within each line to make the margins come out even. When TeX is producing unjustified text, on the other hand, it usually leaves the glue within each line at its natural width. Many typographers prefer unjustified text because its interword spacing is more uniform.

kern. A *kern* indicates a change to the normal spacing between the items of a vertical or horizontal list. A kern can be either positive or negative. By putting a positive kern between two items, you push them further apart by the amount of the kern. By putting a negative kern between two items, you bring them closer together by the amount of the kern. For instance, this text:

```
11\quad 1\kern1pt 1\quad 1\kern-.75pt 1
```

produces letter pairs that look like this:

11   11   11

You can use kerns in vertical mode to adjust the space between particular pairs of lines.

A kern of size d is very similar to a glue item that has size d and no stretch or shrink. Both the kern and the glue insert or remove space between neighboring items. The essential difference is that TeX considers two boxes with only kerns between them to be tied together. That is, TeX won't break a line or a page at a kern unless the kern is immediately followed by glue. Bear this difference in mind when you're deciding whether to use a kern or a glue item for a particular purpose.

TeX automatically inserts kerns between particular pairs of adjacent letters, thus adjusting the space between those letters and enhancing the appearance of your typeset document. For instance, the Computer Modern 10-point roman font contains a kern for the pair 'To' that brings the left edge of the 'o' under the 'T'. Without the kern, you'd get "Top" rather than "Top"—the difference is slight but noticeable. The metrics file (.tfm file) for each font specifies the placement and size of the kerns that TeX automatically inserts when it is setting text in that font.

leaders. You can use *leaders* to fill a space with copies of a pattern, e.g., to put repeated dots between a title and a page number in a table of contents. A leader is a single copy of the pattern. The specification of leaders contains three pieces of information:

(1) what a single leader is
(2) how much space needs to be filled
(3) how the copies of the pattern should be arranged within the space

TeX has three commands for specifying leaders: `\leaders`, `\cleaders`, and `\xleaders` (p. 174). The argument of each command specifies the leader. The command must be followed by glue; the size of the glue specifies how much space is to be filled. The choice of command determines how the leaders are arranged within the space.

Here's an example showing how `\leaders` works:

```
\def\dotting{\leaders\hbox to 1em{\hfil.\hfil}\hfil}
\line{The Political Process\dotting 18}
\line{Bail Bonds\dotting 26}
```

Here we've put the leaders and their associated glue into a macro definition so that we can conveniently use them in two places. This input produces:

The Political Process 18
Bail Bonds 26

The hbox following `\leaders` specifies the leader, namely, an hbox 1 em wide containing a dot at its center. The space is filled with copies of this box, effectively filling it with dots whose centers are 1 em apart. The following `\hfil` (the one at the end of the macro definition) is glue that specifies the space to be filled. In this case it's whatever space is needed to fill out the line. By choosing `\leaders` rather than `\cleaders` or `\xleaders` we've insured that the dots on different lines line up with each other.

In general, the space to be filled acts as a window on the repeated copies of the leader. TeX inserts as many copies as possible, but some space is usually left over—either because of where the leaders fall within the window or because the width of the window isn't an exact multiple of the width of the leader. The difference among the three commands is in how they arrange the leaders within the window and how they distribute any leftover space:

- For `\leaders`, TeX first produces a row of copies of the leader. It then aligns the start of this row with the left end of the innermost box B that is to contain the result of the `\leaders` command. In the two-line example on the above page, B is a box produced by `\line`. Those leaders that fit entirely in the window are placed into

B, and the leftover space at the left and right ends is left empty. The picture is like this:

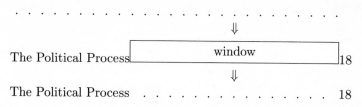

This procedure ensures that in the two-line example on the previous page, the dots in the two lines are vertically aligned (since the reference points of the hboxes produced by \line are vertically aligned).

- For \cleaders, TeX centers the leaders within the window by dividing the leftover space between the two ends of the window. The leftover space is always less than the width of a single leader.
- For \xleaders, TeX distributes the leftover space evenly within the window. In other words, if the leftover space is w and the leader is repeated n times, TeX puts space of width $w/(n+1)$ between adjacent leaders and at the two ends of the leaders. The effect is usually to spread out the leaders a little bit. The leftover space for \xleaders, like that for \cleaders, is always less than the width of a single leader.

So far we've assumed that the leaders consist of hboxes arranged horizontally. Two variations are possible:

(1) You can use a rule instead of an hbox for the leader. TeX makes the rule as wide as necessary to extend across the glue (and the three commands are equivalent).

(2) You can produce vertical leaders that run down the page by including them in a vertical list rather than a horizontal list. In this case you need vertical glue following the leaders.

See pages 223–225 of *The TeXbook* for the precise rules that TeX uses in typesetting leaders.

ligature.   A *ligature* is a single character that replaces a particular sequence of adjacent characters in a typeset document. For example, the word 'office' is typeset as "office", not "office", by high-quality typesetting systems. Knowledge of ligatures is built into the fonts that you use, so there's nothing explicit you need do in order to get TeX to produce them. (You could defeat the ligature in "office", as we did just above, by writing 'of{f}ice' in your input.) TeX is also capable of using its ligature mechanism to typeset the first or last letter of a word differently than the same letter as it would appear in the middle of a word. You can defeat this effect (if you ever encounter it) by using the \noboundary command (p. 101).

Sometimes you may need a ligature from a European language. TEX won't produce these automatically unless you're using a font designed for that language. A number of these ligatures, e.g., 'Æ', are available as commands (see "Letters and ligatures for European alphabets", p. 97).

line break. A *line break* is a place in your document where TEX ends a line as it typesets a paragraph. When TEX processes your document, it collects the contents of each paragraph in a horizontal list. When it has collected an entire paragraph, it analyzes the list to find what it considers to be the best possible line breaks. TEX associates "demerits" with various symptoms of unattractive line breaks—lines that have too much or too little space between words, consecutive lines that end in hyphens, and so forth. It then chooses the line breaks so as to minimize the total number of demerits. See pages 96–101 of *The TEXbook* for a full description of TEX's line-breaking rules.

You can control TEX's choice of line breaks in several ways:

- You can insert a penalty (p. 121) somewhere in the horizontal list that TEX builds as it forms a paragraph. A positive penalty discourages TEX from breaking the line there, while a negative penalty—a bonus, in other words—encourages TEX to break the line there. A penalty of 10000 or more prevents a line break, while a penalty of −10000 or less forces a line break. You can get the same effects with the `\break` and `\nobreak` commands (pp. 120, 121).
- You can tell TEX to allow a hyphen in a particular place by inserting a discretionary hyphen with the `\-` command (p. 126), or otherwise control how TEX hyphenates your document (see "hyphenation", p. 70).
- You can tell TEX to allow a line break after a solidus (/) between two words by inserting `\slash` (p. 122) between them, e.g., 'fur-longs\slash fortnight'.
- You can tell TEX not to break a line between two particular words by inserting a tie (~) between those words.
- You can adjust the penalties associated with line breaking by assigning different values to TEX's line-breaking parameters.
- You can enclose a word or sequence of words in an hbox, thus preventing TEX from breaking the line anywhere within the hbox.

It's useful to know the places where TEX can break a line:

- at glue, provided that:
  (1) the item preceding the glue is one of the following: a box, a discretionary item (e.g., a discretionary hyphen), the end of a math formula, a whatsit, or vertical material produced by `\mark` or `\vadjust` or `\insert`
  (2) the glue is not part of a math formula

When TEX breaks a line at glue, it makes the break at the left edge of the glue space and forgets about the rest of the glue.

- at a kern that's immediately followed by glue, provided that this kern isn't within a math formula
- at the end of a math formula that's immediately followed by glue
- at a penalty, even one within a math formula
- at a discretionary break

When TEX breaks a line, it discards any sequence of glue, kerns, and penalty items that follows the break point. If such a sequence is followed by the beginning of a math formula, it also discards any kern produced by the beginning of the formula.

list. A *list* is a sequence of items (boxes, glue, kerns, etc.) that comprise the contents of an hbox, a vbox, or a math formula. See "horizontal list" (p. 69), "vertical list" (p. 94).

log file. See "file" (p. 62).

macro. A *macro* is a definition that gives a name to a pattern of TEX input text.[11] The name can be either a control sequence or an active character. The pattern is called the "replacement text". The primary command for defining macros is the `\def` control sequence.

As a simple example, suppose that you have a document in which the sequence '$\cos \theta + i \sin \theta$' occurs many times. Instead of writing it out each time, you can define a macro for it:

```
\def\arctheta{\cos \theta + i \sin \theta}
```

Now whenever you need this sequence, you can just "call" the macro by writing '`\arctheta`' and you'll get it. For example, '`$e^{\arctheta}$`' will give you '$e^{\cos \theta + i \sin \theta}$'.

But the real power of macros lies in the fact that a macro can have parameters. When you call a macro that has parameters, you provide arguments that are substituted for those parameters. For example, suppose you write:

```
\def\arc#1{\cos #1 + i \sin #1}
```

The notation `#1` indicates the first parameter of the macro, which in this case has only one parameter. You now can produce a similar form, such as '$\cos 2t + i \sin 2t$', with the macro call '`\arc {2t}`'.

More generally, a macro can have up to nine parameters, which you indicate as '`#1`', '`#2`', etc. in the macro definition. TEX provides two kinds of parameters: delimited parameters and undelimited parameters. Briefly, a delimited parameter has an argument that's delimited, or ended, by a

---

[11] More precisely, the definition gives a name to a sequence of tokens.

specified sequence of tokens (the delimiter), while an undelimited parameter has an argument that doesn't need a delimiter to end it. First we'll explain how macros work when they have only undelimited parameters, and then we'll explain how they work when they have delimited parameters.

If a macro has only undelimited parameters, those parameters must appear one after another in the macro definition *with nothing between them or between the last parameter and the left brace in front of the replacement text.* A call on such a macro consists of the macro name followed by the arguments of the call, one for each parameter. Each argument is either:

- a single token other than a left or right brace, or
- a sequence of tokens enclosed between a left brace and a matching right brace.[12]

When TEX encounters a macro, it expands the macro in its gullet (see "anatomy of TEX", p. 46) by substituting each argument for the corresponding parameter in the replacement text. The resulting text may contain other macro calls. When TEX encounters such an embedded macro call, it expands that call immediately without looking at what follows the call.[13] When TEX's gullet gets to a primitive command that cannot be further expanded, TEX passes that command to TEX's stomach. The order of expansion is sometimes critical, so in order to help you understand it we'll give you an example of TEX at work.

Suppose you provide TEX with the following input:

```
\def\a#1#2{\b#2#1\kern 2pt #1}
\def\b{bb}
\def\c{\char49 cc}
\def\d{dd}
\a\c{e\d} % Call on \a.
```

Then the argument corresponding to #1 is \c, and the argument corresponding to #2 is e\d. TEX expands the macro call in the following steps:

```
\b e\d\c\kern 2pt \c
bbe\d\c\kern 2pt \c
\d\c\kern 2pt \c   ('b', 'b', 'e' sent to stomach)
dd\c\kern 2pt \c
\c\kern 2pt \c   ('d', 'd' sent to stomach)
\char49 cc\kern 2pt \c
\c   ('\char', '4', '9', 'c', 'c', '\kern', '2', 'p', 't' sent to stomach)
\char49 cc
('\char49', 'c', 'c' sent to stomach)
```

---

12 The argument can have nested pairs of braces within it, and each of these pairs can indicate either a group or a further macro argument.

13 In computer science terminology, the expansion is "depth first" rather than "breadth first". Note that you can modify the order of expansion with commands such as `\expandafter`.

Note that the letters 'b', 'c', 'd', and 'e' and the control sequences '\kern' and '\char' are all primitive commands that cannot be expanded further.

A macro can also have "delimited parameters", which can be mixed with the undelimited ones in any combination. The idea of a delimited parameter is that TeX finds the corresponding argument by looking for a certain sequence of tokens that marks the end of the argument—the delimiter. That is, when TeX is looking for such an argument, it takes the argument to be all the tokens from TeX's current position up to but not including the delimiter.

You indicate a delimited parameter by writing '#n' (n must be between 0 and 9) followed by one or more tokens that act as the delimiter. The delimiter extends up to the next '#' or '{'—which makes sense since '#' starts another parameter and '{' starts the replacement text.

The delimiter can't be '#' or '{', so you can tell a delimited parameter from an undelimited one by looking at what comes after it.

If the character after the parameter is '#' or '{', you've got an undelimited parameter; otherwise you've got a delimited one. Note the difference in arguments for the two kinds of parameters—an undelimited parameter is matched either by a single token or by a sequence of tokens enclosed in braces, while a delimited parameter is matched by any number of tokens, even zero.

An example of a macro that uses two delimited parameters is:

```
\def\diet#1 #2.{On #1 we eat #2!}
```

Here the first parameter is delimited by a single space and the second parameter is delimited by a period. If you write:

```
\diet Tuesday turnips.
```

you'll get the text "On Tuesday we eat turnips!". But if the delimiting tokens are enclosed in a group, TeX doesn't consider them as delimiting. So if you write:

```
\diet {Sunday mornings} pancakes.
```

you'll get the text 'On Sunday mornings we eat pancakes!' even though there's a space between 'Sunday' and 'morning'. When you use a space as a delimiter, an end-of-line character ordinarily also delimits the argument since TeX converts the end-of-line to a space before the macro mechanism ever sees it.

Once in a while you might need to define a macro that has '#' as a meaningful character within it. You're most likely to need to do this when you're defining a macro that in turn defines a second macro. What then do you do about the parameters of the second macro to avoid getting TeX confused? The answer is that you write two '#'s for every one that you want when the first macro is expanded. For example, suppose you write the macro definition:

```
\def\first#1{\def\second##1{#1/##1}}
```

Then the call '\first{One}' defines '\second' as:

```
\def\second#1{One/#1}
```

and the subsequent call '\second{Two}' produces the text 'One/Two'.

A number of commands provide additional ways of defining macros (see pp. 230–241). For the complete rules pertaining to macros, see Chapter 20 of *The TeXbook*.

magnification. When TeX typesets your document, it multiplies all dimensions by a magnification factor $f/1000$, where f is the value of the \mag parameter (p. 223). Since the default value of \mag is 1000, the normal case is that your document is typeset just as specified. Increasing the magnification is often useful when you're typesetting a document that will later be photoreduced.

You can also apply magnification to a single font so as to get a smaller or larger version of that font than its "design size". You need to provide the device driver with a shape file (see "font", p. 64) for each magnification of a font that you're using—unless the fonts are built into your printer and your device driver knows about them. When you're defining a font with the \font command (p. 221), you can specify a magnification with the word 'scaled'. For example:

```
\font\largerbold = cmbx10 scaled 2000
```

defines '\largerbold' as a font that is twice as big as cmbx10 (Computer Modern Bold Extended 10-point) and has the character shapes uniformly enlarged by a factor of 2.

Many computer centers find it convenient to provide fonts scaled by a ratio of 1.2, corresponding to magnification values of 1200, 1440, etc. TeX has special names for these values: '\magstep1' for 1200, '\magstep2' for 1440, and so forth up to '\magstep5'. The special value '\magstephalf' corresponds to magnification by $\sqrt{1.2}$, which is visually halfway between '\magstep0' (no magnification) and '\magstep1'. For example:

```
\font\bigbold = cmbx10 scaled \magstephalf
```

You can specify a dimension as it will be measured in the final document independent of magnification by putting 'true' in front of the unit. For instance, '\kern 8 true pt' produces a kern of 8 points whatever the magnification.

margins. The margins of a page define a rectangle that normally contains the printed matter on the page. You can get TeX to print material outside of this rectangle, but only by taking some explicit action that moves the material there. TeX considers headers and footers to lie outside the margins.

The rectangle is defined in terms of its upper-left corner, its width, and its depth. The location of the upper-left corner is defined by the `\hoffset` and `\voffset` parameters (p. 140). The default is to place that corner one inch from the top and one inch from the left side of the page, corresponding to a value of zero for both `\hoffset` and `\voffset`.[14] The width of the rectangle is given by `\hsize` and the depth by `\vsize`.

The implications of these conventions are:

- The left margin is given by `\hoffset` + 1in.
- The right margin is given by the width of the paper minus `\hoffset` + 1in + `\hsize`.
- The top margin is given by `\voffset` + 1in.
- The bottom margin is given by the length of the paper minus `\voffset` + 1in + `\vsize`.

From this information you can see what parameters you need to change in order to change the margins.

Any changes that you make to `\hoffset`, `\voffset`, or `\vsize` become effective the next time TeX starts a page. In other words, if you change them within a page, the change will affect only the *following* pages. If you change `\hsize`, the change will become effective immediately.

mark. A *mark* is an item that you can insert into a horizontal, vertical, or math list and later recover from within your output routine. Marks are useful for purposes such as keeping track of topics to appear in page headers. Each mark has a list of tokens—the "mark text"—associated with it. The `\mark` command (p. 144) expects such a token list as its argument, and appends an item containing that token list (after expansion) to whatever list TeX is currently building. The `\topmark`, `\firstmark`, and `\botmark` commands (p. 144) can be used to retrieve various marks on a page. These commands are most often used in page headers and footers.

Here is a simplified example. Suppose you define a section heading macro as follows:

```
\def\section#1{\medskip{\bf#1}\smallskip\mark{#1}}
% #1 is the name of the section
```

---

[14] This seems to us to be an odd convention. It would have been more natural to have the $(0,0)$ point for `\hoffset` and `\voffset` be at the upper-left corner of the paper and to have set their default values to one inch.

This macro, when called, will produce a section heading in boldface and will also record the name of the section as a mark. You can now define the header for each printed page as follows:

```
\headline = {\ifodd\pageno \hfil\botmark\quad\folio
    \else \folio\quad\firstmark\hfil \fi}
```

Each even (left-hand) page will now have the page number followed by the name of the first section on that page, while each odd (right-hand) page will have the page number followed by the name of the last section on that page. Special cases, e.g., no sections starting on a page, will generally come out correctly because of how `\firstmark` and `\botmark` work.

When you split a page using the `\vsplit` command (p. 149) you can retrieve the mark texts of the first and last marks of the split-off portion with the `\splitfirstmark` and `\splitbotmark` commands (p. 144).

See pages 258–260 of *The TEXbook* for a more precise explanation of how to create and retrieve marks.

math mode. A *math mode* is a mode that TEX is in when it is building a math formula. TEX has two different math modes: text math mode for building a formula to be embedded within a line of text, and display math mode for building a formula to appear on a line by itself. You indicate text math mode by enclosing the formula in $'s, and display math mode by enclosing the formula in $$'s. An important property of both math modes is that *input spaces don't count*. See pages 290–293 of *The TEXbook* for details on how TEX responds to different commands in math mode.

mathcode. A *mathcode* is a number that TEX uses to identify and describe a math character, i.e., a character that has a particular role in a math formula. A mathcode conveys three pieces of information about a character: its font position, its family, and its class. Each of the 256 possible input characters has a mathcode, which is defined by the TEX program but can be changed.

TEX has sixteen families of fonts, numbered 0–15. Each family contains three fonts: one for text size, one for script size, and one for scriptscript size. TEX chooses the size of a particular character, and therefore its font, according to the context. The class of a character specifies its role in a formula (see page 154 of *The TEXbook*). For example, the equals sign '=' is in class 3 (Relation). TEX uses its knowledge of character classes when it is deciding how much space to put between different components of a math formula.

The best way to understand what mathcodes are all about is to see how TEX uses them. So we'll show you what TEX does with a character token t of category code 11 or 12 in a math formula:

(1) It looks up the character's mathcode.

(2) It determines a family f from the mathcode.

(3) It determines the size s from the context.

(4) It selects a font F by picking the font for size s in family f.

(5) It determines a character number n from the mathcode.

(6) It selects as the character c to be typeset the character at position n of font F.

(7) It adjusts the spacing around c according to the class of t and the surrounding context.

(8) It typesets the character c.

The context dependence in items (3) and (7) implies that TEX cannot typeset a math character until it has seen the entire formula containing the math character. For example, in the formula '`$a\over b$`', TEX doesn't know what size the '`a`' should be until it has seen the `\over`.

The mathcode of a character is encoded according to the formula $4096c + 256f + n$, where c is the class of the character, f is its family, and n is its ASCII character code within the family. You can change TEX's interpretation of an input character in math mode by assigning a value to the `\mathcode` table entry (p. 251) for that character. The character must have a category code of 11 (letter) or 12 (other) for TEX to look at its `\mathcode`.

You can define a mathematical character to have a "variable" family by giving it a class of 7. Whenever TEX encounters that character in a math formula, it takes the family of the character to be the current value of the `\fam` parameter (p. 210). A variable family enables you to specify the font of ordinary text in a math formula. For instance, if the roman characters are in family 0, the assignment `\fam = 0` will cause ordinary text in a math formula to be set in roman type rather than in something else like math italic type. If the value of `\fam` is not in the range from 0 to 15, TEX takes the value to be 0, thus making classes 0 and 7 equivalent. TEX sets `\fam` to -1 whenever it enters math mode.

mathematical unit. A *mathematical unit*, denoted by '`mu`', is a unit of distance that is used to specify glue in math formulas. See "muglue" (p. 82).

mode. When TEX is processing your input in its stomach (see "anatomy of TEX", p. 46), it is in one of six *modes*:

- ordinary horizontal mode (assembling a paragraph)
- restricted horizontal mode (assembling an hbox)
- ordinary vertical mode (assembling a page)
- internal vertical mode (assembling a vbox)
- text math mode (assembling a formula that appears in text)
- display math mode (assembling a formula that appears on a line by itself)

The mode describes the kind of entity that TEX is putting together.

Because you can embed one kind of entity within another, e.g., a vbox within a math formula, TeX keeps track not just of one mode but of a whole list of modes (what computer scientists call a "stack"). Suppose that TeX is in mode M and encounters something that puts it into a new mode M'. When it finishes its work in mode M', it resumes what it was doing in mode M.

muglue.   *Muglue* is a kind of glue that you can use only in math formulas. It is measured in `mu` (mathematical units). One `mu` is equal to $1/18$ em, where the size of an em is taken from family 2 of the math fonts. TeX automatically adjusts the size of muglue according to the context. For instance, a glue size of `2mu` is normally smaller within a subscript than it is within ordinary text. You must use the `\mskip` command to produce muglue. For example, '`\mskip 4mu plus 5mu`' produces mathematical glue with natural space of four `mu` and stretch of five `mu`.

number.   In TeX, a *number* is a positive or negative integer. You can write a number in TeX in four different ways:

(1) as an ordinary decimal integer, e.g., `52`
(2) as an octal number, e.g., `'14`
(3) as a hexadecimal number, e.g., `"FF0`
(4) as the code for an ASCII character, e.g., '`)` or '`\)`

Any of these forms can be preceded by '`+`' or '`-`'.

An octal number can have only the digits 0–7. A hexadecimal number can have digits 0–9 and A–F, representing values from 0 to 15. You can't, alas, use lowercase letters when you write a hexadecimal number. If you need an explanation of octal and hexadecimal numbers, you'll find one on pages 43–44 of *The TeXbook*.

A decimal, octal, or hexadecimal number ends at the first character that can't be part of the number. Thus a decimal number ends when TeX sees, say, a letter, even though a letter between '`A`' and '`F`' would not end a hexadecimal number. You can end a number with one or more spaces and TeX will ordinarily ignore them.[15]

The fourth form above specifies a number as the ASCII code for a character. TeX ignores spaces after this form of number also. You can write a number in this form either as '`c` or as '`\c`. The second form, though longer, has the advantage that you can use it with *any* character, even '`\`', '`%`', or '`^^M`'. It does have one rather technical disadvantage: when TeX is expanding a token sequence for a command such as `\edef` or `\write`, occurrences of '`\c`' within numbers will also be expanded if they can be. That's rarely the effect you want.

---

[15] When you're defining a macro that ends in a number, you should always put a space after that number; otherwise TeX may later combine that number with something else.

The following are all valid representations of the decimal number 78:

```
78    +078   "4E   '116   `N    `\N
```

You can't use a number in text by itself since a number isn't a command. However, you can insert the decimal form of a number in text by putting a `\number` command (p. 224) in front of it or the roman numeral form by putting a `\romannumeral` command in front of it.

You can also use decimal constants, i.e., numbers with a fractional part, for specifying dimensions (see "dimension", p. 60). A decimal constant has a decimal point, which can be the first character of the constant. You can use a comma instead of a period to represent the decimal point. A decimal constant can be preceded by a plus or minus sign. Thus '.5in', '-3.22pt', and '+1,5\baselineskip' are valid dimensions. You can't, however, use decimal constants in any context *other* than as the "factor" part of a dimension, i.e., its multiplier.

ordinary mode.   An *ordinary mode* is a mode that TeX is in when it is assembling a paragraph into lines or assembling lines into a page. See "horizontal mode" (p. 69), "vertical mode" (p. 94).

outer.   An *outer* macro is one that you can't use in certain contexts where TeX is processing tokens at high speed. The purpose of making a command outer is to enable TeX to catch errors before it's gone too far. When you define a macro, you can make it outer with the `\outer` command (p. 232).

You cannot use an outer macro in any of the following contexts:

- within an argument to a macro
- in the parameter text or replacement text of a definition
- in the preamble to an alignment
- in the unexecuted part of a conditional test

An outer context is a context in which you can use an outer macro, i.e., it's any context other than the ones just listed.

For example, the following input would be a forbidden use of an outer macro:

```
\leftline{\proclaim Assertion 2. That which is not inner
   is outer.}
```

The `\proclaim` macro (p. 131) is defined in plain TeX to be outer, but it's being used here in a macro argument to `\leftline`.

output routine.   When TeX has accumulated at least enough material to fill up a page, it chooses a breakpoint and places the material before the breakpoint in `\box255`. It then calls the current *output routine*, which processes the material and eventually sends it to the `.dvi` file. The output routine can perform further processing, such as inserting headers, footers, and footnotes. Plain TeX provides a default output routine that inserts a centered page number at the bottom of each page. By providing a different output routine you can achieve such effects as double-column output. You can think of the output routine as having a single responsibility: disposing of the material in `\box255` one way or another.

The current output routine is defined by the value of `\output` (p. 148), which is a list of tokens. When TeX is ready to produce a page, it just expands the token list.

You can make some simple changes to the actions of the plain TeX output routine without actually modifying it. For example, by assigning a list of tokens to `\headline` or `\footline` (p. 143) you can have TeX produce a different header or footer than it ordinarily would.

The output routine is also responsible for collecting any insertions; combining those insertions and any "decorations" such as headers and footers with the main contents of the page and packaging all of this material in a box; and eventually sending that box to the `.dvi` file with the `\shipout` command (p. 148). Although this is what an output routine most often does, a special-purpose output routine might behave differently.

output stream. See "file" (p. 62).

page. TeX processes a document by assembling *pages* one at a time and passing them to the output routine. As it proceeds through your document, TeX maintains a list of lines and other items to be placed on the page. (The lines are actually hboxes.) This list is called the "main vertical list". Periodically TeX goes through a process called "exercising the page builder". The items added to the main vertical list between exercises of the page builder are called "recent contributions".

The page builder first examines the main vertical list to see if it's necessary to ship out a page yet, either because the items on the main vertical list won't all fit on the page or because of an explicit item, such as `\eject` (p. 137), that tells TeX to end the page. If it's not necessary to ship out a page, then the page builder is done for the time being.

Otherwise the page builder analyzes the main vertical list to find what it considers to be the best possible page break. It associates penalties with various kinds of unattractive page breaks—a break that would leave an isolated line at the top or bottom of a page, a break just before a math display, and so forth. It then chooses the least costly page break, where the cost of a break is increased by any penalty associated with that break and by the badness of the page that would result (see page 111 of *The TeXbook* for the cost formula). If it finds several equally costly page breaks, it chooses the last one.

Once the page builder has chosen a page break, it places the items on the list that are before that break into `\box255` and leaves the remaining ones for the next page. It then calls the output routine. `\box255` acts as a mailbox, with the page builder as the sender and the output routine as the receiver. Ordinarily the output routine processes `\box255`, adds other items, such as insertions, headers, and footers, to the page, and ships out the page to the `.dvi` file with a `\shipout` command. (Specialized output routines may behave differently.) From TeX's standpoint, it doesn't matter whether or not the output routine ships out a page; the only responsibility of the output routine is to process `\box255` one way or another.

It's important to realize that the best place to break a page isn't necessarily the last possible place to break the page. Penalties and other considerations may cause the page break to come earlier. Furthermore, TeX appends items to the main vertical list in batches, not just singly. The lines of a paragraph are an example of such a batch. For these reasons the page builder usually has items left over when it breaks a page. These leftover items then form the beginning of the main vertical list for the next page (possibly in the middle of a batch). Because items are carried over from one page to another, you can't assume that as TeX is processing input, the current page number accurately reflects the page on which the corresponding output will appear. See pages 110–114 of *The TeXbook* for a full description of TeX's page-breaking rules.

page break. A *page break* is a place in your document where TeX ends a page and (except at the end of the document) starts a new one. See "page" (p. 84) for the process that TeX goes through in choosing a page break.

You can control TeX's choice of page breaks in several ways:

- You can insert a penalty (p. 136) between two items in the main vertical list. A positive penalty discourages TeX from breaking the page there, while a negative penalty—a bonus, in other words—encourages TeX to break the page there. A penalty of 10000 or more prevents a page break, while a penalty of −10000 or less forces a page break. You can get the same effects with the `\break` and `\nobreak` commands (p. 136).
- You can adjust the penalties associated with page breaking by assigning different values to TeX's page-breaking parameters.
- You can enclose a sequence of paragraphs or other items in the main vertical list within a vbox, thus preventing TeX from breaking the page anywhere within the sequence.

Once TeX has chosen a page break, it places the portion of the main vertical list that precedes the break into `\box255`. It then calls the current output routine to process `\box255` and eventually ships its contents to the `.dvi` file. The output routine must also handle insertions, such as footnotes, that TeX has accumulated while processing the page.

It's useful to know the places where TeX can break a page:

- At glue, provided that the item preceding the glue is a box, a whatsit, a mark, or an insertion. When TeX breaks a page at glue, it makes the break at the top of the glue space and forgets about the rest of the glue.

- At a kern that's immediately followed by glue.
- At a penalty, possibly between the lines of a paragraph.

When TEX breaks a page, it discards any sequence of glue, kerns, and penalty items that follows the break point.

page builder.   See "page" (p. 84).

page layout.   When you're designing a document, you need to decide on its *page layout*: the page size, the margins on all four sides, the headers and footers, if any, that appear at the top and bottom of the page, and the amount of space between the body of the text and the headers or footers. TEX has defaults for all of these. It assumes an $8\frac{1}{2}$-by-11-inch page with margins of approximately one inch on all four sides, no header, and a footer consisting of a centered page number.

The margins are determined jointly by the four parameters \hoffset, \voffset, \hsize, and \vsize (see "margins", page 79, for advice on how to adjust them). The header normally consists of a single line that appears at the top of each page, within the top margin area. You can set it by assigning a token list to the \headline parameter (p. 143). Similarly, the footer normally consists of a single line that appears at the bottom of each page, within the bottom margin area. You can set it by assigning a token list to the \footline parameter (p. 143). For example, the input:

```
\headline = {Baby's First Document\dotfill Page\folio}
\footline = {\hfil}
```

produces a header line like this on each page:

Baby's First Document . . . . Page 19

and no footer line.

You can use marks to place the current topic of a section of text into the header or footer. See "mark" (p. 79) for an explanation of how to do this.

paragraph.   Intuitively, a *paragraph* is a sequence of input lines that's ended by a blank line, by a \par command (p. 110), or by an intrinsically vertical command, such as \vskip. More precisely, a paragraph is a sequence of commands that TEX processes in ordinary horizontal mode. When TEX has collected an entire paragraph, it forms it into a sequence of lines by choosing line breaks (see "line break", p. 74). The result is a list of hboxes with glue, interline penalties, and interspersed vertical material between them. Each hbox is a single line, and the glue is the interline glue.

TEX starts a paragraph when it's in a vertical mode and encounters an inherently horizontal command. In particular, it's in a vertical mode when it's just finished a paragraph, so the horizontal material on the line after a blank input line starts the next paragraph in a natural way. There are many kinds of inherently horizontal commands, but the most common kind is an ordinary character, e.g., a letter.

The `\indent` and `\noindent` commands (pp. 111, 112) are also inherently horizontal commands that tell TEX either to indent or not to indent the beginning of a paragraph. Any other horizontal command in vertical mode causes TEX to do an implicit `\indent`. Once TEX has started a paragraph, it's in ordinary horizontal mode. It first obeys any commands that are in `\everypar`. It then proceeds to collect items for the paragraph until it gets a signal that the paragraph is ended. At the end of the paragraph it resets the paragraph shape parameters `\parshape`, `\hangindent`, and `\looseness`.

TEX ordinarily translates a blank line into `\par`. It also inserts a `\par` into the input whenever it's in horizontal mode and sees an intrinsically vertical command. So ultimately the thing that ends a paragraph is always a `\par` command.

When TEX receives a `\par` command, it first fills out[16] the paragraph it's working on. It then breaks the paragraph into lines, adds the resulting list of items to the enclosing vertical list, and exercises the page builder (in the case where the enclosing vertical list is the main vertical list). If the paragraph was ended by an intrinsically vertical command, TEX then executes that command.

parameter.   The term *parameter* has two different meanings—it can refer either to a TEX parameter or to a macro parameter.

A TEX parameter is a control sequence that names a value. The value of a parameter can be a number, a dimension, an amount of glue or muglue, or a token list. For example, the `\parindent` parameter specifies the distance that TEX skips at the start of an indented paragraph.

You can use the control sequence for a parameter either to retrieve the value of the parameter or to set that value. TEX interprets the control sequence as a request for a value if it appears in a context where a value is expected, and as an assignment otherwise. For example:

```
\hskip\parindent
```

produces horizontal glue whose natural size is given by `\parindent`, while:

```
\parindent = 2pc  % (or \parindent 2pc)
```

---

[16] More precisely, it executes the commands:

```
\unskip \penalty10000 \hskip\parfillskip
```

thus appending items for these commands to the end of the current horizontal list.

sets \parindent to a length of two picas. The assignment:

```
\parindent = 1.5\parindent
```

uses \parindent in both ways. Its effect is to multiply the value of \parindent by 1.5.

You can think of a parameter as a built-in register. You'll find a complete list of the TeX parameters on pages 272–275 of *The TeXbook*.

A macro parameter is a placeholder for text that is to be plugged into the definition of a macro. See "macro" (p. 75) for more information about this kind of parameter.

penalty. A *penalty* is an item that you can include in a horizontal, vertical, or math list in order to discourage TeX from breaking the list at that point or encourage TeX to break the list there. A positive penalty indicates a bad break point, while a negative penalty indicates a good break point. Breaking an ordinary horizontal list produces a line break, while breaking an ordinary vertical list produces a page break. (A penalty has no effect in restricted horizontal or internal vertical mode.)

You can use the \penalty command (pp. 121, 136) to insert a penalty explicitly. A penalty of 10000 or more prevents a break, while a penalty of −10000 or less forces a break.

plain TeX. *Plain TeX* is the form of TeX described in this book and in *The TeXbook*. Plain TeX is part of the standard TeX system, so documents that use only the facilities of plain TeX can usually be transferred from one installation to another without difficulty.

Plain TeX consists of the primitive commands together with a large collection of macros and other definitions. These additional definitions are given in Appendix B of *The TeXbook*. They should also be in the file plain.tex somewhere in your computer system.

primitive. A *primitive* command is one whose definition is built into the TeX computer program. In contrast, a command that is not primitive is defined by a macro or some other form of definition written in TeX itself. The commands in plain TeX consist of the primitive commands together with other commands defined in terms of the primitive ones.

reference point. The *reference point* of a box is the point where the left edge of the box intersects its baseline. When TeX is processing a horizontal or vertical list, it uses the reference points of the boxes in the list to line up those boxes horizontally or vertically (see "box", p. 51).

register. A *register* is a named location for storing a value. It is much like a variable in a programming language. TeX has five kinds of registers, as shown in the following table:

Register type	Contents
box	a box
count	a number
dimen	a dimension
muskip	muglue
skip	glue
toks	a token list

The registers of each type are numbered from 0 to 255. You can access register *n* of category *c* by using the form '\cn', e.g., \muskip192. You can use a register anywhere that information of the appropriate type is called for. For instance, you can use \count12 in any context calling for a number or \skip0 in any context calling for glue.

You put information into a register by assigning something to it:

```
\setbox3 = \hbox{lagomorphs are not mesomorphs}
\count256 = -1
```

The first assignment constructs an hbox and assigns it to box register 3. You can subsequently use '\box3' wherever a box is called for, and you will get just that hbox.[17] The second assignment assigns −1 to count register 256.

A register of a given type, e.g., a glue register, behaves just like a parameter of that type. You retrieve its value or assign to it just as you would with a parameter. Some TeX parameters, e.g., \pageno, are implemented as registers, in fact.

Plain TeX uses many registers for its own purposes, so you should not just pick an arbitrary register number when you need a register. Instead you should ask TeX to reserve a register by using one of the commands \newbox, \newcount, \newdimen, \newmuskip, \newskip, or \newtoks (p. 244). These commands are outer, so you can't use them in a macro definition. If you could, you'd use up a register every time the macro was called and probably run out of registers before long.

Nonetheless you can with some caution use any register temporarily within a group, even one that TeX is using for something else. After TeX finishes executing the commands in a group, it restores the contents of every register to what they were before it started executing the group. When you use an explicitly numbered register inside a group, you must be sure that the register isn't modified by any macro that you might call

---

[17] But note carefully: using a box register also empties it so that its contents become void. The other kinds of registers don't behave that way. You can use the \copy command (p. 164) to retrieve the contents of a box register without emptying it.

within the group. Be especially careful about using arbitrary registers in a group that calls macros that you didn't write yourself.

TeX reserves certain registers for special purposes: `\count0` through `\count9` for page numbering information and `\box255` for the contents of a page just before it is offered to the output routine. Registers `\dimen0`–`\dimen9`, `\skip0`–`\skip9`, `\muskip0`–`\muskip9`, `\box0`–`\box9`, and the 255 registers other than `\box255` are generally available as "scratch" registers. Thus plain TeX provides only one scratch register, `\count255`, for counts. See pages 122 and 346 of *The TeXbook* for conventions to follow in choosing register numbers.

You can examine the contents of registers during a TeX run with the `\showthe` command (p. 253), e.g., with '`\showthe\box0`'.

restricted mode.   A *restricted mode* is a mode that TeX is in when it is assembling an hbox or a vbox. We follow *The TeXbook* in using the term "internal vertical mode" for what you might expect to be "restricted vertical mode". See "horizontal mode" (p. 69) and "vertical mode" (p. 94).

rule.   A *rule* is a solid black rectangle. A rule, like a box, has width, height, and depth. The vertical dimension of the rectangle is the sum of its height and its depth. An ordinary horizontal or vertical straight line is a special case of a rule.

A rule can be either horizontal or vertical. The distinction between a horizontal rule and a vertical one has to do with how you produce the rule, since a vertical rule can be short and fat (and therefore look like a horizontal line), while a horizontal rule can be tall and skinny (and therefore look like a vertical line). TeX's notion of a rule is more general than that of typographers, who think of a rule as a line and would not usually call a square black box a rule.

You can produce a horizontal rule using the `\hrule` command and a vertical rule using the `\vrule` command (p. 172). For example, the control sequence `\hrule` by itself produces a thin rule that runs across the page, like this:

The command '`\vrule height .25in`' produces a vertical rule that runs .25 inches down the page like this:

|

There are two differences between horizontal rules and vertical rules:

(1) For a horizontal rule, TeX defaults the width to the width of the smallest box or alignment that encloses it. For a vertical rule, TeX defaults the height and depth in the same way. (The default is the size that you get if you don't give a size explicitly for that dimension.)

(2) A horizontal rule is an inherently vertical item that cannot participate in a horizontal list, while a vertical rule is an inherently horizontal item that cannot participate in a vertical list. This behavior may seem strange at first but there is good reason for it: a horizontal rule ordinarily runs visually from left to right and thus separates items in a vertical list, while a vertical rule ordinarily runs visually from top to bottom and thus separates items in a horizontal list.

If you construct a rule with three explicit dimensions, it will look the same whether you make it a horizontal rule or a vertical rule. For example, the command '\vrule height1pt depth2pt width3in' produces this horizontal-looking rule:

You'll find a precise statement of TeX's treatment of rules on pages 221–222 of *The TeXbook*.

script size.   *Script size* describes one of the three related fonts in a family. Script size is smaller than text size but larger than scriptscript size. TeX uses script size for subscripts and superscripts, as well as for the numerators and denominators of fractions in text.

scriptscript size.   *Scriptscript size* describes the smallest of the three related fonts in a family. TeX uses scriptscript size for second-order subscripts, superscripts, numerators, and denominators. For example, TeX will use scriptscript size for a subscript on a subscript or for a superscript on a scriptsize numerator.

shrink.   See "glue" (p. 66).

space.   You can cause TeX to put *space* between two items in several ways:

(1) You can write something that TeX treats as a space token: one or more blank characters, the end of a line (the end-of-line character acts like a space), or any command that expands into a space token. TeX generally treats several consecutive spaces as equivalent to a single one, including the case where the spaces include a single end-of-line. (An empty line indicates the end of a paragraph; it causes TeX to generate a \par token.) TeX adjusts the size of this kind of space to suit the length required by the context.

(2) You can write a skip command that produces the glue you specify in the command. The glue can stretch or shrink, producing more or less space. You can have vertical glue as well as horizontal glue. Glue disappears whenever it is next to a line or page break.

(3) You can write a kern. A kern produces a fixed amount of space that does not stretch or shrink and does not disappear at a line or page

break (unless it is immediately followed by glue). The most common use of a kern is to establish a fixed spatial relationship between two adjacent boxes.

Glue and kerns can have negative values. Negative glue or a negative kern between adjacent items brings those items closer together.

stretch. See "glue" (p. 66).

strut. A *strut* is an invisible box whose width is zero and whose height and depth are slightly more than those of a "normal" line of type in the context. Struts are useful for obtaining uniform vertical spacing when TeX's usual line spacing is disabled, e.g., within a math formula or within a horizontal alignment where you've specified `\offinterlineskip`. Because a strut is taller and deeper than everything else on its line, it determines the height and depth of the line. You can produce a strut with the `\strut` command (p. 167) or the `\mathstrut` command (p. 168). You can use `\strut` anywhere, but you can only use `\mathstrut` when TeX is in math mode. A strut in plain TeX has height 8.5 pt and depth 3.5 pt, while a math strut has the height and depth of a left parenthesis in the current style (so it's smaller for subscripts and superscripts).

Here's an example showing how you might use a strut:

```
\vbox{\hsize = 3in \raggedright
   \strut Here is the first of two paragraphs that we're
   setting in a much narrower line length.\strut}
\vbox{\hsize = 3in \raggedright
   \strut Here is the second of two paragraphs that we're
   setting in a much narrower line length.\strut}
```

This input yields:

> Here is the first of two paragraphs that we're
> setting in a much narrower line length.
> Here is the second of two paragraphs that
> we're setting in a much narrower line length.

Without the struts the vboxes would be too close together. Similarly, in the formula:

```
$\overline{x\mathstrut} \otimes \overline{t\mathstrut}$
```

the math struts cause both bars to be set at the same height even though the 'x' and the 't' have different heights:

$$\overline{x} \otimes \overline{t}$$

style. Material in a math formula is set in one of eight *styles*, depending on the context. Knowing about styles can be useful if you want to set part of a formula in a different size of type than the one that TeX has chosen according to its usual rules.

The four primary styles are:

display style   (for formulas displayed on a line by themselves)
text style   (for formulas embedded in ordinary text)
script style   (for superscripts and subscripts)
scriptscript style   (for superscripts on superscripts, etc.)

The other four styles are so-called cramped variants. In these variants superscripts aren't raised as high as usual, and so the formula needs less vertical space than it otherwise would. See pages 140–141 of *The TEXbook* for the details of how TEX selects the style.

TEX chooses a size of type according to the style:

- Display style and text style are set in text size, like 'this'.
- Script style is set in script size, like 'this'.
- Scriptscript style is set in scriptscript size, like 'this'.

See "family" (p. 62) for more information about these three sizes.

TEX doesn't have a "scriptscriptscript" style because such a style would usually have to be set in a size of type too small to read. TEX therefore sets third-order subscripts, superscripts, etc., using the scriptscript style.

Once in a while you may find that TEX has set a formula in a different style than the one you'd prefer. You can override TEX's choice with the `\textstyle`, `\displaystyle`, `\scriptstyle`, and `\scriptscriptstyle` commands (p. 198).

TEX MEX.   (a) A variant of TEX used for mathematical typesetting in Central American countries. (b) A spicy cuisine favored by the TEXnicians of El Paso.

text math.   We use the term *text math* to refer to a math formula set within a line of text, i.e., enclosed in $'s. TEX sets text math in text math mode.

text size.   *Text size* describes the largest of the three related fonts in a family. TEX uses text size for ordinary symbols appearing in math mode.

token.   A *token* is either a single character tagged with a category code, or a control sequence. TEX reads characters from a file using its eyes (see "anatomy of TEX", p. 46) and groups the characters into tokens using its mouth. When a token reaches TEX's stomach, TEX interprets it as a command unless it's part of an argument of a preceding command.

unit of measure.   See "dimension" (p. 60).

vbox.   A *vbox* (vertical box) is a box that TeX constructs by placing the items of a vertical list one after another, top to bottom. A vbox, taken as a unit, is neither inherently horizontal nor inherently vertical, i.e., it can appear as an item of either a vertical list or a horizontal list. You can construct a vbox with the `\vbox` or the `\vtop` command (p. 161). The difference is that for `\vbox`, the reference point of the constructed vbox is derived from that of the last (and usually bottommost) constituent list item, but for `\vtop`, it's that of the first (and usually topmost) constituent list item.

vertical list.   A *vertical list* is a list of items that TeX has produced while it is in one of its vertical modes, i.e., assembling either a vbox or a page. See "vertical mode" below.

vertical mode.   When TeX is assembling either a vbox or the main vertical list from which pages are derived, it is in one of two *vertical modes*: ordinary vertical mode for assembling the main vertical list, and internal vertical mode for assembling vboxes. Whenever TeX is in a vertical mode its stomach (see "anatomy of TeX", p. 46) is constructing a vertical list of items (boxes, glue, penalties, etc.). TeX typesets the items in the list one below another, top to bottom.

A vertical list can't contain any items produced by inherently horizontal commands, e.g., `\hskip` or an ordinary (nonspace) character. [18]

- If TeX is assembling a vertical list in ordinary vertical mode and encounters an inherently horizontal command, it switches to ordinary horizontal mode.
- If TeX is assembling a vertical list in internal vertical mode and encounters an inherently horizontal command, it complains.

Two commands that you might at first think are inherently vertical are in fact inherently horizontal: `\valign` (p. 179) and `\vrule` (p. 172). See page 283 of *The TeXbook* for a list of the inherently horizontal commands.

It's particularly important to be aware that TeX considers an ordinary character other than a space character to be inherently horizontal. If TeX suddenly starts a new paragraph when you weren't expecting it, a likely cause is a character that TeX encountered while in vertical mode. You can convince TeX not to treat that character as inherently horizontal by enclosing it in an hbox since the `\hbox` command, despite its name, is neither inherently horizontal nor inherently vertical.

whatsit.   A *whatsit* is an item of information that tells TeX to carry out some action that doesn't fit into its ordinary scheme of things. A whatsit can appear in a horizontal or vertical list, just like a box or a glue item.

---

[18] TeX *ignores* any space characters that it encounters while it's in a vertical mode.

TEX typesets a whatsit as a box having zero width, height, and depth—in other words, a box that contains nothing and occupies no space.

Three sorts of whatsits are built into TEX:

- The `\openout`, `\closeout`, and `\write` commands (pp. 249, 249) produce a whatsit for operating on an output file. TEX postpones the operation until it next ships out a page to the `.dvi` file (unless the operation is preceded by `\immediate`). TEX uses a whatsit for these commands because they don't have anything to do with what it's typesetting when it encounters them.

- The `\special` command (p. 250) tells TEX to insert certain text directly into the `.dvi` file. As with the `\write` command, TEX postpones the insertion until it next ships out a page to the `.dvi` file. A typical use of `\special` would be to name a graphics file that the device driver should incorporate into your final output.

- When you change languages with the `\language` or `\setlanguage` commands (p. 128), TEX inserts a whatsit that instructs it to use a certain set of hyphenation rules later on when it's breaking a paragraph into lines.

A particular implementation of TEX may provide additional whatsits.

width. The *width* of a box is the amount of horizontal space that it occupies, i.e., the distance from its left edge to its right edge. The typeset material in a box can be wider than the box itself.

5 ▪ Commands for composing paragraphs

This section covers commands that deal with characters, words, lines, and entire paragraphs. For an explanation of the conventions used in this section, see "Descriptions of the commands" (p. 3).

Characters and accents

▪ Letters and ligatures for European alphabets

\AA	Scandinavian letter Å
\aa	Scandinavian letter å
\AE	Æ ligature
\ae	æ ligature
\L	Polish letter Ł
\l	Polish letter ł
\O	Danish/Norwegian letter Ø
\o	Danish/Norwegian letter ø
\OE	Œ ligature
\oe	œ ligature
\ss	German letter ß

These commands produce various letters and ligatures from European alphabets. They are useful for occasional words and phrases in these languages—but if you need to typeset a large amount of text in a European language, you should probably be using a version of TeX adapted to that language.[1]

---

[1] The TeX Users Group (p. 18) can provide you with information about European language versions of TeX.

You'll need a space after these commands when you use them within a word, so that TEX will treat the following letters as part of the word rather than as part of the command. You needn't be in math mode to use these commands.

Example:
```
{\it les \oe vres de Moli\'ere}
```
produces:
  les œvres de Molière

■ Special symbols

☞ \#   pound sign #
   \$ dollar sign $
   \%   percent sign %
   \&   ampersand &
   \˙   underscore _
   \lq   left quote '
   \rq   right quote '
   \lbrack   left bracket [
   \rbrack   right bracket]
   \dag   dagger symbol †
   \ddag   double dagger symbol ‡
   \copyright   copyright symbol ©
   \P   paragraph symbol ¶
   \S   section symbol §

These commands produce various special characters and marks. The first five commands are necessary because TEX by default attaches special meanings to the characters (#, $, %, &, _). You needn't be in math mode to use these commands.

You can use the dollar sign in the Computer Modern italic fonts to get the pound sterling symbol, as shown in the example below.

Example:
```
\dag It'll only cost you \$9.98 over here, but in England
it's {\it \$}24.98.
```
produces:
  †It'll only cost you $9.98 over here, but in England it's £24.98.

\TeX

This command produces the TEX logo. Remember to follow it by \␣ or to enclose it in a group when you want a space after it.

Example:
```
A book about \TeX\ is in your hands.
```
produces:

A book about TEX is in your hands.

\dots

This command produces an ellipsis, i.e., three dots, in ordinary text. It's intended for use in mathematical writing; for an ellipsis between ordinary words, you should use `$\ldots$` (p. 203) instead. Since `\dots` includes its own space, you shouldn't follow it by `\␣`.

Example:
```
The sequence $x_1$, $x_2$, \dots, $x_\infty$
does not terminate.
```
produces:

The sequence x_1, x_2, ..., x_∞ does not terminate.

See also: "Miscellaneous ordinary math symbols" (p. 188).

■ Arbitrary characters

\char ⟨*charcode*⟩

This command produces the character located at position ⟨*charcode*⟩ of the current font.

Example:
```
{\char65} {\char 'A} {\char '\A}
```
produces:

A A A

\mathchar ⟨*mathcode*⟩

This command produces the math character whose class, family, and font position are given by ⟨*mathcode*⟩. It is only legal in math mode.

Example:
```
\def\digger{\mathchar "027F} % Like \spadesuit in plain TeX.
% Class 0, family 2, font position "7F.
$\digger$
```
produces:

♠

See also: `\delimiter` (p. 204).

■ *Accents*

\'   acute accent as in é
\.   dot accent as in ṅ
\=   macron accent as in r̄
\^   circumflex accent as in ô
\'   grave accent as in è
\"   umlaut accent as in ö
\~   tilde accent as in ã
\c   cedilla accent as in ç
\d   underdot accent as in ṛ
\H   Hungarian umlaut accent as in ő
\t   tie-after accent as in u͡u
\u   breve accent as in ř
\v   check accent as in ŏ

These commands produce accent marks in ordinary text. You'll usually need to leave a space after the ones denoted by a single letter (see
"Spaces", p. 12).

Example:
```
Add a soup\c con of \'elan to my pin\~a colada.
```
produces:
    Add a soupçon of élan to my pinã colada.

\i
\j

These commands produce dotless versions of the letters 'i' and 'j'. You
should use them instead of the ordinary 'i' and 'j' when you are putting an
accent above those letters in ordinary text. Use the \imath and \jmath
commands (p. 188) for dotless 'i's and 'j's in math formulas.

Example:
```
long 'i' as in l\=\i fe   \quad \v\j
```
produces:
    long 'i' as in līfe   ǰ

\accent ⟨*charcode*⟩

This command puts an accent over the character following this command.
The accent is the character at position ⟨*charcode*⟩ in the current font.
TEX assumes that the accent has been designed to fit over a character
1 ex high in the same font as the accent. If the character to be accented
is taller or shorter, TEX adjusts the position accordingly. You can change
fonts between the accent and the next character, thus drawing the accent

character and the character to be accented from different fonts. If the accent character isn't really intended to be an accent, TEX won't complain; it will just typeset something ridiculous.

Example:
```
l'H\accent94 otel des Invalides
% Position 94 of font cmr10 has a circumflex accent.
```
produces:
  l'Hôtel des Invalides

See also: Math accents (p. 199).

■ *Defeating boundary ligatures*

\noboundary

You can defeat a ligature or kern that TEX applies to the first or last character of a word by putting \noboundary just before or just after the word. Certain fonts intended for languages other than English contain a special boundary character that TEX puts at the beginning and end of each word. The boundary character occupies no space and is invisible when printed. It enables TEX to provide different typographical treatment to characters at the beginning or end of a word, since the boundary character can be part of a sequence of characters to be kerned or replaced by a ligature. (None of the standard TEX fonts contain this boundary character.) The effect of \noboundary is to delete the boundary character if it's there, thus preventing TEX from recognizing the ligature or kern.

Selecting fonts

■ *Particular fonts*

\fivebf   use 5-point bold font
\fivei   use 5-point math italic font
\fiverm   use 5-point roman font
\fivesy   use 5-point math symbol font
\sevenbf   use 7-point bold font
\seveni   use 7-point math italic font
\sevenrm   use 7-point roman font
\sevensy   use 7-point math symbol font
\tenbf   use 10-point bold text font
\tenex   use 10-point math extension font
\teni   use 10-point math italic font
\tenrm   use 10-point roman text font
\tensl   use 10-point slanted roman font
\tensy   use 10-point math symbol font
\tenit   use 10-point italic font
\tentt   use 10-point typewriter font

These commands cause TEX to typeset the following text in the specified font. Normally you would enclose one of these font-selecting commands in a group, together with the text to be set in the selected font. Outside of a group a font-selecting command is effective until the end of the document (unless you override it with another such command).

Example:
```
See how I've reduced my weight---from
120 lbs.\ to {\sevenrm 140 lbs}.
```
produces:
    See how I've reduced my weight—from 120 lbs. to 140 lbs.

\nullfont

This command selects a font, built into TEX, that has no characters in it. TEX uses it as a replacement for an undefined font in a family of math fonts.

■ *Type styles*

☞ **\bf**   use boldface type
   \it   use italic type
   \rm   use roman type
   \sl   use slanted type
   \tt   use typewriter type

These commands select a type style without changing the typeface or the point size.[2] Normally you would enclose one of these type style commands in a group, together with the text to be set in the selected font. Outside of a group a type style command is effective until the end of the document (unless you override it with another such command).

Example:

```
The Dormouse was {\it not} amused.
```

produces:

The Dormouse was *not* amused.

See also: "Fonts in math formulas" (p. 209).

Uppercase and lowercase

\lccode ⟨*charcode*⟩   [⟨*number*⟩ table entry]
\uccode ⟨*charcode*⟩   [⟨*number*⟩ table entry]

The `\lccode` and `\uccode` values for the 256 possible input characters specify the correspondence between the lowercase and uppercase forms of letters. These values are used by the `\lowercase` and `\uppercase` commands respectively and by TEX's hyphenation algorithm.

TEX initializes the values of `\lccode` and `\uccode` as follows:

- The `\lccode` of a lowercase letter is the ASCII code for that letter.
- The `\lccode` of an uppercase letter is the ASCII code for the corresponding lowercase letter.
- The `\uccode` of an uppercase letter is the ASCII code for that letter.
- The `\uccode` of a lowercase letter is the ASCII code for the corresponding uppercase letter.

---

[2] TEX does not provide predefined commands for changing just the point size, e.g., `\eightpoint`. Supporting such commands would require a great number of fonts, most of which would never be used. Such commands were, however, used in typesetting *The TEXbook*.

■ The \lccode and \uccode of a nonletter are both zero.

Most of the time there's no reason to change these values, but you might want to change them if you're using a language that has more letters than English.

Example:
```
\char\uccode`s \char\lccode`a \char\lccode`M
```
produces:
    Sam

\lowercase – ⟨*token list*⟩ ″
\uppercase – ⟨*token list*⟩ ″

These commands convert the letters in ⟨*token list*⟩, i.e., those tokens with category code 11, to their lowercase and uppercase forms. The conversion of a letter is defined by its \lccode (for lowercase) or \uccode (for uppercase) table value. Tokens in the list that are not letters are not affected—even if the tokens are macro calls or other commands that expand into letters.

Example:
```
\def\x{Cd} \lowercase{Ab\x} \uppercase{Ab\x}
```
produces:
    abCd ABCd

Interword spacing

☞ \␣

This command explicitly produces an interword space called a "control space". A control space is useful when a letter occurs immediately after a control sequence, or in any other circumstance where you don't want two tokens to be run together in the output. The amount of space produced by \␣ is independent of preceding punctuation, i.e., its space factor (p. 107) is 1000.

Incidentally, if you want to print the '␣' character that we've used here to denote a space, you can get it by typing {\tt \char `\ }.

Example:
```
The Dormouse was a \TeX\ expert, but he never let on.
```
produces:
    The Dormouse was a TEX expert, but he never let on.

\space

This command is equivalent to an input space character. It differs from \␣ in that its width *can* be affected by preceding punctuation.

Example:
```
Yes.\space No.\space Maybe.\par
Yes.\␣No.\␣Maybe.
```

produces:

Yes. No. Maybe.
Yes. No. Maybe.

^^M

This construct produces the end of line character. It normally has two effects when TEX encounters it in your input:

(1) It acts as a command, producing either an input space (if it comes at the end of a nonblank line) or a \par token (if it comes at the end of a blank line).

(2) It ends the input line, causing TEX to ignore the remaining characters on the line.

However, ^^M does *not* end the line when it appears in the context '\^^M, denoting the ASCII code for control-M (the number 13). You can change the meaning of ^^M by giving it a different category code. See page 55 for a more general explanation of the ^^ notation.

Example:
```
Hello.^^MGoodbye.
Goodbye again.\par
The \char '\^^M\ character.\par
% The fl ligature is at position 13 of font cmr10
\number '\^^M\ is the end of line code.\par
Again, \number '^^M is the end of line code,
isn't it? % 32 is the ASCII code for a space
```
produces:

Hello. Goodbye again.
The fl character.
13 is the end of line code.
Again, 32isn't it?

☞ ˜

The active character '˜', called a "tie", produces a normal interword space between two words and links those words so that a line break will not occur between them. You should use a tie in any context where a line break would be confusing, e.g., before a middle initial, after an abbreviation such as "Dr.", or after "Fig." in "Fig. 8".

Example:
```
P.D.Q.~Bach (1807--1742), the youngest and most
imitative son of Johann~S. Bach, composed the
{\sl Concerto for Horn and Hardart}.
```

produces:

P.D.Q. Bach (1807–1742), the youngest and most imitative son of Johann S. Bach, composed the *Concerto for Horn and Hardart.*

☞ \/

Every character in a TEX font has an "italic correction" associated with it, although the italic correction is normally zero for a character in an unslanted (upright) font. The italic correction specifies the extra space that's needed when you're switching from a slanted font (not necessarily an italic font) to an unslanted font. The extra space is needed because a slanted character projects into the space that follows it, making the space look too small when the next character is unslanted. The metrics file for a font includes the italic correction of each character in the font.

The \/ command produces an italic correction for the preceding character. You should insert an italic correction when you're switching from a slanted font to an unslanted font, except when the next character is a period or comma.

Example:
```
However, {\it somebody} ate {\it something}: that's clear.

However, {\it somebody\/} ate {\it something\/}:
that's clear.
```

produces:

However, *somebody* ate *something*: that's clear.
However, *somebody* ate *something*: that's clear.

\frenchspacing
\nonfrenchspacing

TEX normally adjusts the spacing between words to account for punctuation marks. For example, it inserts extra space at the end of a sentence and adds some stretch to the glue following any punctuation mark there. The \frenchspacing command tells TEX to make the interword spacing independent of punctuation, while the \nonfrenchspacing command tells TEX to use its normal spacing rules. If you don't specify \frenchspacing, you'll get TEX's normal spacing.

See page 13 for advice on how to control TEX's treatment of punctuation at the end of sentences.

Example:

```
{\frenchspacing  An example: two sentences. Right? No.\par}
{An example: two sentences. Right? No. \par}%
```

produces:

An example: two sentences. Right? No.

An example: two sentences. Right? No.

\obeyspaces

TEX normally condenses a sequence of several spaces to a single space. \obeyspaces instructs TEX to produce a space in the output for each space in the input. \obeyspaces does not cause spaces at the beginning of a line to show up, however; for that we recommend the \obeywhite-space command defined in `eplain.tex` (p. 293). \obeyspaces is often useful when you're typesetting something, computer input for example, in a monospaced font (one in which each character takes up the same amount of space) and you want to show exactly what each line of input looks like.

You can use the \obeylines command (p. 122) to get TEX to follow the line boundaries of your input. \obeylines is often used in combination with \obeyspaces.

Example:

```
These       spaces     are     closed    up
{\obeyspaces but     these    are     not    }.
```

produces:

These spaces are closed up but   these   are   not   .

\spacefactor	[⟨*number*⟩ parameter]
\spaceskip	[⟨*glue*⟩ parameter]
\xspaceskip	[⟨*glue*⟩ parameter]
\sfcode ⟨*charcode*⟩	[⟨*number*⟩ table entry]

These primitive parameters affect how much space TEX puts between two adjacent words, i.e., the interword spacing. The normal interword spacing is supplied by the current font. As TEX is processing a horizontal list, it keeps track of the space factor f in \spacefactor. As it processes each input character c, it updates f according to the value of f_c, the space factor code of c (see below). For most characters, f_c is 1000 and TEX sets f to 1000. (The initial value of f is also 1000.) When TEX sees an interword space, it adjusts the size of that space by multiplying the stretch and shrink of that space by $f/1000$ and $1000/f$ respectively. Thus:

(1) If $f = 1000$, the interword space keeps its normal value.

(2) If $f < 1000$, the interword space gets less stretch and more shrink.

(3) If $f > 1000$, the interword space gets more stretch and less shrink.

In addition, if $f > 2000$ the interword space is further increased by the "extra space" parameter associated with the current font.

Each input character c has an entry in the \sfcode (space factor code) table. The \sfcode table entry is independent of the font. Usually TEX just sets f to f_c after it processes c. However:

- If f_c is zero, TEX leaves f unchanged. Thus a character such as ')' in plain TEX, for which f_c is zero, is essentially transparent to the interword space calculation.

- If $f < 1000 < f_c$, TEX sets f to 1000 rather than to f_c, i.e., it refuses to raise f very rapidly.

The \sfcode value for a period is normally 3000, which is why TEX usually puts extra space after a period (see the rule above for the case $f > 2000$). Noncharacter items in a horizontal list, e.g., vertical rules, generally act like characters with a space factor of 1000.

You can change the space factor explicitly by assigning a different numerical value to \spacefactor. You can also override the normal interword spacing by assigning a different numerical value to \xspaceskip or to \spaceskip:

- \xspaceskip specifies the glue to be used when $f \geq 2000$; in the case where \xspaceskip is zero, the normal rules apply.

- \spaceskip specifies the glue to be used when $f \leq 2000$ or when \xspaceskip is zero; if \spaceskip is zero, the normal rules apply. The stretch and shrink of the \spaceskip glue, like that of the ordinary interword glue, is modified according to the value of f.

See page 76 of *The TEXbook* for the precise rules that TEX uses in calculating interword glue, and pages 285–287 of *The TEXbook* for the adjustments made to \spacefactor after various items in a horizontal list.

Centering and justifying lines

☞ **\centerline** ⟨*argument*⟩
\leftline ⟨*argument*⟩
\rightline ⟨*argument*⟩

The \centerline command produces an hbox exactly as wide as the current line and places ⟨*argument*⟩ at the center of the box. The \leftline and \rightline commands are analogous; they place ⟨*argument*⟩ at the left end or at the right end of the box. If you want to apply one of these commands to several consecutive lines, you must apply it to each one individually. See page 306 for an alternate approach.

Don't use these commands within a paragraph—if you do, TEX probably won't be able to break the paragraph into lines and will complain about an overfull hbox.

Example:
```
\centerline{Grand Central Station}
\leftline{left of Karl Marx}
\rightline{right of Genghis Khan}
```
produces:

> Grand Central Station

left of Karl Marx

> > > right of Genghis Khan

☞ **\line** ⟨*argument*⟩

This command produces an hbox containing ⟨*argument*⟩. The hbox is exactly as wide as the current line, i.e., it extends from the right margin to the left margin.

Example:
```
\line{ugly \hfil suburban \hfil sprawl}
% Without \hfil you'd get an 'underfull box' from this.
```
produces:

ugly   suburban   sprawl

\llap ⟨*argument*⟩
\rlap ⟨*argument*⟩

These commands enable you to produce text that overlaps whatever happens to be to the left or to the right of the current position. \llap backspaces by the width of ⟨*argument*⟩ and then typesets ⟨*argument*⟩. \rlap is similar, except that it typesets ⟨*argument*⟩ first and then backspaces. \llap and \rlap are useful for placing text outside of the current margins. Both \llap and \rlap do their work by creating a box of zero width.

You can also use \llap or \rlap to construct special characters by overprinting, but don't try it unless you're sure that the characters you're using have the same width (which is the case for a monospaced font such as cmtt10, the Computer Modern 10-pointp. 130typewriter font).

Example:

```
\noindent\llap{off left }\line{\vrule $\Leftarrow$
left margin of examples\hfil right margin of examples
$\Rightarrow$\vrule}\rlap{ off right}
```

produces:

off left ⇐ left margin of examples　　　　　　　　right margin of examples ⇒ off right

See also: \hsize (p. 114).

Shaping paragraphs

■ Starting, ending, and indenting paragraphs

\par

This command ends a paragraph and puts TeX into vertical mode, ready to add more items to the page. Since TeX converts a blank line in your input file into a \par token, you don't ordinarily need to type an explicit \par in order to end a paragraph.

An important point is that \par doesn't tell TeX to start a paragraph; it only tells TeX to end a paragraph. TeX starts a paragraph when it is in ordinary vertical mode (which it is after a \par) and encounters an inherently horizontal item such as a letter. As part of its ceremony for starting a paragraph, TeX inserts an amount of vertical space given by the parameter \parskip (p. 141) and indents the paragraph by a horizontal space given by \parindent (p. 113).

You can usually cancel any interparagraph space produced by a \par by giving the command \vskip -\lastskip. It can often be helpful to do this when you're writing a macro that is supposed to work the same way whether or not it is preceded by a blank line.

You can get TeX to take some special action at the start of each paragraph by placing the instructions in \everypar (p. 113).

See pages 283 and 286 of *The TeXbook* for the precise effect of \par.

Example:

```
\parindent = 2em
''Can you row?'' the Sheep asked, handing Alice a pair of
knitting-needles as she was speaking.\par ''Yes, a little%
---but not on land---and not with needles---'' Alice was
starting to say, when suddenly the needles turned into oars.
```

produces:

> "Can you row?" the Sheep asked, handing Alice a pair of knitting-needles as she was speaking.
>
> "Yes, a little—but not on land—and not with needles—" Alice was starting to say, when suddenly the needles turned into oars.

\endgraf

This command is a synonym for the `\par` primitive command. It is useful when you've redefined `\par` but still want access to the original definition of `\par`.

\parfillskip   [⟨*glue*⟩ parameter]

This parameter specifies the horizontal glue that TEX inserts at the end of a paragraph. The default value of `\parfillskip` is `0pt plus 1fil`, which causes the last line of a paragraph to be filled out with blank space. A value of `0pt` forces TEX to end the last line of a paragraph at the right margin.

☞ \indent

If TEX is in vertical mode, as it is after ending a paragraph, this command inserts the `\parskip` interparagraph glue, puts TEX into horizontal mode, starts a paragraph, and indents that paragraph by `\parindent`. If TEX is already in horizontal mode, this command merely produces a blank space of width `\parindent`. Two `\indent`s in a row produce two indentations.

As the example below shows, an `\indent` at a point where TEX would start a paragraph anyway is redundant. When TEX is in vertical mode and sees a letter or some other inherently horizontal command, it starts a paragraph by switching to horizontal mode, doing an `\indent`, and processing the horizontal command.

Example:

```
\parindent = 2em  This is the first in a series of three
paragraphs that show how you can control indentation. Note
that it has the same indentation as the next paragraph.\par
\indent This is the second in a series of three paragraphs.
It has \indent an embedded indentation.\par
\indent\indent This doubly indented paragraph
is the third in the series.
```

produces:

> This is the first in a series of three paragraphs that show how you can control indentation. Note that it has the same indentation as the next paragraph.
>
> This is the second in a series of three paragraphs. It has   an embedded indentation.
>
> This doubly indented paragraph is the third in the series.

☞ **\noindent**

If TeX is in vertical mode, as it is after ending a paragraph, this command inserts the \parskip interparagraph glue, puts TeX into horizontal mode, and starts an unindented paragraph. It has no effect in horizontal mode, i.e., within a paragraph. Starting a paragraph with \noindent thus cancels the indentation by \parindent that would normally occur there.

A common use of \noindent is to cancel the indentation of the first line of a paragraph when the paragraph follows some displayed material.

Example:

```
\parindent = 1em
Tied round the neck of the bottle was a label with the
words \smallskip \centerline{EAT ME}\smallskip
\noindent beautifully printed on it in large letters.
```

produces:

> Tied round the neck of the bottle was a label with the words
>
> EAT ME
>
> beautifully printed on it in large letters.

\textindent ⟨*argument*⟩

This command tells TeX to start a paragraph and indent it by \parindent, as usual. TeX then right-justifies ⟨*argument*⟩ within the indentation and follows it with an en space (half an em). Plain TeX uses this command to typeset footnotes (p. 145) and items in lists (see \item, p. 130).

Example:
```
\parindent = 20pt \textindent{\raise 1pt\hbox{$\bullet$}}%
You are allowed to use bullets in \TeX\ even if
you don't join the militia, and many peace-loving
typographers do so.
```
produces:

> • You are allowed to use bullets in TEX even if you don't join the militia, and many peace-loving typographers do so.

\parindent   [⟨*dimen*⟩ parameter]

This parameter specifies the amount by which the first line of each paragraph is to be indented. As the example below shows, it's a bad idea to set both `\parindent` and `\parskip` to zero since then the paragraph breaks are no longer apparent.

Example:
```
\parindent = 2em This paragraph is indented by 2 ems.
\par \parindent=0pt This paragraph is not indented at all.
\par Since we haven't reset the paragraph indentation,
this paragraph isn't indented either.
```
produces:

> This paragraph is indented by 2 ems.
> This paragraph is not indented at all.
> Since we haven't reset the paragraph indentation, this paragraph isn't indented either.

\everypar   [⟨*token list*⟩ parameter]

TEX performs the commands in ⟨*token list*⟩ whenever it enters horizontal mode, e.g., when it starts a paragraph. By default `\everypar` is empty, but you can take extra actions at the start of every paragraph by putting the commands for those actions into a token list and assigning that token list to `\everypar`.

Example:
```
\everypar = {$\Longrightarrow$\enspace}
Now pay attention!\par
I said, ``Pay attention!''.\par
I'll say it again! Pay attention!
```
produces:

> ⟹ Now pay attention!
> ⟹ I said, "Pay attention!".
> ⟹ I'll say it again! Pay attention!

■ *Shaping entire paragraphs*

☞ **\hsize**   [⟨*dimen*⟩ parameter]

This parameter specifies the current line length, i.e., the usual width of lines in a paragraph starting at the left margin. A great many TEX commands, e.g., \centerline (p. 108) and \hrule (p. 172), implicitly use the value of \hsize. By changing \hsize within a group you can change the width of the constructs produced by such commands.

If you set \hsize within a vbox that contains text, the vbox will have whatever width you've given to \hsize.

Plain TEX sets \hsize to 6.5in.

Example:
```
{\hsize = 3.5in % Set this paragraph 3.5 inches wide.
The hedgehog was engaged in a fight with another hedgehog,
which seemed to Alice an excellent opportunity for
croqueting one of them with the other.\par}%
```
produces:

The hedgehog was engaged in a fight with another hedgehog, which seemed to Alice an excellent opportunity for
croqueting one of them with the other.

$\vdash$ ⌐⌐⌐⌐⌐⌐⌐⌐⌐⌐⌐⌐⌐⌐⌐⌐⌐⌐⌐⌐⌐⌐⌐⌐⌐⌐⌐⌐⌐⌐⌐⌐⌐ ¬ 3.5 in

Example:
```
\leftline{\raggedright\vtop{\hsize = 1.5in
Here is some text that we put into a paragraph that is
an inch and a half wide.}\qquad
\vtop{\hsize = 1.5in Here is some more text that
we put into another paragraph that is an inch and a
half wide.}}
```
produces:

Here is some text that   Here is some more text
we put into a paragraph   that we put into another
that is an inch and a   paragraph that is an
half wide.   inch and a half wide.

☞ **\narrower**

This command makes paragraphs narrower, increasing the left and right margins by \parindent, the current paragraph indentation. It achieves this by increasing both \leftskip and \rightskip by \parindent. Normally you place \narrower at the beginning of a group containing the paragraphs that you want to make narrower. If you forget to enclose \narrower within a group, you'll find that all the rest of your document will have narrow paragraphs.

\narrower affects just those paragraphs that end after you invoke it. If you end a \narrower group before you've ended a paragraph, TeX won't make that paragraph narrower.

Example:

```
{\parindent = 12pt \narrower\narrower\narrower
This is a short paragraph. Its margins are indented
three times as much as they would be
had we used just one ''narrower'' command.\par}
```

produces:

> This is a short paragraph. Its margins are indented three times as much as they would be had we used just one "narrower" command.

\leftskip   [⟨*glue*⟩ parameter]
\rightskip   [⟨*glue*⟩ parameter]

These parameters tell TeX how much glue to place at the left and at the right end of each line of the current paragraph. We'll just explain how \leftskip works since \rightskip is analogous.

You can increase the left margin by setting \leftskip to a fixed nonzero dimension. If you give \leftskip some stretch, you can produce ragged left text, i.e., text that has an uneven left margin.

Ordinarily, you should enclose any assignment to \leftskip in a group together with the affected text in order to keep its effect from continuing to the end of your document. However, it's pointless to change \leftskip's value inside a group that is in turn contained within a paragraph—the value of \leftskip at the *end* of a paragraph is what determines how TeX breaks the paragraph into lines.

Example:

```
{\leftskip = 1in The White Rabbit trotted slowly back
again, looking anxiously about as it went, as if it had
lost something.  {\leftskip = 10in % has no effect
It muttered to itself, ''The Duchess! The Duchess! She'll
get me executed as sure as ferrets are ferrets!''}\par}%
```

produces:

> The White Rabbit trotted slowly back again, looking anxiously about as it went, as if it had lost something. It muttered to itself, "The Duchess! The Duchess! She'll get me executed as sure as ferrets are ferrets!"

Example:

```
\pretolerance = 10000 % Don't hyphenate.
\rightskip = .5in plus 2em
The White Rabbit trotted slowly back again, looking
anxiously about as it went, as if it had lost something.
It muttered to itself, ''The Duchess! The Duchess! She'll
get me executed as sure as ferrets are ferrets!''
```

produces:

> The White Rabbit trotted slowly back again, looking anxiously about as it went, as if it had lost something. It muttered to itself, "The Duchess! The Duchess! She'll get me executed as sure as ferrets are ferrets!"

☞ **\raggedright**
\ttraggedright

These commands cause TeX to typeset your document "ragged right". Interword spaces all have their natural size, i.e., they all have the same width and don't stretch or shrink. Consequently the right margin is generally not even. The alternative, which is TeX's default, is to typeset your document justified, i.e., with uniform left and right margins. In justified text, interword spaces are stretched in order to make the right margin even. Some typographers prefer ragged right because it avoids distracting "rivers" of white space on the printed page.

You should use the \ttraggedright command when typesetting text in a monospaced font and the \raggedright command when typesetting text in any other font.

Most of the time you'll want to apply these commands to an entire document, but you can limit their effects by enclosing them in a group.

Example:

```
\raggedright ''You couldn't have it if you {\it did\/}
want it,'' the Queen said. ''The rule is, jam tomorrow
and jam yesterday---but never jam {\it today\/}.''
''It {\it must\/} come sometimes to 'jam today,%
thinspace'' Alice objected. ''No, it can't'', said the
Queen. ''It's jam every {\it other\/} day: today isn't
any {\it other\/} day.''
```

produces:

> "You couldn't have it if you *did* want it," the Queen said. "The rule is, jam tomorrow and jam yesterday—but never jam *today*." "It *must* come sometimes to 'jam today,'" Alice objected. "No, it can't", said the Queen. "It's jam every *other* day: today isn't any *other* day."

\hang

This command indents the second and subsequent lines of a paragraph by \parindent, the paragraph indentation (p. 113). Since the first line is already indented by \parindent (unless you've cancelled the indentation with \noindent), the entire paragraph appears to be indented by \parindent.

Example:

```
\parindent=24pt \hang  ''I said you {\it looked} like an
egg, Sir,'' Alice gently explained to Humpty Dumpty. ''And
some eggs are very pretty, you know,'' she added.
```

produces:

> "I said you *looked* like an egg, Sir," Alice gently explained to Humpty Dumpty. "And some eggs are very pretty, you know," she added.

\hangafter [⟨*number*⟩ parameter]
\hangindent [⟨*dimen*⟩ parameter]

These two parameters jointly specify "hanging indentation" for a paragraph. The hanging indentation indicates to TeX that certain lines of the paragraph should be indented and the remaining lines should have their normal width. \hangafter determines which lines are indented, while \hangindent determines the amount of indentation and whether it occurs on the left or on the right:

- Let n be the value of \hangafter. If $n < 0$, the first $-n$ lines of the paragraph will be indented. If $n \geq 0$, all but the first n lines of the paragraph will be indented.
- Let x be the value of \hangindent. If $x \geq 0$, the lines will be indented by x on the left. If $x < 0$ the lines will be indented by $-x$ on the right.

When you specify hanging indentation, it applies only to the next paragraph (if you're in vertical mode) or to the current paragraph (if you're in horizontal mode). TeX uses the values of \hangafter and \hangindent at the end of a paragraph, when it breaks that paragraph into lines.

Unlike most of the other paragraph-shaping parameters, \hangafter and \hangindent are reset to their default values at the start of each paragraph, namely, 1 for \hangafter and 0 for \hangindent. If you want to typeset a sequence of paragraphs with hanging indentation, use \everypar (p. 113). If you specify \hangafter and \hangindent as well as \parshape, TeX ignores the \hangafter and \hangindent.

Example:
```
\hangindent=6pc \hangafter=-2
This is an example of a paragraph with hanging indentation.
In this case, the first two lines are indented on the left,
but after that we return to unindented text.
```
produces:

> > This is an example of a paragraph with hanging in-
> > dentation. In this case, the first two lines are indented
> on the left, but after that we return to unindented text.

Example:
```
\hangindent=-6pc \hangafter=1
This is another example of a paragraph with hanging
indentation.  Here, all lines after the first have been
indented on the right. The first line, on the other
hand, has been left unindented.
```
produces:

> This is another example of a paragraph with hanging indentation. Here,
> all lines after the first have been indented on the right.
> The first line, on the other hand, has been left unin-
> dented.

\parshape n $i_1 l_1$ $i_2 l_2$ ... $i_n l_n$

This command specifies the shape of the first n lines of a paragraph—
the next paragraph if you're in vertical mode and the current paragraph
if you're in horizontal mode. The i's and l's are all dimensions. The
first line is indented by i_1 and has length l_1, the second line is indented
by i_2 and has length l_2, and so forth. If the paragraph has more than
n lines, the last indentation/length pair is used for the extra lines. To
achieve special effects such as the one shown here, you usually have to
experiment a lot, insert kerns here and there, and choose your words
to fit the shape.

\parshape, like \hangafter and \hangindent, is effective only for one
paragraph. If you specify \hangafter and \hangindent as well as \par-
shape, TeX ignores the \hangafter and \hangindent.

Example:
```
% A small font and close interline spacing make this work
\smallskip\font\sixrm=cmr6 \sixrm \baselineskip=7pt
\fontdimen3\font = 1.8pt \fontdimen4\font = 0.9pt
\noindent \hfuzz 0.1pt
\parshape 30 0pt 120pt 1pt 118pt 2pt 116pt 4pt 112pt 6pt
108pt 9pt 102pt 12pt 96pt 15pt 90pt 19pt 84pt 23pt 77pt
27pt 68pt 30.5pt 60pt 35pt 52pt 39pt 45pt 43pt 36pt 48pt
27pt 51.5pt 21pt 53pt 16.75pt 53pt 16.75pt 53pt 16.75pt 53pt
16.75pt 53pt 16.75pt 53pt 16.75pt 53pt 16.75pt 53pt 16.75pt
53pt 14.6pt 48pt 24pt 45pt 30.67pt 36.5pt 51pt 23pt 76.3pt
The wines of France and California may be the best
known, but they are not the only fine wines. Spanish
wines are often underestimated, and quite old ones may
be available at reasonable prices. For Spanish wines
the vintage is not so critical, but  the climate of the
Bordeaux region varies greatly from year to year. Some
vintages are not as good as others,
so these years ought to be
s\kern -.1pt p\kern -.1pt e\kern -.1pt c\hfil ially
n\kern .1pt o\kern .1pt t\kern .1pt e\kern .1pt d\hfil:
1962, 1964, 1966.  1958, 1959, 1960, 1961, 1964,
1966 are also good California vintages.
Good luck finding them!
```
produces:

The wines of France and California
may be the best known, but they
are not the only fine wines. Spanish wines are often underestimated,
and quite old ones may be available at reasonable prices. For
Spanish wines the vintage is
not so critical, but the cli-
mate of the Bordeaux re-
gion varies greatly from
year to year. Some
vintages are not as
good as others,
so these years
ought to be
specially
noted:
1962,
1964,
1966.
1958,
1959,
1960,
1961,
1964,
1966
are also
good Cal-
ifornia vintages.
Good luck finding them!

\prevgraf   [⟨*number*⟩ parameter]

In horizontal mode, this parameter specifies the number of lines in the paragraph so far; in vertical mode, it specifies the number of lines in the previous paragraph. TₑX only sets \prevgraf after it has finished breaking some text into lines, i.e., at a math display or at the end of a paragraph. See page 103 of *The TₑXbook* for more details about it.

\vadjust – ⟨*vertical mode material*⟩ ″

This command inserts the specified ⟨*vertical mode material*⟩ just after the output line containing the position where the command occurs. You can use it, for instance, to cause a page eject or to insert extra space after a certain line.

Example:

```
Some of these words are \vadjust{\kern8pt\hrule} to be
found above the line and others are to be found below it.
```

produces:

Some of these words are to be found above the line and others are to

───

be found below it.

See also: \parindent (p. 113), \parskip (p. 141), \everypar (p. 113).

Line breaks

■ Encouraging or discouraging line breaks

\break

This command forces a line break. Unless you do something to fill out the line, you're likely to get an "underfull hbox" complaint. \break can also be used in vertical mode.

Example:

```
Fill out this line\hfil\break and start another one.\par
% Use \hfil here to fill out the line.
This line is underfull---we ended it\break prematurely.
% This line causes an 'underfull hbox' complaint.
```

produces:
> Fill out this line
> and start another one.
> This   line   is   underfull—we   ended   it
> prematurely.

\nobreak

This command prevents a line break where it otherwise might occur.
\nobreak can also be used in vertical mode.

Example:
```
Sometimes you'll encounter a situation where
a certain space\nobreak\qquad must not get lost.
```
produces:
> Sometimes you'll encounter a situation where a certain space   must
> not get lost.

\allowbreak

This command tells TeX to allow a line break where one could not ordinarily occur. It's most often useful within a math formula, since TeX is reluctant to break lines there. \allowbreak can also be used in vertical mode.

Example:
```
Under most circumstances we can state with some confidence
that $2+2\allowbreak=4$, but skeptics may disagree.
\par For such moronic automata, it is not difficult to
analyze the input/\allowbreak output behavior in the limit.
```
produces:
> Under most circumstances we can state with some confidence that $2+2$
> $=4$, but skeptics may disagree.
> For such moronic automata, it is not difficult to analyze the input/
> output behavior in the limit.

\penalty ⟨*number*⟩

This command produces a penalty item. The penalty item makes TeX more or less willing to break a line at the point where that item occurs. A negative penalty, i.e., a bonus, encourages a line break; a positive penalty discourages a line break. A penalty of 10000 or more prevents a break altogether, while a penalty of −10000 or less forces a break. \penalty can also be used in vertical mode.

Example:
```
\def\break{\penalty -10000 } % as in plain TeX
\def\nobreak{\penalty 10000 } % as in plain TeX
\def\allowbreak{\penalty 0 } % as in plain TeX
```

\obeylines

TeX normally treats an end of line as a space. \obeylines instructs TeX to treat each end of line as an end of paragraph, thus forcing a line break. \obeylines is often useful when you're typesetting verse or computer programs. If any of your lines are longer than the effective line length (\hsize − \parindent), however, you may get an extra line break within those lines.

Because TeX inserts the \parskip glue (p. 141) between lines controlled by \obeylines (since it thinks each line is a paragraph), you should normally set \parskip to zero when you're using \obeylines.

You can use the \obeyspaces command (p. 107) to get TeX to take spaces within a line literally. \obeylines and \obeyspaces are often used together.

Example:
```
\obeylines
''Beware the Jabberwock, my son!
\quad The jaws that bite, the claws that catch!
Beware the Jubjub bird, and shun
\quad The frumious Bandersnatch!''
```
produces:

"Beware the Jabberwock, my son!
    The jaws that bite, the claws that catch!
Beware the Jubjub bird, and shun
    The frumious Bandersnatch!"

☞ \slash

This command produces a solidus (/) and also tells TeX that it can break the line after the solidus, if necessary.

Example:
```
Her oldest cat, while apparently friendly to most people,
had a Jekyll\slash Hyde personality when it came to mice.
```
produces:

Her oldest cat, while apparently friendly to most people, had a Jekyll/ Hyde personality when it came to mice.

■ *Line breaking parameters*

\pretolerance   [⟨*number*⟩ parameter]
\tolerance   [⟨*number*⟩ parameter]

These parameters determine the badness that TEX will tolerate on each line when it is choosing line breaks for a paragraph. The badness is a measure of how far the interword spacing deviates from the ideal. \pretolerance specifies the tolerable badness for line breaks without hyphenation; \tolerance specifies the tolerable badness for line breaks with hyphenation. The tolerable badness can be exceeded in either of two ways: a line is too tight (the interword spaces are too small) or it is too loose (the interword spaces are too big).

- If TEX must set a line too tightly, it lets the line end before the right margin and complains about an "underfull hbox".
- If TEX must set a line too loosely, it lets the line run past the right margin and complains about an "overfull hbox".

TEX chooses line breaks in the following steps:

(1) It attempts to choose line breaks without hyphenating. If none of the resulting lines have a badness exceeding \pretolerance, the line breaks are acceptable and the paragraph can now be set.

(2) Otherwise, it tries another set of line breaks, this time allowing hyphenation. If none of the resulting lines have a badness exceeding \tolerance, the new set of line breaks is acceptable and the paragraph can now be set.

(3) Otherwise, it adds \emergencystretch (see below) to the stretch of each line and tries again.

(4) If none of these attempts have produced an acceptable set of line breaks, it sets the paragraph with one or more overfull hboxes and complains about them.

Plain TEX sets \tolerance to 200 and \pretolerance to 100. If you set \tolerance to 10000, TEX becomes infinitely tolerant and accepts any spacing, no matter how bad (unless it encounters a word that won't fit on a line, even with hyphenation). Thus by changing \tolerance you can avoid overfull and underfull hboxes, but at the cost of making the spacing worse. By making \pretolerance larger you can get TEX to avoid hyphenation (and also run faster), again at the cost of possibly worse spacing. If you set \pretolerance to −1, TEX will not even try to set the paragraph without hyphenation.

The \hbadness parameter (p. 170) determines the level of badness that TEX will tolerate before it complains, but \hbadness does not affect the way that TEX typesets your document. The \hfuzz parameter (p. 171) determines the amount that an hbox can exceed its specified width before TEX considers it to be erroneous.

\emergencystretch   [⟨*dimen*⟩ parameter]

By setting this parameter to be greater than zero, you can make it easier for TEX to typeset your document without generating overfull hboxes. This is a better alternative than setting `\tolerance=10000`, since that tends to produce really ugly lines. If TEX can't typeset a paragraph without exceeding `\tolerance`, it will try again, adding `\emergencystretch` to the stretch of each line. The effect of the change is to scale down the badness of each line, enabling TEX to make spaces wider than they would otherwise be and thus choose line breaks that are as good as possible under the circumstances.

\looseness   [⟨*number*⟩ parameter]

This parameter gives you a way to change the total number of lines in a paragraph from what they optimally would be. `\looseness` is so named because it's a measure of how loose the paragraph is, i.e., how much extra space there is in it.

Normally, `\looseness` is 0 and TEX chooses line breaks in its usual way. But if `\looseness` is, say, 3, TEX does the following:

(1) It chooses line breaks normally, resulting in a paragraph of n lines.

(2) It discards these line breaks and tries to find a new set of line breaks that gives the paragraph $n + 3$ lines. (Without the previous step, TEX wouldn't know the value of n.)

(3) If the previous attempt results in lines whose badness exceeds `\tolerance`, it tries to get $n + 2$ lines—and if that also fails, $n + 1$ lines, and finally n lines again.

Similarly, if looseness is $-n$, TEX attempts to set the paragraph with n fewer lines than normal. The easiest way for TEX to make a paragraph one line longer is to put a single word on the excess line. You can prevent this by putting a tie (p. 105) between the last two words of the paragraph.

Setting `\looseness` is the best way to force a paragraph to occupy a given number of lines. Setting it to a negative value is useful when you're trying to increase the amount of text you can fit on a page. Similarly, setting it to a positive value is useful when you're trying to decrease the amount of text on a page.

TEX sets `\looseness` to 0 when it ends a paragraph, after breaking the paragraph into lines. If you want to change the looseness of several paragraphs, you must do it individually for each one or put the change into `\everypar` (p. 113).

\linepenalty   [⟨*number*⟩ parameter]

This parameter specifies demerits that TEX assesses for each line break when it is breaking a paragraph into lines. The penalty is independent of where the line break occurs. Increasing the value of this parameter causes TEX to try harder to set a paragraph with a minimum number of lines, even at the cost of other aesthetic considerations such as avoiding overly tight interword spacing. Demerits are in units of badness squared, so you need to assign a rather large value to this parameter (in the thousands) for it to have any effect. Plain TEX sets \linepenalty to 10.

\adjdemerits   [⟨*number*⟩ parameter]

This parameter specifies additional demerits that TEX attaches to a breakpoint between two adjacent lines that are "visually incompatible". Such a pair of lines makes a paragraph appear uneven. Incompatibility is evaluated in terms of the tightness or looseness of lines:

(1) A line is tight if its glue needs to shrink by at least 50%.
(2) A line is decent if its badness is 12 or less.
(3) A line is loose if its glue needs to stretch by more than 50%.
(4) A line is very loose if its glue needs to stretch so much that its badness exceeds 100.

Two adjacent lines are visually incompatible if their categories are not adjacent, e.g., a tight line is next to a loose one or a decent line is next to a very loose one.

Demerits are in units of badness squared, so you need to assign a rather large value to this parameter (in the thousands) for it to have any effect. Plain TEX sets \adjdemerits to 10000.

\exhyphenpenalty   [⟨*number*⟩ parameter]

This parameter specifies the penalty that TEX attaches to a breakpoint at an explicit hyphen such as the one in "helter-skelter". Increasing this parameter has the effect of discouraging TEX from ending a line at an explicit hyphen. Plain TEX sets \exhyphenpenalty to 50.

\hyphenpenalty   [⟨*number*⟩ parameter]

This parameter specifies the penalty that TEX attaches to a breakpoint at an implicit hyphen. Implicit hyphens can come from TEX's hyphenation dictionary or from discretionary hyphens that you've inserted with \- (p. 126). Increasing this parameter has the effect of discouraging TEX from hyphenating words. Plain TEX sets \hyphenpenalty to 50.

\doublehyphendemerits   [⟨*number*⟩ parameter]

This parameter specifies additional demerits that TEX attaches to a breakpoint when that breakpoint leads to two consecutive lines that end in a hyphen. Increasing the value of this parameter has the effect of discouraging TeX from hyphenating two lines in a row. Demerits are in units of badness squared, so you need to assign a rather large value to this parameter (in the thousands) for it to have any effect. Plain TeX sets `\doublehyphendemerits` to 10000.

\finalhyphendemerits   [⟨*number*⟩ parameter]

This parameter specifies additional demerits that TeX attaches to a breakpoint that causes the next to last line of a paragraph to end with a hyphen. Such a hyphen is generally considered to be unaesthetic because of the possible blank space from a short last line beneath it. Increasing the value of this parameter has the effect of discouraging TeX from ending the next to the last line with a hyphen. Demerits are in units of badness squared, so you need to assign a rather large value to this parameter (in the thousands) for it to have any effect. Plain TeX sets `\finalhyphendemerits` to 5000.

\binoppenalty   [⟨*number*⟩ parameter]

This parameter specifies the penalty for breaking a math formula after a binary operator when the formula appears in a paragraph. Plain TeX sets `\binoppenalty` to 700.

\relpenalty   [⟨*number*⟩ parameter]

This parameter specifies the penalty for breaking a math formula after a relation when the formula appears in a paragraph. Plain TeX sets `\relpenalty` to 500.

■ *Hyphenation*

☞   \-

The `\-` command inserts a "discretionary hyphen" into a word. The discretionary hyphen allows TeX to hyphenate the word at that place. TeX isn't obliged to hyphenate there—it does so only if it needs to. This command is useful when a word that occurs in one or two places in your document needs to be hyphenated, but TeX can't find an appropriate hyphenation point on its own.

Example:
```
Alice was exceedingly reluctant to shake hands first
with either Twee\-dle\-dum or Twee\-dle\-dee, for
fear of hurting the other one's feelings.
```

produces:

Alice was exceedingly reluctant to shake hands first with either Twee-
dledum or Tweedledee, for fear of hurting the other one's feelings.

\discretionary – ⟨*pre-break text*⟩ ″ – ⟨*post-break text*⟩ ″ – ⟨*no-break text*⟩ ″
This command specifies a "discretionary break", namely, a place where
TeX can break a line. It also tells TeX what text to put on either side
of the break.

- If TeX does not break there, it uses the ⟨*no-break text*⟩.
- If TeX does break there, it puts the ⟨*pre-break text*⟩ just before the
  break and the ⟨*post-break text*⟩ just after the break.

Just as with \-, TeX isn't obligated to break a line at a discretionary
break. In fact, \- is ordinarily equivalent to \discretionary{-}{}{}.

TeX sometimes inserts discretionary breaks on its own. For example, it
inserts \discretionary{}{}{} after an explicit hyphen or dash.

Example:
```
% An ordinary discretionary hyphen (equivalent to \-):
\discretionary{-}{}{}
% A place where TeX can break a line, but should not
% insert a space if the line isn't broken there, e.g.,
% after a dash:
\discretionary{}{}{}
% Accounts for German usage: 'flicken', but 'flik-
% ken':
German ``fli\discretionary{k-}{k}{ck}en''
```

\hyphenation – ⟨*word*⟩ ␣ . . . ␣ ⟨*word*⟩ ″
TeX keeps a dictionary of exceptions to its hyphenation rules. Each dictionary entry indicates how a particular word should be hyphenated. The
\hyphenation command adds words to the dictionary. Its argument is a
sequence of words separated by blanks. Uppercase and lowercase letters
are equivalent. The hyphens in each word indicate the places where TeX
can hyphenate that word. A word with no hyphens in it will never be
hyphenated. However, you can still override the hyphenation dictionary
by using \- in a particular occurrence of a word. You need to provide all
the grammatical forms of a word that you want TeX to handle, e.g., both
the singular and the plural.

Example:
```
\hyphenation{Gry-phon my-co-phagy}
\hyphenation{man-u-script man-u-scripts piz-za}
```

\uchyph   [⟨*number*⟩ parameter]
A positive value of \uchyph (uppercase hyphenation) permits hyphenation of words, such as proper names, that start with a capital letter.
A zero or negative value inhibits such hyphenation. Plain TEX sets
\uchyph to 1, so TEX normally tries to hyphenate words that start with
a capital letter.

\showhyphens – ⟨*word*⟩ ␣ . . . ␣ ⟨*word*⟩ "
This command isn't normally used in documents, but you can use it
at your terminal to see how TEX would hyphenate some random set of
words. The words, with hyphenations indicated, appear both in the log
and at your terminal. You'll get a complaint about an underfull hbox—
just ignore it.

Example:
```
\showhyphens{threshold quizzical draughts argumentative}
```
produces in the log:
```
Underfull \hbox (badness 10000) detected at line 0
[] \tenrm thresh-old quizzi-cal draughts ar-gu-men-ta-tive
```

\language   [⟨*number*⟩ parameter]
Different languages have different sets of hyphenation rules. This parameter determines the set of hyphenation rules that TEX uses. By changing
\language you can get TEX to hyphenate portions of text or entire documents according to the hyphenation rules appropriate to a particular
language. Your local information about TEX will tell you if any additional sets of hyphenation rules are available (besides the ones for English) and what the appropriate values of \language are. The default
value of \language is 0.

TEX sets the current language to 0 at the start of every paragraph,
and compares \language to the current language whenever it adds a
character to the current paragraph. If they are not the same, TEX adds a
whatsit indicating the language change. This whatsit is the clue in later
processing that the language rules should change.

\setlanguage ⟨*number*⟩
This command sets the current language to ⟨*number*⟩ by inserting the
same whatsit that you'd get by changing \language. However, it does
not change the value of \language.

\lefthyphenmin   [⟨*number*⟩ parameter]
\righthyphenmin   [⟨*number*⟩ parameter]
These parameters specify the smallest word fragments that TEX allows
at the left and at the right end of a hyphenated word. Plain TEX de-

faults them to 2 and 3 respectively; these are the recommended values for English.

\hyphenchar *⟨font⟩*   [*⟨number⟩* parameter]

TeX doesn't necessarily use the '-' character at hyphenation points. Instead, it uses the \hyphenchar of the current font, which is usually '-' but need not be. If a font has a negative \hyphenchar value, TeX won't hyphenate words in that font.

Note that *⟨font⟩* is a control sequence that names a font, not a *⟨font-name⟩* that names font files. Beware: an assignment to \hyphenchar is *not* undone at the end of a group. If you want to change \hyphenchar locally, you'll need to save and restore its original value explicitly.

Example:
```
\hyphenchar\tenrm = '-
    % Set hyphenation for tenrm font to '-'.
\hyphenchar\tentt = -1
    % Don't hyphenate words in font tentt.
```

\defaulthyphenchar   [*⟨number⟩* parameter]

When TeX reads the metrics file for a font in response to a \font command, it sets the font's \hyphenchar to \defaulthyphenchar. If the value of \defaulthyphenchar is not in the range 0–255 when you load a font, TeX won't hyphenate any words in that font unless you override the decision by setting the font's \hyphenchar later on. Plain TeX sets \defaulthyphenchar to 45, the ASCII code for '-'.

Example:
```
\defaulthyphenchar = '-
    % Assume '-' is the hyphen, unless overridden.
\defaulthyphenchar = -1
    % Don't hyphenate, unless overridden.
```

See also: \pretolerance (p. 123).

Section headings, lists, and theorems

☞ **\beginsection** *⟨argument⟩* **\par**

You can use this command to begin a major subdivision of your document. *⟨argument⟩* is intended to serve as a section title. \beginsection surrounds ⟨*argument*⟩ by extra vertical space and sets it in boldface, left-justified. You can produce the \par that ends ⟨*argument*⟩ with a blank line.

Example:
```
$\ldots$  till she had brought herself down to nine
inches high.


\beginsection Section 6. Pig and Pepper


For a minute or two she stood looking at the house $\ldots$
```
produces:

... till she had brought herself down to nine inches high.

Section 6. Pig and Pepper

For a minute or two she stood looking at the house ...

\item ⟨*argument*⟩
\itemitem ⟨*argument*⟩

These commands are useful for creating itemized lists. The entire paragraph following ⟨*argument*⟩ is indented by \parindent (for \item) or by 2\parindent (for \itemitem). (See page 113 for an explanation of \parindent.) Then ⟨*argument*⟩, followed by an en space, is placed just to the left of the text of the first line of the paragraph so that it falls within the paragraph indentation as specified by \parindent.

If you want to include more than one paragraph in an item, put \item{} in front of the additional paragraphs.

Example:
```
{\parindent = 18pt
\noindent Here is what we require:
\item{1.}Three eggs in their shells,
but with the yolks removed.
\item{2.}Two separate glass cups containing:
\itemitem{(a)}One-half cup {\it used} motor oil.
\itemitem{(b)}One cup port wine, preferably French.
\item{3.}Juice and skin of one turnip.}
```
produces:

Here is what we require:

1. Three eggs in their shells, but with the yolks removed.
2. Two separate glass cups containing:
   (a) One-half cup *used* motor oil.
   (b) One cup port wine, preferably French.
3. Juice and skin of one turnip.

☞   **\proclaim** ⟨*argument*⟩.␣⟨*general text*⟩ **\par**

This command "proclaims" a theorem, lemma, hypothesis, etc. It sets ⟨*argument*⟩ in boldface type and the following paragraph in italics. ⟨*argument*⟩ must be followed by a period and a space token, which serve to set off ⟨*argument*⟩ from ⟨*general text*⟩. ⟨*general text*⟩ consists of the text up to the next paragraph boundary, except that you can include multiple paragraphs by putting them within braces and ending a paragraph after the closing right brace.

Example:

```
\proclaim Theorem 1.
What I say is not to be believed.

\proclaim Corollary 1. Theorem 1 is false.\par
```

produces:

Theorem 1. *What I say is not to be believed.*

Corollary 1. *Theorem 1 is false.*

6 Commands for composing pages

This section covers commands that deal with pages, their components, and the output routine. For an explanation of the conventions used in this section, see "Descriptions of the commands" (p. 3).

Interline and interparagraph spaces

\baselineskip [⟨*glue*⟩ parameter]
\lineskiplimit [⟨*dimen*⟩ parameter]
\lineskip [⟨*glue*⟩ parameter]

These three parameters jointly determine how much space TeX leaves between consecutive boxes of an ordinary vertical list, e.g., the lines of a paragraph. This space is called "interline glue". It is also inserted between the component boxes of a vbox constructed in internal vertical mode.

In the usual case, when the boxes aren't abnormally high or deep, TeX makes the distance from the baseline of one box to the baseline of the next one equal to \baselineskip. It does this by inserting interline glue equal to \baselineskip minus the depth of the upper box (as given by \prevdepth) and the height of the lower box. But if this interline glue would be less than \lineskiplimit, indicating that the two boxes are too close together, TeX inserts the \lineskip glue instead.[1] See pages 79–80 of *The TeXbook* for a precise description.

---

[1] TeX actually accounts for the beginning of a vertical list by setting \prevdepth to $-1000\,$pt and testing \prevdepth before *every* box. If \prevdepth $\leq -1000\,$pt it does not insert any interline glue.

Note that \baselineskip and \lineskip measure *different things*: the distance between baselines on the one hand and the distance between the bottom of one box and the top of the next box on the other hand. See page 78 of *The TEXbook* for further details. The first example below shows the effects of \lineskiplimit.

You can obtain the effect of double spacing by doubling the value of \baselineskip as illustrated in the second example below. A change to \baselineskip at any point before the end of a paragraph affects the entire paragraph.

Example:
```
\baselineskip = 11pt \lineskiplimit = 1pt
\lineskip = 2pt plus .5pt
Sometimes you'll need to typeset a paragraph that has
tall material, such as a mathematical formula,  embedded
within it.  An example of such a formula is $n \choose k$.
Note the extra space above and below this line as
compared with the other lines.
(If the formula didn't project below the line,
we'd only get extra space above the line.)
```
produces:

Sometimes you'll need to typeset a paragraph that has tall material, such as a mathematical formula, embedded within it. An example of such a formula is $\binom{n}{k}$. Note the extra space above and below this line as compared with the other lines. (If the formula didn't project below the line, we'd only get extra space above the line.)

Example:
```
\baselineskip = 2\baselineskip % Start double spacing.
```

\prevdepth   [⟨*dimen*⟩ parameter]

When TEX adds a box to a vertical list, it sets \prevdepth to the depth of that box. TEX sets \prevdepth to -1000 pt at the start of a vertical list, indicating that the usual interline glue should be suppressed.

\normalbaselineskip   [⟨*glue*⟩ parameter]
\normallineskiplimit   [⟨*dimen*⟩ parameter]
\normallineskip   [⟨*glue*⟩ parameter]
\normalbaselines

The three parameters contain values for \baselineskip, \lineskip, and \lineskiplimit respectively. The \normalbaselines command sets \baselineskip, \lineskip, and \lineskiplimit to the values contained in the three parameters.

\offinterlineskip

This command tells TEX to stop inserting interline glue from now on. Unless you want it to be in effect for the rest of the document (which you probably don't), you should enclose it in a group together with the text you want it to affect. Its main purpose is to let you do interline spacing yourself, e.g., using struts, without interference from TEX's normal interline glue. \offinterlineskip is often useful when you're constructing a horizontal alignment.

Example:
```
\def\entry#1:#2 {\strut\quad#1\quad&\quad#2\quad\cr}
\offinterlineskip \tabskip = 0pt \halign{%
\vrule\quad\hfil#\hfil\quad\vrule&
    \quad\hfil#\hfil\quad\vrule\cr
\noalign{\hrule}
\vphantom{\vrule height 2pt}&\cr \noalign{\hrule}
\entry \it Opera:\it Composer
\vphantom{\vrule height 2pt}&\cr \noalign{\hrule}
\vphantom{\vrule height 2pt}&\cr
\entry Fidelio:Beethoven
\entry Peter Grimes:Britten
\entry Don Giovanni:Mozart
\vphantom{\vrule height 2pt}&\cr \noalign{\hrule}}
```
produces:

Opera	*Composer*
Fidelio	Beethoven
Peter Grimes	Britten
Don Giovanni	Mozart

\nointerlineskip

This command tells TEX not to insert interline glue in front of the next line. It has no effect on subsequent lines.

\openup ⟨*dimen*⟩

This command increases \baselineskip by ⟨*dimen*⟩. An \openup command before the end of a paragraph affects the entire paragraph, so you shouldn't use \openup to change \baselineskip within a paragraph. \openup is most useful for typesetting tables and math displays—a little extra space between rows often makes them more readable.

Example:
```
Alice picked up the White King very gently, and lifted him
across more slowly than she had lifted the Queen; but before
she put him on the table, she thought she might well dust
him a little, he was so covered with ashes.
\openup .5\baselineskip % 1.5 linespacing.
```
produces:

Alice picked up the White King very gently, and lifted him across more slowly than she had lifted the Queen; but before she put him on the table, she thought she might well dust him a little, he was so covered with ashes.

Page breaks

■ Encouraging or discouraging page breaks

\break
This command forces a page break. Unless you do something to fill out the page, you're likely to get an underfull vbox. \break can also be used in horizontal mode.

\nobreak
This command prevents a page break where it otherwise might occur. \nobreak can also be used in horizontal mode.

\allowbreak
This command tells TeX to allow a page break where one could not ordinarily occur. \allowbreak can also be used in horizontal mode.

\penalty ⟨*number*⟩
This command produces a penalty item. The penalty item makes TeX more or less willing to break a page at the point where that item occurs. A negative penalty, i.e., a bonus, encourages a page break; a positive penalty discourages a page break. A penalty of 10000 or more prevents a break

altogether, while a penalty of -10000 or less forces a break. `\penalty` can also be used in horizontal mode.

Example:

```
\def\break{\penalty-10000 } % as in plain TeX
\def\nobreak{\penalty10000 } % as in plain TeX
\def\allowbreak{\penalty0 } % as in plain TeX
```

\goodbreak

This command ends a paragraph and also indicates to TeX that this is a good place to break the page.

\smallbreak
\medbreak
\bigbreak

These commands indicate increasingly desirable places for TeX to break a page. They also cause TeX to insert a `\smallskip`, `\medskip`, or `\bigskip` (p. 154) if the page break doesn't actually happen. TeX suppresses this skip if it occurs just after an equal or larger skip.

☞ ### \eject
\supereject

These commands force a page break at the current position and end the current paragraph. If you don't precede them with `\vfil` (p. 157), TeX will try to stretch out the page contents (and will probably complain about an underfull vbox). The `\supereject` command, in addition, instructs the plain TeX output routine to force out any leftover insertions, such as long footnotes, so that they are produced before any more input is processed. Thus `\supereject` is a good command to use at the end of each chapter or other major unit of your document.

\filbreak

This command provides a kind of conditional page break. It tells TeX to break the page—but not if the text up to a later `\filbreak` also fits on the same page. By enclosing a paragraph in a pair of `\filbreak`s, you can ensure that TeX will keep a paragraph on a single page if it can. You should not use `\filbreak` within a paragraph, since it forces TeX into vertical mode and thus ends the paragraph. See page 266 for more advice on this subject.

\raggedbottom
\normalbottom

Normally TeX tries hard to ensure that all pages have the same depth, i.e., that their bottom margins are equal. The `\raggedbottom` command tells TEX to allow some variability among the bottom margins on different pages. It's often appropriate to use \raggedbottom when you have material that contains large blocks of material that should not be split across pages. The \normalbottom command cancels the effect of \raggedbottom.

■ Page breaking parameters

\interlinepenalty   [⟨*number*⟩ parameter]
This parameter specifies the penalty for breaking a page between the lines of a paragraph. By setting it to 10000 you can force all page breaks to occur between paragraphs, provided that the pages have enough stretch so that TEX can still compose them decently. Plain TEX leaves \interlinepenalty at 0.

\clubpenalty   [⟨*number*⟩ parameter]
This parameter specifies the penalty for breaking a page just after the first line of a paragraph. A line by itself at the bottom of a page is called a "club line". Plain TEX sets \clubpenalty to 150.

\widowpenalty   [⟨*number*⟩ parameter]
This parameter specifies the penalty for breaking a page just before the last line of a paragraph. A line by itself at the top of a page is called a "widow line". Plain TEX sets \widowpenalty to 150.

\displaywidowpenalty   [⟨*number*⟩ parameter]
This parameter specifies the penalty for breaking a page just before the last line of a partial paragraph that immediately precedes a math display. Plain TEX sets \displaywidowpenalty to 50.

\predisplaypenalty   [⟨*number*⟩ parameter]
This parameter specifies the penalty for breaking a page just before a math display. Plain TEX sets \predisplaypenalty to 10000.

\postdisplaypenalty   [⟨*number*⟩ parameter]
This parameter specifies the penalty for breaking a page just after a math display. Plain TEX leaves \postdisplaypenalty at 0.

\brokenpenalty   [⟨*number*⟩ parameter]

This parameter specifies the penalty for breaking a page just after a line that ends in a discretionary item (usually a hyphen). \brokenpenalty applies to page breaking, while \hyphenpenalty (p. 125) applies to line breaking. Plain TEX sets \brokenpenalty to 100.

\insertpenalties   [⟨*number*⟩ parameter]

This parameter contains the sum of certain penalties that TEX accumulates as it is placing insertions onto the current page. These penalties are incurred when TEX is processing an \insert command and discovers that a previous insertion of the same kind on this page has been split, leaving part of it for subsequent pages. See pages 123–125 of *The TEXbook* for the details of this calculation.

\insertpenalties has an entirely different meaning during an output routine—it's the number of insertions that have been seen but that don't fit on the current page (see page 125 of *The TEXbook*).

\floatingpenalty   [⟨*number*⟩ parameter]

This parameter specifies the penalty that TEX adds to \insertpenalties when the page builder is adding an insertion to the current page and discovers that a previous insertion of the same kind on this page has been split, leaving part of it for subsequent pages. Plain TEX leaves \floatingpenalty at 0.

\pagegoal   [⟨*dimen*⟩ parameter]

This parameter specifies the desired height for the current page. TEX sets \pagegoal to the current value of \vsize when it first puts a box or an insertion on the current page. You can shorten a page while TEX is working on it by changing the value of \pagegoal—even if the new value is less than the height of the material already on that page. TEX will just put the extra material on the next page. But remember—\pagegoal is reset to \vsize again when TEX starts the next page.

\pagetotal   [⟨*dimen*⟩ parameter]

This parameter specifies the accumulated natural height of the current page. TEX updates \pagetotal as it adds items to the main vertical list.

\pagedepth   [⟨*dimen*⟩ parameter]

This parameter specifies the depth of the current page. TEX updates \pagedepth as it adds items to the main vertical list.

\pageshrink   [⟨*dimen*⟩ parameter]

This parameter specifies the amount of shrink in the accumulated glue on the current page. TₑX updates \pageshrink as it adds items to the main vertical list.

\pagestretch   [⟨*dimen*⟩ parameter]
\pagefilstretch   [⟨*dimen*⟩ parameter]
\pagefillstretch   [⟨*dimen*⟩ parameter]
\pagefilllstretch   [⟨*dimen*⟩ parameter]

These four parameters together specify the amount of stretch in the glue on the current page. The amount of stretch has the form $n_0 + n_1\mathtt{fil} + n_2\mathtt{fill} + n_3\mathtt{filll}$, with the four parameters giving the values of the four n_i. TₑX updates these parameters as it adds items to the main vertical list.

Page layout

■ *Page description parameters*

\hsize   [⟨*dimen*⟩ parameter]

This parameter specifies the current line length. See page 114 for a more complete explanation.

\vsize   [⟨*dimen*⟩ parameter]

This parameter specifies the current vertical extent of a page. TₑX examines it only when it is starting a page. Thus if you change \vsize in the middle of a page, your change won't affect anything until the following page. If you want to change the vertical extent of a page when you're in the middle of it, you should assign the new height to \pagegoal (p. 139) instead. (If you want the change to affect the following pages too, you should change *both* \vsize and \pagegoal.) Plain TₑX sets \vsize to 8.9in.

\hoffset   [⟨*dimen*⟩ parameter]
\voffset   [⟨*dimen*⟩ parameter]

TₑX normally takes the "origin" of a page, that is, the point where it starts printing, as being one inch down from the top of the page and one inch to the right of the left end of the page.[2] The values of \hoffset and \voffset give the horizontal and vertical offset of the actual origin from this point. Thus if \hoffset and \voffset are both zero, TeX uses its normal origin.

Example:
```
  \hoffset = -.3in
      % Start printing .7 inches from left edge of paper.
  \voffset = 1in
      % Start printing 2 inches from top edge of paper.
```

\topskip   [⟨*glue*⟩ parameter]

This parameter specifies the glue that TeX inserts at the top of each page in order to keep the tops of pages even. The top of the page is considered to be at the baseline of an imaginary line of text just above the top line of the page. The \topskip glue comes between the top of the page and the top of the first box on the page. TeX adjusts the glue produced by \topskip so that the distance between the top of the page and the baseline of the first box on the page is \baselineskip (p. 133). But if the first box is so tall that its top would land above the top of the page, TeX sets \topskip for that page to zero.

To understand better the effect of these rules, assume that \topskip has no stretch or shrink and that the first item on the page is indeed a box. Then if the height of that box is no greater than \topskip, its baseline will be \topskip from the top of the page independently of its height. On the other hand, if the height of the box is d greater than \topskip, its baseline will be $\texttt{\textbackslash topskip} + d$ from the top of the page. See pages 113–114 of *The TeXbook* for the remaining details of how \topskip works. Plain TeX sets \topskip to 10pt.

\parskip   [⟨*glue*⟩ parameter]

This parameter specifies the "paragraph skip", i.e., the vertical glue that TeX inserts at the start of a paragraph. See \par (p. 110) for more information about what happens when TeX starts a paragraph. Plain TeX sets \parskip to 0pt plus 0.1pt.

\maxdepth   [⟨*dimen*⟩ parameter]

This parameter specifies the maximum depth of the bottom box on a page. It is related to \boxmaxdepth (p. 163). If the depth of the bottom box on a page exceeds \maxdepth, TeX moves the box's reference point

---

[2] TeX itself is indifferent to where the origin of the page is, but this information has to be built into the device drivers that convert .dvi files into printable form so that different devices will yield the same results.

down so that it's \maxdepth from the bottom of that box. Without this adjustment, the bottom box on a page could extend well into the bottom margin or even off the page entirely. Plain TEX sets \maxdepth to 4pt.

■ *Page numbers*

\pageno   [⟨*number*⟩ parameter]
This parameter contains the current page number as an integer. The page number is normally negative for front-matter pages that are numbered with small roman numerals instead of arabic numerals. If you change the page number within a page, the changed number will be used in any headers or footers that appear on that page. The actual printing of page numbers is handled by TEX's output routine, which you can modify.

    Plain TEX keeps the page number in the register \count0. (\pageno is, in fact, a synonym for \count0.) Whenever it ships out a page to the .dvi file, TEX displays the current value of \count0 on your terminal so that you can tell which page it is working on. It's possible to use registers \count1–\count9 for nested levels of page numbers (you must program this yourself). If any of these registers are nonzero, TEX displays them on your terminal also.[3]

Example:
```
This explanation appears on page \number\pageno\
of our book.
```
produces:
    This explanation appears on page 142 of our book.

Example:
```
\pageno = 30 % Number the next page as 30.
Don't look for this explanation on page \number\pageno.
```
produces:
    Don't look for this explanation on page 30.

\advancepageno
This command adds 1 to the page number n in \pageno if $n \geq 0$ and subtracts 1 from it if $n < 0$.

☞ \nopagenumbers
By default, plain TEX produces a footer containing a centered page number. This command tells TEX to produce a blank footer instead.

---

[3] More precisely, it displays all registers in sequence from \count0 to \count9, but omits trailing zero registers. For instance, if the values of \count0–\count3 are $(17, 0, 0, 7)$ and the others are 0, TEX displays the page number as [17.0.0.7].

\folio

This command produces the current page number, whose value is the number n contained in \pageno. If $n \geq 0$, TEX produces n as a decimal number, while if $n < 0$, TEX produces $-n$ in lowercase roman numerals.

Example:

```
This explanation appears on page \folio\ of the book.
```

produces:

This explanation appears on page 143 of the book.

■ *Header and footer lines*

\headline   [⟨*token list*⟩ parameter]
\footline   [⟨*token list*⟩ parameter]

These parameters contain, respectively, the current headline (header) and the current footline (footer). The plain TEX output routine places the headline at the top of each page and the footline at the bottom of each page. The default headline is empty and the default footline is a centered page number.

The headline and footline should both be as wide as \hsize (use \hfil, p. 157, for this if necessary). You should always include a font-setting command in these lines, since the current font is unpredictable when TEX is calling the output routine. If you don't set the font explicitly, you'll get whatever font TEX was using when it broke the page.

You shouldn't try to use \headline or \footline to produce multiline headers or footers. Although TEX won't complain, it will give you something that's very ugly. See page 274 for a method of creating multiline headers or footers.

Example:

```
\headline = {\tenrm My First Reader\hfil Page \folio}
```

produces:

My First Reader   Page 10
(*at the top of page 10*)

Example:

```
\footline = {\tenit\ifodd\pageno\hfil\folio
            \else\folio\hfil\fi}
% Produce the page number in ten-point italic at
% the outside bottom corner of each page.
```

■ *Marks*

\mark – ⟨*text*⟩ ″

This command causes TEX to append a mark containing ⟨*mark text*⟩ to whatever list it is currently constructing. Generally you shouldn't use \mark within an "inner" construct such as a math formula or a box you've built with an \hbox, \vbox, or \vtop command, because TEX won't see the mark when it's constructing the main box of the page. But if you use \mark in ordinary horizontal mode or directly in an hbox that's part of the main vertical list, the mark migrates out to the main vertical list. See pages 259–260 of *The TEXbook* for examples showing how \mark can be used.

\firstmark
\botmark
\topmark

These commands expand to the mark text in an item generated by an earlier \mark command. The mark text has the form of a token list. TEX sets the values of these commands when it finishes placing the contents of a page into \box255, just before calling the output routine as part of its page breaking actions. TEX determines these values as follows:

- \firstmark contains the tokens of the first mark on the page.
- \botmark contains the tokens of the last mark on the page.
- \topmark contains the tokens of the mark that is in effect at the very top of the page. That mark is the last mark that *preceded* the page, i.e., the \botmark of the previous page. It is empty if no marks preceded the page.

If a page has no marks on it, TEX will set \firstmark and \botmark to the same mark as \topmark, i.e., the most recent preceding mark. The table at the bottom of page 258 of *The TEXbook* illustrates the relation among \firstmark, \botmark, and \topmark.

\splitfirstmark
\splitbotmark

These commands expand to the mark text generated by an earlier \mark command that produced an item in the item list of a vbox *V*. The mark text has the form of a token list. When TEX splits *V* in response to a \vsplit command (p. 149), it sets the values of these commands as follows:

- \splitfirstmark contains the tokens of the first mark in the item list of *V*.

- \splitbotmark contains the tokens of the last mark in the item list of V.

These commands produce no tokens if there was no preceding \vsplit, or if the most recent preceding \vsplit didn't contain any marks.

Insertions

■ Footnotes

☞ **\footnote** $\langle argument_1 \rangle$ $\langle argument_2 \rangle$
\vfootnote $\langle argument_1 \rangle$ $\langle argument_2 \rangle$
These commands produce footnotes. $\langle argument_1 \rangle$ is the "reference mark" for the footnote and $\langle argument_2 \rangle$ is its text. The text can be several paragraphs long if necessary and can contain constructs such as math displays, but it shouldn't contain any insertions (such as other footnotes).

You shouldn't use these commands inside a subformula of a math formula, in a box within a box being contributed to a page, or in an insertion of any kind. If you're unsure whether these restrictions apply, you can be safe by only using \footnote and \vfootnote directly within a paragraph or between paragraphs.

These restrictions aren't as severe as they seem because you can use \vfootnote to footnote most anything. Both \footnote and \vfootnote insert the reference mark in front of the footnote itself, but \vfootnote doesn't insert the reference mark into the text. Thus, when you use \vfootnote you can explicitly insert the reference mark wherever it belongs without concern about the context and place the \vfootnote in the next paragraph. If you find that the footnote lands on the page following the one where it belongs, move the \vfootnote back to the previous paragraph. There are rare circumstances where you'll need to alter the text of your document in order to get a footnote to appear on the same page as its reference mark.

Example:
```
To quote the mathematician P\'olya is a ploy.\footnote
*{This is an example of an anagram, but not a strict one.}
```
produces:
To quote the mathematician Pólya is a ploy.*

$\vdots$

---

* This is an example of an anagram, but not a strict one.

Example:
```
$$f(t)=\sigma\sigma t\;\raise 1ex \hbox{\dag}$$
\vfootnote \dag{The $\sigma\sigma$ notation was explained in
the previous section.}
```
produces:

$$f(t) = \sigma\sigma t\ ^\dagger$$

$$\vdots$$

_____

† The $\sigma\sigma$ notation was explained in the previous section.

■ General insertions

\topinsert ⟨*vertical mode material*⟩ **\endinsert**
\midinsert ⟨*vertical mode material*⟩ **\endinsert**
\pageinsert ⟨*vertical mode material*⟩ **\endinsert**

These commands produce different forms of insertions that instruct (or allow) TEX to relocate the ⟨*vertical mode material*⟩:

- \topinsert attempts to put the material at the top of the current page. If it won't fit there, \topinsert will move the material to the next available top of page.
- \midinsert attempts to put the material at the current position. If it won't fit there, \midinsert will move the material to the next available top of page.
- \pageinsert puts the material by itself on the next page. To avoid an underfull page, be sure to end the inserted material with \vfil or fill out the excess space some other way.

The ⟨*vertical mode material*⟩ is said to be "floating" because TEX can move it from one place to another. Insertions are very useful for material such as figures and tables because you can position such material where you want it without knowing where the page breaks will fall.

Each of these commands implicitly ends the current paragraph, so you should use them only between paragraphs. You should not use them within a box or within another insertion. If you have several insertions competing for the same space, TEX will retain their relative order.

Example:
```
\pageinsert
% This text will appear on the following page, by itself.
This page is reserved for a picture of the Queen of Hearts
sharing a plate of oysters with the Walrus and
the Carpenter.
\endinsert
```

\endinsert

This command ends an insertion started by \topinsert, \midinsert, or \pageinsert.

\insert ⟨*number*⟩ – ⟨*vertical mode material*⟩ ″

This primitive command provides the underlying mechanism for constructing insertions, but it is hardly ever used outside of a macro definition. The definitions of the \footnote, \vfootnote, \topinsert, \midinsert, and \pageinsert commands are all built around \insert.

When you design insertions for a document, you should assign a different integer code[4] n to each kind of insertion, using the \newinsert command (p. 244) to obtain the integer codes. The \insert command itself appends the ⟨*vertical mode material*⟩ to the current horizontal or vertical list. Your output routine is responsible for moving the inserted material from where it resides in \box n to an output page.

TEX groups together all insertions having the same code number. Each insertion code n has four registers associated with it:

- \box n is where TEX accumulates the material for insertions with code n. When TEX breaks a page, it puts into \box n as much insertion n material as will fit on the page. Your output routine should then move this material to the actual page. You can use \ifvoid (p. 238) to test if there is any material in \box n. If not all the material fits, TEX saves the leftovers for the next page.

- \count n is a magnification factor f. When TEX is computing the vertical space occupied on the page by insertion n material, it multiplies the vertical extent of this material by $f/1000$. Thus you would ordinarily set f to 500 for a double-column insertion and to 0 for a marginal note.

- \dimen n specifies the maximum amount of insertion n material that TEX will put on a single page.

- \skip n specifies extra space that TEX allocates on the page if the page contains any insertion n material. This space is in addition

---

[4] *The TEXbook* uses the term "class" for a code. We use a different term to avoid confusion with the other meaning of "class" (p. 56).

to the space occupied by the insertion itself. For example, it would account for the space on a page above the footnotes (if there are any).

TEX sets \box *n*, and you should set the other three registers so that TEX can correctly compute the vertical space required by the insertion. See pages 122–125 of *The TEXbook* for further details of how TEX processes this command and of how insertions interact with page breaking.

See also: \floatingpenalty (p. 139).

Modifying the output routine

\output   [⟨*token list*⟩ parameter]
This parameter contains the current output routine, i.e., the token list that TEX expands when it finds a page break. TEX puts the page into \box255, so \output is responsible for doing something with \box255— either shipping it out or putting it somewhere else. The output routine is also responsible for attaching things such as headers and footers.

\plainoutput
This command invokes plain TEX's output routine. Plain TEX sets \output to a token list containing the single token \plainoutput.

\shipout ⟨*box*⟩
This command instructs TEX to send ⟨*box*⟩ to the .dvi file. TEX expands any \write command in ⟨*box*⟩ as part of \shipout. The principal use of \shipout is in the output routine, but you can use it anywhere.

\deadcycles   [⟨*number*⟩ parameter]
This parameter contains the number of times that TEX has initiated the output routine since the last time it did a \shipout.[5] If \deadcycles gets too big, you've probably gotten TEX into a loop, e.g., one where the page builder is trying the same page break over and over again.

\maxdeadcycles   [⟨*number*⟩ parameter]
If the value of \deadcycles exceeds the value of \maxdeadcycles, TEX assumes that the output routine has gotten into a loop. TEX then complains and runs its own simple output routine, equivalent to \shipout

---

[5] More precisely, TEX sets \deadcyles to 0 whenever it executes \shipout and increments it by 1 whenever it executes \output.

\box255, that is likely to break the loop. Plain TeX sets \maxdeadcycles to 25.

\outputpenalty   [⟨*number*⟩ parameter]

TeX sets this parameter when it breaks a page. If the breakpoint was at a penalty item, TeX removes the penalty item and sets \outputpenalty to the penalty value at the breakpoint; otherwise it sets \outputpenalty to 0.

Suppose that you are undoing a page break in order to break the page at a different place than the one that TeX has just chosen. In order to reconstruct the page, you need to recreate the penalty at TeX's chosen breakpoint. You can accomplish this with the command \penalty \outputpenalty.

\holdinginserts   [⟨*number*⟩ parameter]

If this parameter is greater than 0 when TeX is processing a page break, TeX will refrain from processing insertions. Setting this parameter to 1 can be useful when you're writing an output routine that needs to reprocess the contents of the page, e.g., an output routine that uses a value of \vsize (p. 140) different from the one used by the page builder.

Splitting vertical lists

\vsplit ⟨*number*⟩ **to** ⟨*dimen*⟩

This command causes TeX to split the box numbered ⟨*number*⟩, which we'll call B_2, into two parts. It uses the same algorithm that it would use if B_2 was a page and it was breaking that page; the division point then corresponds to the page break that it would find. The box B_2 must be a vbox, not an hbox. TeX puts the material preceding the division point into another box B_1 and leaves the material after the division point in B_2. The \vsplit command then produces B_1. Normally you'd assign B_1 to a different box register, as in the example below. If the division point is at the end of B_2, B_2 will be empty after the \vsplit.

TeX employs its usual page-breaking algorithm for the split. It uses ⟨*dimen*⟩ for \pagegoal, the desired height of B_1. The vertical extent of B_1 may not be exactly ⟨*dimen*⟩ because TeX may not be able to achieve its page goal perfectly. TeX does not consider insertions in calculating the split, so insertions in the original vertical list of B_2 will be retained but won't affect the split point.

Example:
```
\setbox 20 = \vsplit 30 to 7in
% Split off the first seven inches or so of material from
% box 30 and place that material in box 20.
```

\splitmaxdepth   [⟨*dimen*⟩ parameter]

This parameter specifies the maximum allowable depth of a box resulting from a \vsplit. \splitmaxdepth plays the same role that \maxdepth (p. 141) plays for a page.

\splittopskip   [⟨*glue*⟩ parameter]

This parameter specifies the glue that TEX inserts at the top of a box resulting from a \vsplit. \splittopskip plays the same role that \topskip (p. 141) plays for a page.

See also: \splitbotmark, \splitfirstmark (p. 144).

7 Commands for horizontal and vertical modes

This section covers commands that have corresponding or identical forms for both horizontal and vertical modes. These commands provide boxes, spaces, rules, leaders, and alignments. For an explanation of the conventions used in this section, see "Descriptions of the commands" (p. 3).

Producing space

■ Fixed-width horizontal space

\thinspace

This command produces a positive kern whose width is one-sixth of an em (p. 60) i.e., it causes TeX to move its position right by that amount. It is useful when you have a nested quotation, for example, and you want to separate the levels of quotes. TeX won't break a line at a \thinspace.

Example:
```
``\thinspace`A quote.'\thinspace''\par
24,\thinspace 29--31,\thinspace 45,\thinspace 102
```
produces:
  "'A quote.'"
  24, 29–31, 45, 102

\negthinspace

This command produces a negative kern whose width is one-sixth of an em (p. 60), i.e., it causes TeX to move its position left by that amount.

It is useful for bringing together characters that are a little too far apart. TEX won't break a line at a `\negthinspace`.

Example:

```
The horror, the horror\negthinspace, the horror of it all!
```

produces:

The horror, the horror, the horror of it all!

\enspace

This command produces a kern whose width is one en (half of an em, see page 60). TEX won't break a line at an `\enspace` unless it's followed by glue. In a bulleted list, the bullets are usually separated from the following text by an `\enspace`.

Example:

```
Lemma 1.\enspace There exists a white rabbit.
```

produces:

Lemma 1. There exists a white rabbit.

☞ \enskip
\quad
\qquad

Each of these commands produces a glob of horizontal glue that can neither stretch nor shrink. TEX can break a line at such glue. The width of these glues (which are relative to the current font) are as follows for `cmr10`, the default plain TEX font:

Command	Space	Illustration
\enskip	$1/2$ em	→| |←
\quad	1 em	→| |←
\qquad	2 em	→| |←

Example:

```
en\enskip skip; quad\quad skip; qquad\qquad skip
```

produces:

en skip; quad skip; qquad skip

■ *Fixed-length vertical space*

☞ \smallskip
\medskip
\bigskip

These commands produce successively larger amounts of vertical space:

smallskip	medskip	bigskip

\smallskip skips by 3 points and can stretch or shrink by 1 point. \med-skip is equivalent to two \smallskips and \bigskip is equivalent to two \medskips.

These commands end a paragraph since they are inherently vertical. The skips that they produce are in addition to the normal inter-paragraph skip.

Example:

Hop \smallskip skip \medskip and \bigskip jump.

produces:

Hop

skip

and

jump.

\smallskipamount   [⟨*glue*⟩ parameter]
\medskipamount   [⟨*glue*⟩ parameter]
\bigskipamount   [⟨*glue*⟩ parameter]

These parameters specify the amounts of glue produced by the \small-skip, \medskip, and \bigskip commands. By changing these parameters you change the effect of the commands. The default values (for plain TeX) correspond to a quarter of a linespace, half a linespace, and a full linespace. We recommend that you maintain this ratio by changing these values whenever you change \baselineskip (p. 133).

■ *Variable-size space*

☞ **\hskip** ⟨*dimen₁*⟩ **plus** ⟨*dimen₂*⟩ **minus** ⟨*dimen₃*⟩
\vskip ⟨*dimen₁*⟩ **plus** ⟨*dimen₂*⟩ **minus** ⟨*dimen₃*⟩

These commands produce horizontal and vertical glue respectively. In the simplest and most common case when only ⟨*dimen₁*⟩ is present, \hskip skips to the right by ⟨*dimen₁*⟩ and \vskip skips down the page by ⟨*dimen₁*⟩. More generally, these commands produce glue whose natural size is ⟨*dimen₁*⟩, whose stretch is ⟨*dimen₂*⟩, and whose shrink is ⟨*dimen₃*⟩. Either the **plus** ⟨*dimen₂*⟩, the **minus** ⟨*dimen₃*⟩, or both can be omitted. If both are present, the **plus** must come before the **minus**. An omitted value is taken to be zero. Any of the ⟨*dimen*⟩s can be negative.

You can use \hskip in math mode, but you can't use mu units (see "mathematical unit", p. 81) for any of the dimensions. If you want mu units, use \mskip (p. 215) instead.

Example:
```
\hbox to 2in{one\hskip 0pt plus .5in two}
```
produces:

one   two

┌─────────────────────────────────┐ 2 in

Example:
```
\hbox to 2in{Help me! I can't fit
{\hskip 0pt minus 2in} inside this box!}
```
produces:

Help me! I can't fitnside this box!

┌─────────────────────────────────┐ 2 in

Example:
```
\vbox to 4pc{\offinterlineskip% Just show effects of \vskip.
   \hbox{one}\vskip 0pc plus 1pc \hbox{two}
      \vskip .5pc \hbox{three}}
```
produces:

one

two
three

\hglue ⟨*glue*⟩
\vglue ⟨*glue*⟩

The \hglue command produces horizontal glue that won't disappear at a line break; the \vglue command produces vertical glue that won't disappear at a page break. In other respects these commands are just like \hskip and \vskip. You can use \vglue to produce blank space at the top of a page, e.g., above a title on the first page of a document, but \topglue (p. 156) is usually better for this purpose.

\topglue   [⟨*glue*⟩ parameter]

This command[1] causes the space from the top of the page to the top of the first box on the page to be ⟨*glue*⟩ precisely. The top of the page is considered to be at the baseline of an imaginary line of text just above the top line of the page. More precisely, it's a distance \topskip above the origin as given by \hoffset and \voffset.

---

[1] \topglue was added to TeX in version 3.0, later than the other enhancements introduced by new TeX (p. 18). It is first described in the *eighteenth* edition of *The TeXbook*.

This command is useful because TEX ordinarily adjusts the glue produced by \topskip in a complex way. By using \topglue you can control the position of the first box on the page without worrying about those adjustments.

\kern ⟨*dimen*⟩

The effect of this command depends on the mode that TEX is in when it encounters it:

- In a horizontal mode, TEX moves its position to the right (for a positive kern) or to the left (for a negative kern).
- In a vertical mode, TEX moves its position down the page (for a positive kern) or up the page (for a negative kern).

Thus a positive kern produces empty space while a negative kern causes TEX to back up over something that it's already produced. This notion of a kern is different from the notion of a kern in some computerized typesetting systems—in TEX, positive kerns push two letters *apart* instead of bringing them closer together.

A kern is similar to glue, except that (a) a kern can neither stretch nor shrink, and (b) TEX will only break a line or a page at a kern if the kern is followed by glue and is not part of a math formula. If TEX finds a kern at the end of a line or a page, it discards the kern. If you want to get the effect of a kern that never disappears, use \hglue or \vglue.

You can use \kern in math mode, but you can't use mu units (see "mathematical unit", p. 81) for ⟨*dimen*⟩. If you want mu units, use \mkern (p. 215) instead.

Example:
```
\centerline{$\Downarrow$}\kern 3pt % a vertical kern
\centerline{$\Longrightarrow$\kern 6pt % a horizontal kern
   {\bf Heed my warning!}\kern 6pt % another horizontal kern
   $\Longleftarrow$}
\kern 3pt % another vertical kern
\centerline{$\Uparrow$}
```
produces:

$$\Downarrow$$
$$\Longrightarrow \textbf{ Heed my warning! } \Longleftarrow$$
$$\Uparrow$$

\hfil   **\vfil**
\hfill   **\vfill**

These commands produce infinitely stretchable horizontal and vertical glue that overwhelms any finite stretch that may be present.   \hfil and \hfill produce horizontal glue, while \vfil and \vfill produce vertical glue.

\hfill is infinitely larger than \hfil. If both \hfill and \hfil appear in the same box, the \hfill will consume all the available extra space and the \hfil will be effectively ignored. \hfill can in turn be overwhelmed by \hskip 0pt plus 1filll. The glue produced by \hfil and \hfill never shrinks.

The behavior of \vfil and \vfill is analogous.

Example:
    \hbox to 2in{Left\hfil Middle \hfil Right}
produces:

Left   Middle   Right

⌐ ' ' ' ' ' | ' ' ' ' ' ' ¬ 2 in

Example:
    \hbox to 2in{Left\hfil Middle \hfill Right}
produces:

LeftMiddle   Right

⌐ ' ' ' ' ' | ' ' ' ' ' ' ¬ 2 in

Example:
    \leftline{%
    \vbox to 4pc{%
        \hbox{Top}\vfil\hbox{Middle}\vfil \hbox{Bottom}}\quad
    \vbox to 4pc{%
        \hbox{Top}\vfil\hbox{Middle}\vfill\hbox{Bottom}}}
produces:

Top   Top
           Middle
Middle

Bottom   Bottom

\hss
\vss

These commands produce horizontal and vertical glue that is both infinitely stretchable and infinitely shrinkable. The glue can shrink to a negative distance, producing the effect of backspacing along a line (for \hss) or moving back up a page (for \vss).

Example:
    \line{text\hfil\hbox to 0pt{margin\hss}}
    % 'margin\hss' shrinks to the zero width of the hbox.
produces:

text   margin

Example:
```
\vbox to 1pc{\hrule width 6pc % Top of box.
    \hbox{1} \vskip 1pc\hbox to 2pc{\hfil 2}
    % The \vss absorbs the extra distance produced by \vskip.
    \vss \hbox to 3pc{\hfil 3}
    \hrule width 6pc}% Bottom of box.
```
produces:

```
I ‾‾‾‾‾‾‾‾‾‾
      3
‾‾‾‾‾‾‾‾‾‾‾‾
    2
```

\hfilneg
\vfilneg

These commands cancel the effect of a preceding \hfil or \vfil. While
\hfil and \vfil produce infinitely stretchable positive glue, \hfilneg
and \vfilneg produce infinitely stretchable negative glue. (Thus, n
\hfilnegs cancel n \hfils, and similarly for \vfilneg.) The main use of
\hfilneg and \vfilneg is to counteract the effect of an \hfil or \vfil
inserted by a macro.

   \hfilneg and \vfilneg have the curious property that if they are the
only infinitely stretchable glue in a box, they produce exactly the same
effect as \hfil and \vfil.

Example:
```
\leftline{\hfil on the right\hfilneg}
% Cancel the \hfil that \leftline produces to the right
% of its argument.
```
produces:

on the right

Example:
```
\def\a{\hbox to 1pc{\hfil 2}\vfil}
\vbox to 4pc{\hbox{1} \vfil \a
    \vfilneg \hbox to 2pc{\hfil 3}}
```
produces:
```
1


  2
   3
```

See also: \hbadness and \vbadness (p. 170), \hfuzz and \vfuzz (p. 171),
"leaders" (p. 72).

Manipulating boxes

■ Constructing hboxes and vboxes

\hbox – ⟨*horizontal mode material*⟩ ″
\hbox to ⟨*dimen*⟩ – ⟨*horizontal mode material*⟩ ″
\hbox spread ⟨*dimen*⟩ – ⟨*horizontal mode material*⟩ ″
This command produces an hbox (horizontal box) containing ⟨*horizontal mode material*⟩. The braces around ⟨*horizontal mode material*⟩ define a group. TEX doesn't break the ⟨*horizontal mode material*⟩ into lines, since it's in restricted horizontal mode when it's assembling the box. TEX won't change the size of the box once it's been produced.

\hbox is often useful when you want to keep some text all on one line. If your use of \hbox prevents TEX from breaking lines in an acceptable way, TEX will complain about an overfull hbox.

The width of the hbox depends on the arguments to \hbox:

- If you specify only ⟨*horizontal mode material*⟩, the hbox will have its natural width.
- If you specify **to** ⟨*dimen*⟩, the width of the hbox will be ⟨*dimen*⟩.
- If you specify **spread** ⟨*dimen*⟩, the width of the hbox will be its natural width plus ⟨*dimen*⟩, i.e., the hbox will be spread out by ⟨*dimen*⟩.

The \hfil command (p. 157) is useful for filling out an hbox with empty space when the material in the box isn't as wide as the width of the box.

Example:
```
\hbox{ugly suburban sprawl}
\hbox to 2in{ugly \hfil suburban \hfil sprawl}
\hbox spread 1in {ugly \hfil suburban \hfil sprawl}
% Without \hfil in the two preceding lines,
% you'd get 'underfull hbox'es.
```
produces:
```
ugly suburban sprawl
ugly        suburban        sprawl
ugly            suburban            sprawl
```
3 in

\vtop ⟨*vertical mode material*⟩
\vtop to ⟨*dimen*⟩ – ⟨*vertical mode material*⟩ ″
\vtop spread ⟨*dimen*⟩ – ⟨*vertical mode material*⟩ ″
\vbox – ⟨*vertical mode material*⟩ ″
\vbox to ⟨*dimen*⟩ – ⟨*vertical mode material*⟩ ″
\vbox spread ⟨*dimen*⟩ – ⟨*vertical mode material*⟩ ″

These commands produce a vbox (vertical box) containing ⟨*vertical mode material*⟩. The braces around ⟨*vertical mode material*⟩ define a group. TeX is in internal vertical mode when it's assembling the box. TeX won't change the size of the box once it's been produced.

The difference between \vtop and \vbox lies in where TeX puts the reference point of the constructed vbox. Ordinarily, the reference point gotten from \vtop tends to be at or near the top of the constructed vbox, while the reference point gotten from \vbox tends to be at or near the bottom of the constructed vbox. Thus a row of vboxes all constructed with \vtop will tend to have their tops nearly in a line, while a row of vboxes all constructed with \vbox will tend to have their bottoms nearly in a line.

\vtop and \vbox are often useful when you want to keep some text together on a single page. (For this purpose, it usually doesn't matter which command you use.) If your use of these commands prevents TeX from breaking pages in an acceptable way, TeX will complain that it's found an overfull or underfull vbox while \output is active.

The height of a vbox depends on the arguments to \vtop or \vbox. For \vbox, TeX determines the height as follows:

- If you specify only ⟨*vertical mode material*⟩, the vbox will have its natural height.
- If you specify **to** ⟨*dimen*⟩, the height of the vbox will be ⟨*dimen*⟩.
- If you specify **spread** ⟨*dimen*⟩, the height of the vbox will be its natural height plus ⟨*dimen*⟩, i.e., the height of the vbox will be stretched vertically by ⟨*dimen*⟩.

For \vtop, TeX constructs the box using its rules for \vbox and then apportions the vertical extent between the height and the depth as described below.

Ordinarily, the width of a constructed vbox is the width of the widest item inside it.[2] The rules for apportioning the vertical extent between the height and the depth are more complicated:

- For \vtop, the height is the height of its first item, if that item is a box or rule. Otherwise the height is zero. The depth is whatever vertical extent remains after the height is subtracted.

---

[2] More precisely, it's the distance from the reference point to the rightmost edge of the constructed vbox. Therefore, if you move any of the items right using \moveright or \moveleft (with a negative distance), the constructed vbox might be wider.

- For \vbox, the depth is the depth of its last item, if that item is a box or rule. Otherwise the depth is zero. The height is whatever vertical extent remains after the depth is subtracted.[3]

The \vfil command (p. 157) is useful for filling out a vbox with empty space when the material in the box isn't as tall as the vertical extent of the box.

Example:

```
\hbox{\hsize = 10pc \raggedright\parindent = 1em
\vtop{In this example, we see how to use vboxes to
produce the effect of double columns.  Each vbox
contains two paragraphs, typeset according to \TeX's
usual rules except that it's ragged right.\par
This isn't really the best way to get true double
columns because the columns}
\hskip 2pc
\vtop{\noindent
aren't balanced and we haven't done anything to choose
the column break automatically or even to fix up the
last line of the first column.\par
However, the technique of putting running text into a
vbox is very useful for placing that text where you
want it on the page.}}
```

produces:

In this example, we see how to use vboxes to produce the effect of double columns. Each vbox contains two paragraphs, typeset according to TeX's usual rules except that it's ragged right.

This isn't really the best way to get true double columns because the columns

aren't balanced and we haven't done anything to choose the column break automatically or even to fix up the last line of the first column.

However, the technique of putting running text into a vbox is very useful for placing that text where you want it on the page.

---

[3] In fact, there's a further complication. Suppose that after the depth has been determined using the two rules that follow, the depth turns out to be greater than \boxmaxdepth. Then the depth is reduced to \boxmaxdepth and the height is adjusted accordingly.

Example:
```
\hbox{\hsize = 1in \raggedright\parindent = 0pt
\vtop to .75in{\hrule This box is .75in deep. \vfil\hrule}
\qquad
\vtop{\hrule This box is at its natural depth. \vfil\hrule}
\qquad
\vtop spread .2in{\hrule This box is .2in deeper than
                 its natural depth.\vfil\hrule}}
```
produces:

This box is
.75in deep.

This box is
at its natural
depth.

This box is .2in
deeper than its
natural depth.

Example:
```
% See how \vbox lines up boxes at their bottoms
% instead of at their tops.
\hbox{\hsize = 1in \raggedright
\vbox to .5in{\hrule This box is .5in deep.\vfil\hrule}
\qquad
\vbox to .75in{\hrule This box is .75in deep.\vfil\hrule}}
```
produces:

This box is
.75in deep.

This box is .5in
deep.

\boxmaxdepth   [⟨*dimen*⟩ parameter]

This parameter contains a dimension D. TEX will not construct a box whose depth exceeds D. If you produce a box whose depth d would exceed D, TEX will transfer the excess depth to the height of the box, effectively moving the reference point of the box down by $d - D$. If you set \boxmaxdepth to zero, TEX will line up a row of vboxes so that their bottom boundaries all lie on the same horizontal line. Plain TEX sets \boxmaxdepth to \maxdimen (p. 244), so \boxmaxdepth won't affect your boxes unless you change it.

\underbar ⟨*argument*⟩

This command puts ⟨*argument*⟩ into an hbox and underlines it without regard to anything that protrudes below the baseline of the box.

Example:
```
\underbar{Why not learn \TeX?}
```
produces:

Why not learn T_EX?

\everyhbox   [⟨*token list*⟩ parameter]
\everyvbox   [⟨*token list*⟩ parameter]

These parameters contain token lists that T_EX expands at the start of every hbox or vbox that it constructs. Any items resulting from the expansion then become the beginning of the list of items for the box. By default these token lists are empty.

■ Setting and retrieving the contents of boxes

\setbox ⟨*register*⟩ = ⟨*box*⟩
\box ⟨*register*⟩

These commands respectively set and retrieve the contents of the box register whose number is ⟨*register*⟩. Note that you set a box register a little differently than you set the other kinds of registers: you use \setbox n = rather than \box n =.

Retrieving the contents of a box register with these commands has the side effect of emptying it, so that the box register become void. If you don't want that to happen, you can use \copy (see below) to retrieve the contents. You should use \box in preference to \copy when you don't care about what's in a box register after you've used it, so as not to exhaust T_EX's memory by filling it with obsolete boxes.

Example:
```
\setbox0 = \hbox{mushroom}
\setbox1 = \vbox{\copy0\box0\box0}
\box1
```
produces:
mushroom
mushroom

\copy ⟨*register*⟩

This command produces a copy of box register ⟨*register*⟩. This command is useful when you want to retrieve the contents of a box register but don't want to destroy the contents. (Retrieving the register contents with `\box` makes the register void.)

Example:
```
\setbox0 = \hbox{good }
Have a \copy0 \box0 \box0 day!
```
produces:

Have a good good day!

`\unhbox` ⟨*register*⟩
`\unvbox` ⟨*register*⟩

These commands produce the list contained in box register ⟨*register*⟩ and make that box register void. `\unhbox` applies to box registers containing hboxes and `\unvbox` applies to box registers containing vboxes. You should use these commands in preference to `\unhcopy` and `\unvcopy` (see below) when you don't care about what's in the box register after you've used it, so as not to exhaust TeX's memory by filling it with obsolete boxes.

Example:
```
\setbox0=\hbox{The Mock Turtle sighed deeply, and
drew the back of one flapper across his eyes. }
\setbox1=\hbox{He tried to speak, but sobs choked
                his voice. }
\unhbox0 \unhbox1
% \box0 \box1 would set two hboxes side by side
% (and produce a badly overfull line).
\box1 % produces nothing
```
produces:

The Mock Turtle sighed deeply, and drew the back of one flapper across his eyes. He tried to speak, but sobs choked his voice.

`\unhcopy` ⟨*register*⟩
`\unvcopy` ⟨*register*⟩

These commands produce the list contained in box register ⟨*register*⟩ and leave the contents of the register undisturbed. `\unhcopy` applies to box registers containing hboxes and `\unvcopy` applies to box registers containing vboxes.

Example:

```
\setbox0=\hbox{The Mock Turtle sighed deeply, and
drew the back of one flapper across his eyes. }
\setbox1=\hbox{He tried to speak, but sobs choked his
        voice. }
\unhcopy0 \unhcopy1\par\noindent
% \box0 \box1 would set two hboxes side by side
% (and produce a badly overfull line).
\box1 % Produces an hbox (which can't be broken).
```

produces:

The Mock Turtle sighed deeply, and drew the back of one flapper across his eyes. He tried to speak, but sobs choked his voice.

He tried to speak, but sobs choked his voice.

See also: \wd, \dp, \ht (p. 167).

■ Shifting boxes

\moveleft ⟨*dimen*⟩ ⟨*box*⟩
\moveright ⟨*dimen*⟩ ⟨*box*⟩

These commands move ⟨*box*⟩ left or right by ⟨*dimen*⟩ (which can be negative). You can only apply \moveleft and \moveright to a box that's in a vertical list.

Example:

```
\vbox{\vbox{Phoebe}\vbox{walked}%
\moveleft 20pt\vbox{a}\moveright 20pt\vbox{crooked}%
\vbox{mile.}}
```

produces:

Phoebe
walked

a

     crooked
mile.

\lower ⟨*dimen*⟩ ⟨*box*⟩
\raise ⟨*dimen*⟩ ⟨*box*⟩

These commands move ⟨*box*⟩ up or down by ⟨*dimen*⟩ (which can be negative). You can only apply \raise and \lower to a box that's in a horizontal list.

Example:

```
Are you feeling \lower 6pt \hbox{depressed} about the
                \raise 6pt \hbox{bump} on your nose?
```

produces:

Are you feeling _{depressed} about the ^{bump} on your nose?

■ Dimensions of box registers

\ht ⟨*register*⟩	[⟨*dimen*⟩ parameter]
\dp ⟨*register*⟩	[⟨*dimen*⟩ parameter]
\wd ⟨*register*⟩	[⟨*dimen*⟩ parameter]

These parameters refer to the height, depth, and width respectively of box register ⟨*register*⟩. You can use them to find out the dimensions of a box. You can also change the dimensions of a box, but it's a tricky business; if you want to be adventurous you can learn all about it from pages 388–389 of *The TEXbook*.

Example:

```
\setbox0 = \vtop{\hbox{a}\hbox{beige}\hbox{bunny}}%
The box has width \the\wd0, height \the\ht0,
and depth \the\dp0.
```

produces:

The box has width 27.2223pt, height 4.30554pt, and depth 25.94444pt.

■ Struts, phantoms, and empty boxes

\strut

This command produces a box whose width is zero and whose height (8.5pt) and depth (3.5pt) are those of a more or less typical line of type in `cmr10`, the default plain TEX font. Its main use is in forcing lines to have the same height when you've disabled TEX's interline glue with \offinterlineskip or a similar command, e.g., when you're constructing an alignment. If the natural height of a line is too short, you can bring it up to standard by including a \strut in the line. The strut will force the height and depth of the line to be larger, but it won't print anything or consume any horizontal space.

If you're setting type in a font that's bigger or smaller than `cmr10`, you should redefine `\strut` for that context.

Example:
```
\noindent % So we're in horizontal mode.
\offinterlineskip % So we get the inherent spacing.
% The periods in this vbox are not vertically equidistant.
\vtop{\hbox{.}\hbox{.(}\hbox{.x}
   \hbox{.\vrule height 4pt depth 0pt}}\qquad
% The periods in this vbox are vertically equidistant
% because of the struts.
\vtop{\hbox{.\strut}\hbox{.(\strut}\hbox{.x\strut}
   \hbox{.\vrule height 4pt depth 0pt\strut}}
```
produces:

\mathstrut

This command produces a phantom formula whose width is zero and whose height and depth are the same as those of a left parenthesis. `\mathstrut` is in fact defined as `\vphantom(`. Its main use is for getting radicals, underbars, and overbars to line up with other radicals, underbars, and overbars in a formula. It is much like `\strut` (p. 167), except that it adjusts itself to the different styles that can occur in math formulas.

Example:
```
$$\displaylines{
\overline{a_1a_2} \land \overline{b_1b_2}
\quad{\rm versus}\quad \overline{a_1a_2\mathstrut}
   \land \overline{b_1b_2\mathstrut}\cr
\sqrt{\epsilon} + \sqrt{\xi} \quad{\rm versus}\quad
\sqrt{\epsilon\mathstrut} + \sqrt{\xi\mathstrut}\cr}$$
```
produces:

$$\overline{a_1a_2} \land \overline{b_1b_2} \quad \text{versus} \quad \overline{a_1a_2} \land \overline{b_1b_2}$$

$$\sqrt{\epsilon} + \sqrt{\xi} \quad \text{versus} \quad \sqrt{\epsilon} + \sqrt{\xi}$$

\phantom ⟨argument⟩

This command produces an empty box having the same size and placement that ⟨argument⟩ would have were it typeset. One use of `\phantom` is for reserving space for a symbol that for some reason needs to be drawn in by hand.

Example:
```
$1\phantom{9}2$
```
produces:

1 2

\hphantom ⟨argument⟩
\vphantom ⟨argument⟩

These commands produce phantom boxes that don't print anything:

- \hphantom produces a box with the same width as ⟨argument⟩ but zero height and depth.
- \vphantom produces a box with the same height and depth as ⟨argument⟩ but zero width.

Their main purpose is to force a subformula to have a certain minimum horizontal or vertical dimension.

Example:
```
$$\left[\vphantom{u\over v}t\right] \star
      \left[{u\over v}\right]\quad
   \{\hphantom{xx}\}$$
```
produces:

$$\left[t\right] \star \left[\frac{u}{v}\right] \quad \{ \quad \}$$

\smash ⟨argument⟩

This command typesets ⟨argument⟩, but forces the height and depth of its containing box to be zero. You can use \smash and \vphantom in combination to give a subformula any height and depth that you wish.

Example:
```
$${\smash{r_m \brace r_n}\vphantom{r}} \Longrightarrow r$$
```
produces:

$$\left\{ \begin{matrix} r_m \\ r_n \end{matrix} \right\} \Longrightarrow r$$

\null

This command produces an empty hbox.

Example:
```
\setbox0 = \null
The null box \null has width \the\wd0, height \the\ht0,
and depth \the\dp0.
```
produces:
    The null box has width 0.0pt, height 0.0pt, and depth 0.0pt.

■ *Parameters pertaining to malformed boxes*

\overfullrule   [⟨*dimen*⟩ parameter]
This parameter specifies the width of the rule that TEX appends to an
overfull hbox. Plain TEX sets it to **5pt**.

\hbadness   [⟨*number*⟩ parameter]
\vbadness   [⟨*number*⟩ parameter]
These parameters specify the thresholds of horizontal and vertical badness for reporting underfull or overfull boxes. **\hbadness** applies to
hboxes and **\vbadness** applies to vboxes. If the badness of a constructed
box exceeds the threshold, TEX will report an error. If you raise the
thresholds (the plain TEX defaults are both 1000), TEX will be less likely
to complain. Note that the settings of **\hbadness** and **\vbadness** have
no effect on the appearance of your typeset document; they only affect
the error messages that you get. See page 302 of *The TEXbook* for a precise description of how TEX decides when to complain about an overfull
or underfull box.

Example:
```
\hbadness = 10000 % Suppress any hbadness complaints.
\hbox to 2in{a b}\par
\hbadness = 500 % Report hbadness exceeding 500.
\hbox to 2in{a\hskip 0pt plus .5in b}
```
produces in the log:
```
Underfull \hbox (badness 5091) detected at line 4
\tenrm a b

\hbox(6.94444+0.0)x144.54, glue set 3.70787
.\tenrm a
.\glue 0.0 plus 36.135
.\tenrm b
```

\badness
This command yields the numerical value of the badness of the box (either
horizontal or vertical) that TEX has most recently produced. If the box

was overfull, \badness will be 1000000; in all other cases it will be between 0 and 10000.

\hfuzz   [⟨*dimen*⟩ parameter]
\vfuzz   [⟨*dimen*⟩ parameter]

These parameters specify the amount that a box can exceed its natural size before TeX considers it to be overfull. \hfuzz applies to hboxes and \vfuzz applies to vboxes. Plain TeX sets both parameters to 0.1pt.

Example:
```
\hfuzz = .5in
\hbox to 2in{This box is longer than two inches.}
% No error results
```
produces:

This box is longer than two inches.

⌐ ᵎ ᵎ ᵎ ᵎ ⌐ ᵎ ᵎ ᵎ ⌐ ᵎ ᵎ ᵎ ⌐ ᵎ ᵎ ᵎ ⌐ ᵎ ᵎ ᵎ ⌐ 3 in

See also: \tolerance (p. 123).

Retrieving the last item from a list

\lastkern
\lastskip
\lastpenalty
\lastbox

These control sequences yield the value of the last item on the current list. They aren't true commands because they can only appear as part of an argument. If the last item on the list isn't of the indicated type, they yield a zero value (or an empty box, in the case of \lastbox). For example, if the last item on the current list is a kern, \lastkern yields the dimension of that kern; if it isn't a kern, it yields a dimension of 0.

Using \lastbox has the additional effect of removing the last box from the list. If you want the original \lastbox to remain on the list, you have to add a copy of it to the list. \lastbox is not permitted in a math list or in the main vertical list.

These control sequences are most useful after macro calls that migh' have inserted entities of the indicated kinds.

Example:
```
\def\a{two\kern 15pt}
one \a\a\hskip 2\lastkern three\par
% Get three times as much space before 'three'.
\def\a{\hbox{two}}
one \a
\setbox0 = \lastbox % Removes 'two'.
three \box0.
```
produces:

one two   two   three

one three two.

\unkern
\unskip
\unpenalty

If the last item on the current list is of type kern, glue, or penalty respectively, these commands remove it from that list. If the item isn't of the right type, these commands have no effect. Like **\lastbox**, you can't apply them to lists in math mode or to the main vertical list. These commands are most useful after a macro call that is known to have inserted a specific item that you don't want there. TEX doesn't provide an **\unbox** command because **\lastbox** produces nearly the same effect.

Rules and leaders

\hrule
\hrule **height** ⟨*dimen*⟩ **width** ⟨*dimen*⟩ **depth** ⟨*dimen*⟩
\vrule
\vrule **width** ⟨*dimen*⟩ **height** ⟨*dimen*⟩ **depth** ⟨*dimen*⟩

The **\hrule** command produces a horizontal rule; the **\vrule** command produces a vertical rule. You can specify any or all of the width, height, and depth of the rule—TEX supplies default values for those that you omit. You can give the dimensions of the rule in any order; the forms listed above show just two of the possible combinations. You can even give a dimension of a given kind more than once—if you do, the last one is the one that counts.

If you don't specify the width of a horizontal rule, the rule is extended horizontally to the boundaries of the innermost box or alignment that contains the rule. If you don't specify the height of a horizontal rule, it defaults to `0.4pt`; if you don't specify the depth of a horizontal rule, it defaults to `0pt`.

If you don't specify the width of a vertical rule, it defaults to `0.4pt`. If you don't specify the height or the depth of a vertical rule, the rule is extended to the boundary of the innermost box or alignment that contains the rule.

TeX treats a horizontal rule as an inherently vertical item and a vertical rule as an inherently horizontal item. Thus a horizontal rule is legal only in a vertical mode, while a vertical rule is legal only in a horizontal mode. If this seems surprising, visualize it—a horizontal rule runs from left to right and separates vertical items in a sequence, while a vertical rule runs up and down and separates horizontal items in a sequence.

Example:
```
\hrule\smallskip
\hrule width 2in \smallskip
\hrule width 3in height 2pt \smallskip
\hrule width 3in depth 2pt
```
produces:

Example:
```
% Here you can see how the baseline relates to the
% height and depth of an \hrule.
\leftline{
   \vbox{\hrule width .6in height 5pt depth 0pt}
   \vbox{\hrule width .6in height 0pt depth 8pt}
   \vbox{\hrule width .6in height 5pt depth 8pt}
   \vbox{\hbox{ baseline}\kern 3pt \hrule width .6in}
}
```
produces:

baseline

Example:
```
\hbox{( {\vrule} {\vrule width 8pt} )}
\hbox {( {\vrule height 13pt depth 0pt}
   {\vrule height 13pt depth 7pt} x)}
% the parentheses define the height and depth of each of the
% two preceding boxes; the 'x' sits on the baseline
```
produces:

☞ **\leaders** ⟨*box or rule*⟩ ⟨*skip command*⟩
\cleaders ⟨*box or rule*⟩ ⟨*skip command*⟩
\xleaders ⟨*box or rule*⟩ ⟨*skip command*⟩

These commands produce leaders, i.e., they fill a horizontal or vertical space with copies of a pattern (see "leaders", p. 72). The ⟨*box*⟩ or ⟨*rule*⟩ specifies a leader, i.e., a single copy of the pattern, while the ⟨*skip command*⟩ specifies a window to be filled with a row or a column of the leaders. The pattern is repeated as many times as will fit into the window. If ⟨*skip command*⟩ is a horizontal skip, the window contains a row of leaders and TeX must be in a horizontal mode; if ⟨*skip command*⟩ is a vertical skip, the window contains a column of leaders and TeX must be in a vertical mode.

The commands differ in how they arrange the repeated pattern in the space and where they put any leftover space:

- For **\leaders**, TeX aligns a row of leaders with the left end of the innermost box B that is to contain the result of the **\leaders** command. It aligns a column of leaders with the top of B. Those leaders that fall entirely within the window are retained. Any leftover space at the top and bottom of the window is left empty.
- For **\cleaders**, the leaders are centered within the window.
- For **\xleaders** the pattern is uniformly distributed throughout the window. If the leftover space is l and the leader is repeated n times, TeX puts space of width or height $l/(n+1)$ between adjacent leaders and at the two ends (left and right or top and bottom) of the leaders.

Example:
```
\def\pattern{\hbox to 15pt{\hfil.\hfil}}
\line{Down the Rabbit-Hole {\leaders\pattern\hfil} 1}
\line{The Pool of Tears {\leaders\pattern\hfil} 9}
\line{A Caucus-Race and a Long Tale {\cleaders\pattern
    \hfil} 19}
\line{Pig and Pepper {\xleaders\pattern\hfil} 27}
```
produces:

Down the Rabbit-Hole 1
The Pool of Tears 9
A Caucus-Race and a Long Tale 19
Pig and Pepper 27

Example:
```
\def\bulletfill{\vbox to 3ex{\vfil\hbox{$\bullet$}\vfil}}%
\def\mybox{\vbox to 1in}
\def\myrule{\hrule width 4pt}\hsize=2in
\hrule \line{%
  \mybox{\myrule depth 8pt \leaders\bulletfill\vfill}
  \hfil
  \mybox{\myrule depth 15pt \leaders\bulletfill\vfill}
  \hfil
  \mybox{\myrule depth 18pt \cleaders\bulletfill\vfill}
  \hfil
  \mybox{\myrule depth 12pt \xleaders\bulletfill\vfill}%
}\hrule
```
produces:

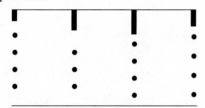

\dotfill
\hrulefill

These commands respectively fill the enclosing horizontal space with a row of dots on the baseline and with a horizontal line on the baseline. It's usually a good idea to leave a space between \dotfill or \hrulefill and any text that precedes or follows it (see the example below).

Example:
```
\hbox to 3in{Start {\dotfill} Finish}
\hbox to 3in{Swedish {\hrulefill} Finnish}
```
produces:

Start .... Finish

Swedish ⎯⎯⎯⎯⎯⎯⎯⎯⎯⎯⎯⎯⎯ Finnish

\leftarrowfill
\rightarrowfill

These commands fill the enclosing horizontal space with left-pointing or right-pointing arrows.

Example:
```
\hbox to 3in{\vrule \rightarrowfill \ 3 in
             \leftarrowfill\vrule}
```
produces:

|————————————→ 3 in ←————————————|

Alignments

■ Tabbing alignments

\+ ⟨*text*⟩ **&** ⟨*text*⟩ **&** ··· **\cr**
\tabalign

These commands begin a single line in a tabbed alignment. The only difference between \+ and \tabalign is that \+ is an outer macro—you can't use it when TEX is reading tokens at high speed (see "outer", p. 83).

If you place an '&' at a position to the right of all existing tabs in a tabbing alignment, the '&' establishes a new tab at that position.

Example:
```
\cleartabs % Nullify any previous \settabs.
\+ {\bf if }$a[i] < a[i+1]$ &{\bf then}&\cr
\+&&$a[i] := a[i+1]$;\cr
\+&&{\it found }$:=$ {\bf true};\cr
\+&{\bf else}\cr
\+&&{\it found }$:=$ {\bf false};\cr
\+&{\bf end if};\cr
```
produces:

if $a[i] < a[i+1]$ **then**
$\qquad\qquad\qquad a[i] := a[i+1];$
$\qquad\qquad\qquad$ *found* := **true**;
$\qquad\quad$ **else**
$\qquad\qquad\qquad$ *found* := **false**;
$\qquad\quad$ **end if**;

\settabs ⟨*number*⟩ **\columns**
\settabs \+ ⟨*sample line*⟩ **\cr**

The first form of this command defines a set of tab stops for a tabbing alignment. It tells TEX to set the tab stops so as to divide each line into

⟨*number*⟩ equal parts. TEX takes the length of a line to be `\hsize`, as usual. You can make the alignment narrower by decreasing `\hsize`.

Example:
```
{\hsize = 3in \settabs 3 \columns
\+$1$&one&first\cr
\+$2$&two&second\cr
\+$3$&three&third\cr}
```
produces:

1	one	first
2	two	second
3	three	third

⌐ ' ' ' | ' ' ' ' | ' ' ' ' | ' ' ' ' | ' ' ' ⌐ 3 in

The second form of this command defines tab stops by setting the tab stops at the positions indicated by the '`&`'s in the sample line. The sample line itself does not appear in the output. When you use this form you'll usually want to put material into the sample line that is somewhat wider than the widest corresponding material in the alignment, in order to produce space between the columns. That's what we've done in the example below. The material following the last tab stop is irrelevant, since TEX does not need to position anything at the place where the `\cr` appears.

The tab settings established by `\settabs` remain in effect until you issue a new `\settabs` command or end a group containing the `\settabs` command. This is true for both forms of the command.

Example:
```
% The first line establishes the template.
\settabs \+$1$\qquad & three\quad & seventh\cr
\+$1$&one&first\cr
\+$2$&two&second\cr
\+$3$&three&third\cr
```
produces:

1	one	first
2	two	second
3	three	third

\cleartabs

This command clears all the tabs to the right of the current column. Its main use is in applications such as typesetting computer programs in which the tab positions change from line to line.

See also: `\cr`, `\endline`, `\crcr` (p. 180).

■ *General alignments*

\halign – ⟨*preamble*⟩ **\cr** ⟨*row*⟩ **\cr** ... ⟨*row*⟩ **\cr** ″
\halign to ⟨*dimen*⟩– ⟨*preamble*⟩ **\cr** ⟨*row*⟩ **\cr** ... ⟨*row*⟩ **\cr** ″
\halign spread ⟨*dimen*⟩– ⟨*preamble*⟩ **\cr** ⟨*row*⟩ **\cr** ... ⟨*row*⟩ **\cr** ″

This command produces a horizontal alignment consisting of a sequence of rows, where each row in turn contains a sequence of column entries. TEX adjusts the widths of the column entries to accommodate the widest one in each column.

A horizontal alignment can only appear when TEX is in a vertical mode. We recommend that you first study alignments in general (p. 44) before you attempt to use this command.

An alignment consists of a preamble followed by the text to be aligned. The preamble, which describes the layout of the rows that follow, consists of a sequence of column templates, separated by '&' and ended by \cr. Each row consists of a sequence of column entries, also separated by '&' and ended by \cr. Within a template, '#' indicates where TEX should insert the corresponding text of a column entry. In contrast, \settabs uses a fixed implicit template of '#', i.e., it just inserts the text as is.

TEX typesets each column entry in restricted horizontal mode, i.e., as the contents of an hbox, and implicitly encloses it in a group.

The **to** form of this command instructs TEX to make the width of the alignment be ⟨*dimen*⟩, adjusting the space between columns as necessary. The **spread** form of this command instructs TEX to make the alignment wider by ⟨*dimen*⟩ than its natural width. These forms are like the corresponding forms of \hbox (p. 160).

See \tabskip (p. 184) for an example using the **to** form.

Example:
```
\tabskip = 1em \halign{%
   \hfil\it#\hfil&\hfil#\hfil&#&\hfil\$#\cr
   United States&Washington&dollar&1.00\cr
   France&Paris&franc&0.174\cr
   Israel&Jerusalem&shekel&0.507\cr
   Japan&Tokyo&yen&0.0829\cr}
```
produces:

United States	Washington	dollar	$1.00
France	Paris	franc	$0.174
Israel	Jerusalem	shekel	$0.507
Japan	Tokyo	yen	$0.0829

\valign – ⟨*preamble*⟩ **\cr** ⟨*column*⟩ **\cr** ... ⟨*column*⟩ **\cr** ″
\valign to ⟨*dimen*⟩ – ⟨*preamble*⟩ **\cr** ⟨*column*⟩ **\cr** ... ⟨*column*⟩ **\cr** ″
\valign spread ⟨*dimen*⟩ – ⟨*preamble*⟩ **\cr** ⟨*column*⟩ **\cr** ... ⟨*column*⟩ **\cr** ″

This command produces a vertical alignment consisting of a sequence of columns, where each column in turn contains a sequence of row entries. TeX adjusts the heights of the row entries to accommodate the tallest one in each row.

A vertical alignment can only appear when TeX is in a horizontal mode. Because vertical alignments are (a) conceptually somewhat difficult and (b) not often used, we recommend that you learn about alignments in general (p. 44) and the \halign command (see above) before you attempt to use the \valign command.

An alignment consists of a preamble followed by the text to be aligned. The preamble, which describes the layout of the columns that follow, consists of a sequence of row templates, separated by '&' and ended by \cr. Each column consists of a sequence of row entries, also separated by '&' and ended by \cr. Within a template, '#' indicates where TeX should insert the corresponding text of a row entry.

TeX typesets each row entry in internal vertical mode, i.e., as the contents of a vbox, and implicitly encloses the entry in a group. It always gives the vbox zero depth. Any text or other horizontal mode material in a row entry then puts TeX into ordinary horizontal mode. (This is just an application of the general rules for TeX's behavior in internal vertical mode.) The usual paragraphing parameters apply in this case: the row entry has an initial indentation of \parindent (p. 113) and its lines have the \leftskip and \rightskip (p. 115) glue appended to them.

Note in particular that a row entry containing text has a width of \hsize (p. 114). Unless you reset \hsize to the row width that you want, you're likely to encounter overfull hboxes, or find that the first column takes up the width of the entire page, or both.

Normally, you need to include a strut in each template so that the rows don't come out crooked as a result of the varying heights of the entries in the alignment. You can produce a strut with the \strut command.

The **to** form of this command instructs TeX to make the vertical extent of the alignment be ⟨*dimen*⟩, adjusting the space between rows as necessary. The **spread** form of this command instructs TeX to make the alignment taller by ⟨*dimen*⟩ than its natural height. These forms are like the corresponding forms of \vbox (p. 161).

Example:
```
{\hsize=1in \parindent=0pt
\valign{#\strut&#\strut&#\strut&#\strut\cr
   bernaise&curry&hoisin&hollandaise\cr
   ketchup&marinara&mayonnaise&mustard\cr
   rarebit&tartar\cr}}
```
produces:

bernaise	ketchup	rarebit
curry	marinara	tartar
hoisin	mayonnaise	
hollandaise	mustard	

Example:
```
% same thing but without struts (shows why you need them)
{\hsize=1in \parindent=0pt
\valign{#&#&#&#\cr
   bernaise&curry&hoisin&hollandaise\cr
   ketchup&marinara&mayonnaise&mustard\cr
   rarebit&tartar\cr}}
```
produces:

bernaise	ketchup	rarebit
curry	marinara	tartar
hoisin	mayonnaise	
hollandaise	mustard	

\ialign

This command behaves just like \halign, except that it first sets the \tabskip glue to zero and sets \everycr empty.

\cr

This command ends the preamble of a horizontal or vertical alignment, a row of a horizontal or tabbing alignment, or a column of a vertical alignment. You can cause TeX to take certain actions whenever it sees a \cr by setting the value of the \everycr parameter (p. 185).

\endline

This command is a synonym for the \cr command. It is useful when you've redefined \cr but still need access to the original definition.

\crcr

This command behaves just like \cr, except that TeX ignores it if it comes immediately after a \cr or a \noalign. Its main application is as a safety measure to avoid a misleading error message caused by a macro that expects an argument ending in \cr. If you put \crcr after the '#*n*' that denotes such an argument in the macro's definition, the macro will work properly whether or not the argument ends with \cr.

\omit

This command tells TEX to ignore a template in a horizontal or vertical alignment while processing a particular column or row entry respectively. \omit must appear as the first item in a column or row entry; in effect, it overrides the template from the preamble with the simple template '#'.

Example:
```
\tabskip = 2em\halign{%
   \hfil\it#\hfil&\hfil#\hfil&#&\hfil\$#\cr
   United States&Washington&dollar&1.00\cr
   \omit \dotfill France\dotfill&Paris&franc&0.174\cr
   Israel&Jerusalem&shekel&0.507\cr
   Japan&Tokyo&yen&0.0829\cr}
```
produces:

United States	Washington	dollar	$1.00
…France…	Paris	franc	$0.174
Israel	Jerusalem	shekel	$0.507
Japan	Tokyo	yen	$0.0829

Example:
```
{\hsize=1.2in \parindent=0pt
\valign{(#)\strut&(#)\strut&(#)\strut&(#)\strut\cr
   bernaise&curry&hoisin&hollandaise\cr
   ketchup&\omit\strut{\bf MARINARA!}&mayonnaise&mustard\cr
   rarebit&tartar\cr}}
```
produces:

(bernaise)	(ketchup)	(rarebit)
(curry)	**MARINARA!**	(tartar)
(hoisin)	(mayonnaise)	
(hollandaise)	(mustard)	

\span

The meaning of this command depends on whether it appears in a preamble or in an alignment entry.

- Normally, TEX does not expand tokens in the preamble when it reads them. Putting \span in front of a token in the preamble causes that token to be expanded immediately according to TEX's usual rules of macro expansion.

- Putting \span instead of '&' between two column or row entries causes those columns or rows to be combined. For a horizontal alignment, the width of the combined column is the sum of the widths of the component columns. For a vertical alignment, the height of the combined row is the sum of the heights of the component rows. The template of the combined column or combined row forms a single group, so font-setting commands preceding a \span affect everything up to the next '&'.

\span is rarely useful by itself outside of a template, but it provides the basic mechanism for defining \multispan.

\multispan ⟨number⟩

This command tells TeX that the following ⟨number⟩ columns in a row of a horizontal alignment, or ⟨number⟩ rows in a column of a vertical alignment, should be combined into a single column or row (as with \span) and that their templates should be omitted (as with \omit).

Example:
```
\tabskip = 13pt\halign{%
   \hfil\it#\hfil&\hfil#\hfil&#&\hfil\$#\cr
   United States&Washington&dollar&1.00\cr
   France&Paris&franc&0.174\cr
   Israel&Jerusalem &
      \multispan 2 \hfil\it(no information)\hfil \cr
   Japan&Tokyo&yen&0.0829\cr}
```
produces:

United States	Washington	dollar	$1.00
France	Paris	franc	$0.174
Israel	Jerusalem	*(no information)*	
Japan	Tokyo	yen	$0.0829

Example:
```
{\hsize=1.2in \parindent=0pt
\valign{(#)\strut&(#)\strut&(#)\strut&(#)\strut\cr
   bernaise&curry&hoisin&hollandaise\cr
   \multispan 3$$\left\{{{\rm ketchup}\atop{\rm marinara}}
      \right\}$$&mustard\cr
   rarebit&tartar\cr}}
```
produces:

(bernaise)   (rarebit)

(curry)   ⎧ ketchup ⎫   (tartar)

(hoisin)   ⎩ marinara ⎭

(hollandaise)   (mustard)

\noalign – ⟨*vertical mode material*⟩ ″
\noalign – ⟨*horizontal mode material*⟩ ″

This command inserts ⟨*vertical mode material*⟩ after the current row of a horizontal alignment or ⟨*horizontal mode material*⟩ after the current column of a vertical alignment. The material can be text, glue, a rule, or anything else.

The most common use of \noalign is to put extra space after a row or column. If you want to put extra space after *every* row of a horizontal alignment, use \openup (p. 135).

Example:
```
\halign{%
   \hfil\it#\hfil\tabskip=2em&\hfil#\hfil&#&
      \hfil\$#\tabskip=0em\cr
% The \tabskip changes prevent the rule below
% from sticking out.
United States&Washington&dollar&1.00\cr
France&Paris&franc&0.174\cr
\noalign{\smallskip\hrule\smallskip}
Israel&Jerusalem&shekel&0.507\cr
Japan&Tokyo&yen&0.0829\cr}
```
produces:

United States	Washington	dollar	\$1.00
France	Paris	franc	\$0.174
Israel	Jerusalem	shekel	\$0.507
Japan	Tokyo	yen	\$0.0829

Example:
```
{\hsize=1in \parindent=0pt
\valign{#\strut&#\strut&#\strut&#\strut\cr
   \noalign{\vrule width 2pt\quad}
   bernaise&curry&hoisin&hollandaise\cr
   \noalign{\vrule width 2pt\quad}
   ketchup&marinara&mayonnaise&mustard\cr
   \noalign{\vrule width 2pt\quad}
   rarebit&tartar\cr
   \noalign{\vrule width 2pt\quad}}}
```
produces:

bernaise
curry
hoisin
hollandaise

ketchup
marinara
mayonnaise
mustard

rarebit
tartar

\tabskip   [⟨*glue*⟩ parameter]

This parameter specifies the amount of horizontal or vertical glue that
TEX puts between the columns of a horizontal alignment or between the
rows of a vertical alignment. TEX also puts the \tabskip glue to the left
of the first column and to the right of the last column of a horizontal
alignment, and above the first row and below the last row of a vertical
alignment. You can change \tabskip within a template—the change will
affect the glue associated with all the following &'s as well as the glue after
the last row or column.

Example:
```
\halign to 3.5in{%
   \hfil\it#\tabskip = 2em plus 8pt
      \hfil&\hfil#\hfil&#\tabskip = 1em
      &\hfil\$#\tabskip = 0em\cr
   United States&Washington&dollar&1.00\cr
   France&Paris&franc&0.174\cr
   Israel&Jerusalem&shekel&0.507\cr
   Japan&Tokyo&yen&0.0829\cr}
```
produces:

United States	Washington	dollar	$1.00
France	Paris	franc	$0.174
Israel	Jerusalem	shekel	$0.507
Japan	Tokyo	yen	$0.0829

Example:
```
{\hsize = 1in \parindent=0pt \tabskip=5pt
\valign{#\strut&#\strut\tabskip = 3pt
   &#\strut&#\strut\cr
   bernaise&curry&hoisin&hollandaise\cr
   ketchup&marinara&mayonnaise&mustard\cr
   rarebit&tartar\cr}}
```
produces:

bernaise	ketchup	rarebit
curry	marinara	tartar
hoisin	mayonnaise	
hollandaise	mustard	

\hidewidth

This command tells TEX to ignore the width of the next column entry in
a horizontal alignment. It's useful when you have an entry that is longer
than most of the others in the same column, and you'd rather have that
entry stick out of the column than make all the entries in the column

wider. If the `\hidewidth` is at the left of the entry, the entry sticks out to the left; if the `\hidewidth` is at the right of the entry, the entry sticks out to the right.

Example:
```
\tabskip = 25pt\halign{%
    \hfil\it#\hfil&\hfil#\hfil&#&\hfil\$#\cr
    United States&\hidewidth Washington&
        dollar&1.00\cr
    France&Paris&franc&0.174\cr
    Israel&Jerusalem&shekel&0.507\cr
    Japan&Tokyo&yen&0.0829\cr}
```
produces:

United States	Washington	dollar	$1.00
France	Paris	franc	$0.174
Israel	Jerusalem	shekel	$0.507
Japan	Tokyo	yen	$0.0829

\everycr   [⟨*token list*⟩ parameter]

TEX expands ⟨*token list*⟩ whenever it executes a `\cr`—at the end of every preamble, at the end of every row of a horizontal alignment, and at the end of every column of a vertical alignment. The `\everycr` commands are expanded just after the `\cr`. Thus you can cause TEX to execute certain commands at the end of a preamble, row, or column by assigning a list of those commands to `\everycr`.

The `\everycr` tokens shouldn't include any commands other than `\noalign`. That's because the `\everycr` tokens will reappear after the last `\cr` of the alignment. A command other than `\noalign` will then make TEX think that it's starting a new row or column. TEX will complain about a missing `\cr`, insert a `\cr`, insert the `\everycr` tokens again, and repeat these actions indefinitely.

Example:
```
\everycr={\noalign{\smallskip\hrule\smallskip}}
\halign{#\tabskip = 11pt&\hfil#\hfil&\hfil#\hfil
        \tabskip = 0pt\cr
    $1$&one&first\cr
    $2$&two&second\cr
    $3$&three&third\cr}
```
produces:

1	one	first
2	two	second
3	three	third

8 ▪ Commands for composing math formulas

This section covers commands for constructing math formulas. For an explanation of the conventions used in this section, see "Descriptions of the commands" (p. 3).

Simple parts of formulas

▪ *Greek letters*

☞

α	\alpha	μ	\mu	σ	\sigma
β	\beta	ν	\nu	ς	\varsigma
χ	\chi	ω	\omega	Σ	\Sigma
δ	\delta	Ω	\Omega	τ	\tau
Δ	\Delta	ϕ	\phi	θ	\theta
ϵ	\epsilon	φ	\varphi	ϑ	\vartheta
ε	\varepsilon	Φ	\Phi	Θ	\Theta
η	\eta	π	\pi	υ	\upsilon
γ	\gamma	ϖ	\varpi	Υ	\Upsilon
Γ	\Gamma	Π	\Pi	ξ	\xi
ι	\iota	ψ	\psi	Ξ	\Xi
κ	\kappa	Ψ	\Psi	ζ	\zeta
λ	\lambda	ρ	\rho		
Λ	\Lambda	ϱ	\varrho		

These commands produce Greek letters suitable for mathematics. You can only use them within a math formula, so if you need a Greek letter within ordinary text you must enclose it in dollar signs ($). TeX does not have commands for Greek letters that look like their roman counterparts, since you can get them by using those roman counterparts. For example, you can get a lowercase omicron in a formula by writing the letter 'o', i.e., '{\rm o}' or an uppercase beta ('B') by writing '{\rm B}'.

Don't confuse the following letters:

- \upsilon ('υ'), {\rm v} ('v'), and \nu ('ν').
- \varsigma ('ς') and \zeta ('ζ').

You can get slanted capital Greek letters by using the math italic (\mit) font.

TeX treats Greek letters as ordinary symbols when it's figuring how much space to put around them.

Example:
```
If $\rho$ and $\theta$ are both positive, then $f(\theta)
-{\mit \Gamma}_{\theta} < f(\rho)-{\mit \Gamma}_{\rho}$.
```
produces:
If ρ and θ are both positive, then $f(\theta) - \Gamma_\theta < f(\rho) - \Gamma_\rho$.

■ *Miscellaneous ordinary math symbols*

☞

∞	\infty	$\exists$	\exists	∂	\partial
$\Re$	\Re	$\forall$	\forall	$\surd$	\surd
$\Im$	\Im	$\hbar$	\hbar	$\wp$	\wp
$\angle$	\angle	ℓ	\ell	$\flat$	\flat
$\triangle$	\triangle	$\aleph$	\aleph	$\sharp$	\sharp
$\backslash$	\backslash	$\imath$	\imath	$\natural$	\natural
$\vert$	\vert	$\jmath$	\jmath	$\clubsuit$	\clubsuit
$\Vert$	\—	∇	\nabla	$\diamondsuit$	\diamondsuit
$\Vert$	\Vert	$\neg$	\neg	$\heartsuit$	\heartsuit
$\emptyset$	\emptyset	$\neg$	\lnot	$\spadesuit$	\spadesuit
$\bot$	\bot	'	' (apostrophe)		
$\top$	\top	$\prime$	\prime		

These commands produce various symbols. They are called "ordinary symbols" to distinguish them from other classes of symbols such as relations. You can only use an ordinary symbol within a math formula, so if you need an ordinary symbol within ordinary text you must enclose it in dollar signs ($).

The commands \imath and \jmath are useful when you need to put an accent on top of an 'i' or a 'j'.

An apostrophe (') is a short way of writing a superscript \prime. (The \prime command by itself generates a big ugly prime.)

The \| and \Vert commands are synonymous, as are the \neg and \lnot commands. The \vert command produces the same result as '|'.

The symbols produced by \backslash, \vert, and \Vert are delimiters. These symbols can be produced in larger sizes by using \bigm et al. (p. 211).

Example:

```
The Knave of $\heartsuit$s, he stole some tarts.
```

produces:

The Knave of $\heartsuit$s, he stole some tarts.

Example:

```
If $\hat\imath < \hat\jmath$ then $i' \leq j^\prime$.
```

produces:

If $\hat{\imath} < \hat{\jmath}$ then $i' \leq j'$.

Example:

```
$${{x-a}\over{x+a}}\biggm\backslash{{y-b}\over{y+b}}$$
```

produces:

$$\frac{x-a}{x+a} \Bigg\backslash \frac{y-b}{y+b}$$

■ Binary operations

$\vee$	\vee	$\cdot$	\cdot	$\triangleleft$	\triangleleft
$\wedge$	\wedge	$\diamond$	\diamond	$\triangleright$	\triangleright
$\amalg$	\amalg	$\bullet$	\bullet	$\bigtriangledown$	\bigtriangledown
$\cap$	\cap	$\circ$	\circ	$\bigtriangleup$	\bigtriangleup
$\cup$	\cup	$\bigcirc$	\bigcirc	$*$	\ast
$\uplus$	\uplus	$\odot$	\odot	$\star$	\star
$\sqcap$	\sqcap	$\ominus$	\ominus	$\times$	\times
$\sqcup$	\sqcup	$\oplus$	\oplus	$\div$	\div
$\dagger$	\dagger	$\oslash$	\oslash	$\setminus$	\setminus
$\ddagger$	\ddagger	$\otimes$	\otimes	$\wr$	\wr
$\land$	\land	$\pm$	\pm		
$\lor$	\lor	$\mp$	\mp		

These commands produce the symbols for various binary operations. Binary operations are one of TeX's classes of math symbols. TeX puts different amounts of space around different classes of math symbols. When TeX needs to break a line of text within a math formula, it will consider placing the break after a binary operation—but only if the operation is at the outermost level of the formula, i.e., not enclosed in a group.

In addition to these commands, TeX also treats '+' and '−' as binary operations. It considers '/' to be an ordinary symbol, despite the fact that mathematically it is a binary operation, because it looks better with less space around it.

Example:
```
$$z = x \div y \quad \hbox{if and only if} \quad
z \times y = x \;\hbox{and}\; y \neq 0$$
```
produces:

$$z = x \div y \quad \text{if and only if} \quad z \times y = x \text{ and } y \neq 0$$

*

The ***** command indicates a discretionary multiplication symbol ($\times$), which is a binary operation. This multiplication symbol behaves like a discretionary hyphen when it appears in a formula within text. That is, TeX will typeset the **\times** symbol *only* if the formula needs to be broken at that point. There's no point in using ***** in a displayed formula since TeX never breaks displayed formulas on its own.

Example:
```
Let $c = a\*b$. In the case that $c=0$ or $c=1$, let
$\Delta$ be $(\hbox{the smallest $q$})\*(\hbox{the
largest $q$})$ in the set of approximate $\tau$-values.
```
produces:

Let $c = ab$. In the case that $c = 0$ or $c = 1$, let Δ be (the smallest q) $\times$ (the largest q) in the set of approximate τ-values.

■ Relations

$\asymp$	\asymp	$\gg$	\gg	$\bowtie$	\bowtie
$\cong$	\cong	$\ll$	\ll	$\propto$	\propto
$\dashv$	\dashv	$\models$	\models	$\approx$	\approx
$\vdash$	\vdash	$\ne$	\ne	$\sim$	\sim
$\perp$	\perp	$\neq$	\neq	$\simeq$	\simeq
$\mid$	\mid	$\notin$	\notin	$\frown$	\frown
$\parallel$	\parallel	$\in$	\in	$\smile$	\smile
$\doteq$	\doteq	$\ni$	\ni	$\subset$	\subset
$\equiv$	\equiv	$\ni$	\owns	$\subseteq$	\subseteq
$\ge$	\ge	$\prec$	\prec	$\supset$	\supset
$\geq$	\geq	$\preceq$	\preceq	$\supseteq$	\supseteq
$\le$	\le	$\succ$	\succ	$\sqsubseteq$	\sqsubseteq
$\leq$	\leq	$\succeq$	\succeq	$\sqsupseteq$	\sqsupseteq

These commands produce the symbols for various relations. Relations are one of TeX's classes of math symbols. TeX puts different amounts of space around different classes of math symbols. When TeX needs to break a line of text within a math formula, it will consider placing the break after a relation—but only if the relation is at the outermost level of the formula, i.e., not enclosed in a group.

In addition to the commands listed here, TeX treats '=' and the "arrow" commands (p. 192) as relations.

Certain relations have more than one command that you can use to produce them:

- '$\geq$' (\ge and \geq).
- '$\leq$' (\le and \leq).
- '$\neq$' (\ne, \neq, and \not=).
- '$\ni$' (\ni and \owns).

You can produce negated relations by prefixing them with \not, as follows:

$\not\asymp$	**\not\asymp**	$\not\leq$	**\not\leq**	$\neq$	**\not\simeq**
$\not\cong$	**\not\cong**	$\not\prec$	**\not\prec**	$\not\subset$	**\not\subset**
$\not\equiv$	**\not\equiv**	$\not\preceq$	**\not\preceq**	$\not\subseteq$	**\not\subseteq**
$\neq$	**\not=**	$\not\succ$	**\not\succ**	$\not\supset$	**\not\supset**
$\not\geq$	**\not\ge**	$\not\succeq$	**\not\succeq**	$\not\supseteq$	**\not\supseteq**
$\not\geq$	**\not\geq**	$\not\approx$	**\not\approx**	$\not\sqsubseteq$	**\not\sqsubseteq**
$\not\leq$	**\not\le**	$\not\sim$	**\not\sim**	$\not\sqsupseteq$	**\not\sqsupseteq**

Example:
```
We can show that $AB \perp AC$, and that
$\triangle ABF \not\sim \triangle ACF$.
```
produces:
We can show that $AB \perp AC$, and that $\triangle ABF \not\sim \triangle ACF$.

■ *Left and right delimiters*

☞
{	**\lbrace**	[	**\lbrack**	⌈	**\lceil**
{	**\\-**	]	**\rbrack**	⌉	**\rceil**
}	**\rbrace**	⟨	**\langle**	⌊	**\lfloor**
}	**\"**	⟩	**\rangle**	⌋	**\rfloor**

These commands produce left and right delimiters. Mathematicians use delimiters to indicate the boundaries between parts of a formula. Left delimiters are also called "openings", and right delimiters are also called "closings". Openings and closings are two of TeX's classes of math symbols. TeX puts different amounts of space around different classes of math symbols. You might expect the space that TeX puts around openings and closings to be symmetrical, but in fact it isn't.

Some left and right delimiters have more than one command that you can use to produce them:

- '{' (\lbrace and \{)
- '}' (\rbrace and \})
- '[' (\lbrack and '[')
- ']' (\rbrack and ']')

You can also use the left and right bracket characters (in either form) outside of math mode.

In addition to these commands, TEX treats '(' as a left delimiter and ')' as a right delimiter.

You can have TEX choose the size for a delimiter by using \left and \right (p. 204). Alternatively, you can get a delimiter of a specific size by using one of the \bigx commands (see \big et al., p. 211).

Example:
```
The set $\{\,x \mid x>0\,\}$ is empty.
```
produces:
The set $\{\, x \mid x > 0 \,\}$ is empty.

■ Arrows

←	\leftarrow		↼	\leftharpoondown
←	\gets		⇁	\rightharpoondown
⇐	\Leftarrow		↽	\leftharpoonup
→	\rightarrow		⇀	\rightharpoonup
→	\to		⇌	\rightleftharpoons
⇒	\Rightarrow		↦	\mapsto
↔	\leftrightarrow		⟼	\longmapsto
⇔	\Leftrightarrow		↓	\downarrow
⟵	\longleftarrow		⇓	\Downarrow
⟸	\Longleftarrow		↑	\uparrow
⟶	\longrightarrow		⇑	\Uparrow
⟹	\Longrightarrow		↕	\updownarrow
⟷	\longleftrightarrow		⇕	\Updownarrow
⟺	\Longleftrightarrow		↗	\nearrow
⟺	\iff		↘	\searrow
↩	\hookleftarrow		↖	\nwarrow
↪	\hookrightarrow		↙	\swarrow

These commands provide arrows of different kinds. They are classified as relations (p. 190). The vertical arrows in the list are also delimiters, so you can make them larger by using \big et al. (p. 211).

The command \iff differs from \Longleftrightarrow in that it produces extra space to the left and right of the arrow.

You can place symbols or other legends on top of a left or right arrow with \buildrel (p. 202).

Example:
```
$$f(x)\mapsto f(y) \iff x \mapsto y$$
```
produces:

$$f(x) \mapsto f(y) \iff x \mapsto y$$

■ Named mathematical functions

☞

cos	**\cos**	sinh	**\sinh**	hom	**\hom**
sin	**\sin**	tanh	**\tanh**	ker	**\ker**
tan	**\tan**	det	**\det**	inf	**\inf**
cot	**\cot**	dim	**\dim**	sup	**\sup**
csc	**\csc**	exp	**\exp**	lim	**\lim**
sec	**\sec**	ln	**\ln**	lim inf	**\liminf**
arccos	**\arccos**	log	**\log**	lim sup	**\limsup**
arcsin	**\arcsin**	lg	**\lg**	max	**\max**
arctan	**\arctan**	arg	**\arg**	min	**\min**
cosh	**\cosh**	deg	**\deg**	Pr	**\Pr**
coth	**\coth**	gcd	**\gcd**		

These commands set the names of various mathematical functions in roman type, as is customary. If you apply a superscript or subscript to one of these commands, TeX will in most cases typeset it in the usual place. In display style, TeX typesets superscripts and subscripts on \det, \gcd, \inf, \lim, \liminf, \limsup, \max, \min, \Pr, and \sup as though they were limits, i.e., directly above or directly below the function name.

Example:
```
$\cos^2 x + \sin^2 x = 1\qquad\max_{a \in A} g(a) = 1$
```
produces:

$$\cos^2 x + \sin^2 x = 1 \qquad \max_{a \in A} g(a) = 1$$

\bmod

This command produces a binary operation for indicating a modulus within a formula.

Example:
```
$$x = (y+1) \bmod 2$$
```
produces:

$$x = (y + 1) \bmod 2$$

\pmod

This command provides a notation for indicating a modulus in parentheses at the end of a formula.

Example:

```
$$x \equiv y+1 \pmod 2$$
```

produces:

$$x \equiv y + 1 \quad (\text{mod } 2)$$

■ Large operators

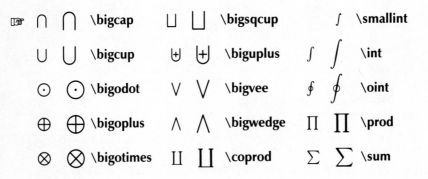

☞ ∩ ⋂ \bigcap	⊔ ⨆ \bigsqcup	∫ \smallint
∪ ⋃ \bigcup	⊎ ⨄ \biguplus	∫ ∫ \int
⊙ ⨀ \bigodot	∨ ⋁ \bigvee	∮ ∮ \oint
⊕ ⨁ \bigoplus	∧ ⋀ \bigwedge	∏ ∏ \prod
⊗ ⨂ \bigotimes	⨿ ∐ \coprod	Σ ∑ \sum

These commands produce various large operator symbols. TEX produces the smaller size when it's in text style and the larger size when it's in display style. Operators are one of TEX's classes of math symbols. TEX puts different amounts of space around different classes of math symbols.

The large operator symbols with '`big`' in their names are different from the corresponding binary operations (see p. 189) such as \cap (∩) since they usually appear at the beginning of a formula. TEX uses different spacing for a large operator than it does for a binary operation.

Don't confuse '$\sum$' (\sum) with 'Σ'(\Sigma) or confuse '$\prod$' (\prod) with 'Π' (\Pi). \Sigma and \Pi produce capital Greek letters, which are smaller and have a different appearance.

A large operator can have limits. The lower limit is specified as a subscript and the upper limit as a superscript.

Example:

```
$$\bigcap_{k=1}^r (a_k \cup b_k)$$
```

produces:

$$\bigcap_{k=1}^{r} (a_k \cup b_k)$$

Example:
```
$${\int_0^\pi \sin^2 ax\,dx} = {\pi \over 2}$$
```
produces:

$$\int_0^\pi \sin^2 ax\,dx = \frac{\pi}{2}$$

\limits

When it's in text style, TeX normally places limits after a large operator. This command tells TeX to place limits above and below a large operator rather than after it.

If you specify more than one of \limits, \nolimits, and \display-limits, the last command rules.

Example:
```
Suppose that $\bigcap\limits_{i=1}^Nq_i$ contains at least
two elements.
```
produces:

Suppose that $\bigcap\limits_{i=1}^N q_i$ contains at least two elements.

\nolimits

When it's in display style, TeX normally places limits above and below a large operator. (The \int operator is an exception—TeX places limits for \int after the operator in all cases.) This command tells TeX to place limits after a large operator rather than above and below it.

If you specify more than one of \limits, \nolimits, and \display-limits, the last command rules.

Example:
```
$$\bigcap\nolimits_{i=1}^Nq_i$$
```
produces:

$$\bigcap\nolimits_{i=1}^N q_i$$

\displaylimits

This command tells TeX to follow its normal rules for placement of limits:

(1) Limits on \int are placed after the operator.
(2) Limits on other large operators are placed after the operator in text style.
(3) Limits on other large operators are placed above and below the operator in display style.

It's usually simpler to use \limits or \nolimits to produce a specific effect, but \displaylimits is sometimes useful in macro definitions.

Note that plain TEX defines `\int` as a macro that sets `\nolimits`, so `\int\displaylimits` in text style restores the `\limits` convention.

If you specify more than one of `\limits`, `\nolimits`, and `\display-limits`, the last command rules.

Example:
```
$$a(\lambda) = {1 \over {2\pi}} \int\displaylimits
_{-\infty}^{+\infty} f(x)e^{-i\lambda x}\,dx$$
```
produces:

$$a(\lambda) = \frac{1}{2\pi} \int\limits_{-\infty}^{+\infty} f(x)e^{-i\lambda x}\,dx$$

■ Punctuation

\cdotp
\ldotp

These two commands respectively produce a centered dot and a dot positioned on the baseline. They are valid only in math mode. TEX treats them as punctuation, putting no extra space in front of them but a little extra space after them. In contrast, TEX puts an equal amount of space on both sides of a centered dot generated by the `\cdot` command (p. 189).

Example:
```
$x \cdotp y \quad x \ldotp y \quad x \cdot y$
```
produces:

$x \cdotp y \quad x.y \quad x \cdot y$

\colon

This command produces a colon punctation symbol. It is valid only in math mode. The difference between `\colon` and the colon character (:) is that ':' is an operator, so TEX puts extra space to the left of it whereas it doesn't put extra space to the left of `\colon`.

Example:
```
$f \colon t \quad f : t$
```
produces:

$f{:}t \quad f : t$

Superscripts and subscripts

☞ · $\langle argument\rangle$ ˆ $\langle argument\rangle$
\sb $\langle argument\rangle$ \sp $\langle argument\rangle$

The commands in each column are equivalent. The commands in the first column typeset $\langle argument\rangle$ as a subscript, and those in the second column typeset $\langle argument\rangle$ as a superscript. The \sb and \sp commands are mainly useful if you're working on a terminal that lacks an underscore or caret, or if you've redefined '_' or 'ˆ' and need access to the original definition. These commands are also used for setting lower and upper limits on summations and integrals.

If a subscript or superscript is not a single token, you need to enclose it in a group. TEX does not prioritize subscripts or superscripts, so it will reject formulas such as a_i_j, aˆiˆj, or aˆi_j.

Subscripts and superscripts are normally typeset in script style, or in scriptscript style if they are second-order, e.g., a subscript on a subscript or a superscript on a a subscript. You can set *any* text in a math formula in a script or scriptscript style with the \scriptstyle and \scriptscriptstyle commands (p. 198).

You can apply a subscript or superscript to any of the commands that produce named mathematical functions in roman type (see p. 193). In certain cases (again, see p. 193) the subscript or superscript appears directly above or under the function name as shown in the examples of \lim and \det below.

Example:
```
$x_3 \quad t_{\max} \quad a_{i_k} \quad \sum_{i=1}^n{q_i}
    \quad x^3\quad e^{t \cos\theta}\quad r^{x^2}\quad
    \int_0^\infty{f(x)\,dx}$
$$\lim_{x \leftarrow 0} f(x)\qquad
    \det^{z \in A}\qquad \sin^2 t$$
```
produces:

$$x_3 \quad t_{\max} \quad a_{i_k} \quad \sum_{i=1}^n q_i \quad x^3 \quad e^{t \cos\theta} \quad r^{x^2} \quad \int_0^\infty f(x)\,dx$$

$$\lim_{x \leftarrow 0} f(x) \qquad \overset{z \in A}{\det} \qquad \sin^2 t$$

■ *Selecting and using styles*

\textstyle
\scriptstyle
\scriptscriptstyle
\displaystyle
These commands override the normal style and hence the font that TEX
uses in setting a formula. Like font-setting commands such as \it, they
are in effect until the end of the group containing them. They are useful
when TEX's choice of style is inappropriate for the formula you happen
to be setting.

Example:
```
$t+{\scriptstyle t + {\scriptscriptstyle t}}$
```
produces:

$t + t{+}t$

\mathchoice – $\langle math_1 \rangle$ ″ – $\langle math_2 \rangle$ ″ – $\langle math_3 \rangle$ ″ – $\langle math_4 \rangle$ ″
This command tells TEX to typeset one of the subformulas $\langle math_1 \rangle$,
$\langle math_2 \rangle$, $\langle math_3 \rangle$, or $\langle math_4 \rangle$, making its choice according to the current style. That is, if TEX is in display style it sets the \mathchoice
as $\langle math_1 \rangle$; in text style it sets it as $\langle math_2 \rangle$; in script style it sets it as
$\langle math_3 \rangle$; and in scriptscript style it sets it as $\langle math_4 \rangle$.

Example:
```
\def\mc{{\mathchoice{D}{T}{S}{SS}}}
The strange formula $\mc_{\mc_\mc}$ illustrates a
mathchoice.
```
produces:
The strange formula $T_{S_{ss}}$ illustrates a mathchoice.

\mathpalette $\langle argument_1 \rangle$ $\langle argument_2 \rangle$
This command provides a convenient way of producing a math construct
that works in all four styles. To use it, you'll normally need to define
an additional macro, which we'll call \build. The call on \mathpalette
should then have the form \mathpalette\build$\langle argument \rangle$.

\build tests what style TEX is in and typesets $\langle argument \rangle$ accordingly. It should be defined to have two parameters. When you call
\mathpalette, it will in turn call \build, with #1 being a command
that selects the current style and #2 being $\langle argument \rangle$. Thus, within the
definition of \build you can typeset something in the current style by
preceding it with '#1'. See page 360 of *The TEXbook* for examples of using

\mathpalette and page 151 of *The TEXbook* for a further explanation of how it works.

Compound symbols

■ Math accents

☞ \acute   acute accent as in $\acute{x}$
\b   bar-under accent as in $\underline{x}$
\bar   bar accent as in $\bar{x}$
\breve   breve accent as in $\breve{x}$
\check   check accent as in $\check{x}$
\ddot   double dot accent as in $\ddot{x}$
\dot   dot accent as in $\dot{x}$
\grave   grave accent as in $\grave{x}$
\hat   hat accent as in $\hat{x}$
\widehat   wide hat accent as in $\widehat{x+y}$
\tilde   tilde accent as in $\tilde{x}$
\widetilde   wide tilde accent as in $\widetilde{z+a}$
\vec   vector accent as in $\vec{x}$

These commands produce accent marks in math formulas. You'll ordinarily need to leave a space after any one of them. A wide accent can be applied to a multicharacter subformula; TEX will center the accent over the subformula. The other accents are usefully applied only to a single character.

Example:
```
$\dot t^n \qquad \widetilde{v_1 + v_2}$
```
produces:
$$\dot{t}^n \qquad \widetilde{v_1 + v_2}$$

\mathaccent ⟨*mathcode*⟩
This command tells TEX to typeset a math accent whose family and character code are given by ⟨*mathcode*⟩. (TEX ignores the class of the mathcode.) See Appendix G of *The TEXbook* for the details of how TEX positions such an accent. The usual way to use \mathaccent is to put it in a macro definition that gives a name to a math accent.

Example:
```
\def\acute{\mathaccent "7013}
```

See also: "Accents" (p. 100).

■ *Fractions and other stacking operations*

☞ **\over**
\atop
\above ⟨*dimen*⟩
\choose
\brace
\brack

These commands stack one subformula on top of another one. We will explain how **\over** works, and then relate the other commands to it.

\over is the command that you'd normally use to produce a fraction. If you write something in one of the following forms:

$$\mathtt{\$\$}\langle formula_1\rangle\mathtt{\backslash over}\langle formula_2\rangle\mathtt{\$\$}$$
$$\mathtt{\$}\langle formula_1\rangle\mathtt{\backslash over}\langle formula_2\rangle\mathtt{\$}$$
$$\mathtt{\backslash left}\langle delim\rangle\langle formula_1\rangle\mathtt{\backslash over}\langle formula_2\rangle\mathtt{\backslash right}\langle delim\rangle$$
$$\mathtt{\{}\langle formula_1\rangle\mathtt{\backslash over}\langle formula_2\rangle\mathtt{\}}$$

you'll get a fraction with numerator ⟨*formula₁*⟩ and denominator ⟨*formula₂*⟩, i.e., ⟨*formula₁*⟩ over ⟨*formula₂*⟩. In the first three of these forms the **\over** is not implicitly contained in a group; it absorbs everything to its left and to its right until it comes to a boundary, namely, the beginning or end of a group.

You can't use **\over** or any of the other commands in this group more than once in a formula. Thus a formula such as:

```
$$a \over n \choose k$$
```

isn't legal. This is not a severe restriction because you can always enclose one of the commands in braces. The reason for the restriction is that if you had two of these commands in a single formula, TEX wouldn't know how to group them.

The other commands are similar to **\over**, with the following exceptions:

- **\atop** leaves out the fraction bar.
- **\above** provides a fraction bar of thickness ⟨*dimen*⟩.
- **\choose** leaves out the fraction bar and encloses the construct in parentheses. (It's called "choose" because $\binom{n}{k}$ is the notation for the number of ways of choosing k things out of n things.)
- **\brace** leaves out the fraction bar and encloses the construct in braces.
- **\brack** leaves out the fraction bar and encloses the construct in brackets.

Example:
```
$${n+1 \over n-1}        \qquad {n+1 \atop n-1}    \qquad
  {n+1 \above 2pt n-1} \qquad {n+1 \choose n-1} \qquad
  {n+1 \brace n-1}        \qquad {n+1 \brack n-1}$$
```
produces:

$$\frac{n+1}{n-1} \qquad \begin{matrix} n+1 \\ n-1 \end{matrix} \qquad \frac{n+1}{n-1} \qquad \binom{n+1}{n-1} \qquad \left\{ \begin{matrix} n+1 \\ n-1 \end{matrix} \right\} \qquad \left[\begin{matrix} n+1 \\ n-1 \end{matrix} \right]$$

\overwithdelims $\langle delim_1 \rangle$ $\langle delim_2 \rangle$
\atopwithdelims $\langle delim_1 \rangle$ $\langle delim_2 \rangle$
\abovewithdelims $\langle delim_1 \rangle$ $\langle delim_2 \rangle$ $\langle dimen \rangle$

Each of these commands stacks one subformula on top of another one and surrounds the entire construct with $\langle delim_1 \rangle$ on the left and $\langle delim_2 \rangle$ on the right. These commands follow the same rules as \over, \atop, and \above. The $\langle dimen \rangle$ in \abovewithdelims specifies the thickness of the fraction bar.

Example:
```
$${m \overwithdelims () n}\qquad
  {m \atopwithdelims || n}\qquad
  {m \abovewithdelims \{\} 2pt n}$$
```
produces:

$$\left(\frac{m}{n} \right) \qquad \left| \begin{matrix} m \\ n \end{matrix} \right| \qquad \left\{ \frac{m}{n} \right\}$$

\cases

This command produces the mathematical form that denotes a choice among several cases. Each case has two parts, separated by '&'. TeX treats the first part as a math formula and the second part as ordinary text. Each case must be followed by \cr.

Example:
```
$$g(x,y) = \cases{f(x,y),&if $x<y$\cr
                  f(y,x),&if $x>y$\cr
                  0,&otherwise.\cr}$$
```
produces:

$$g(x,y) = \begin{cases} f(x,y), & \text{if } x < y \\ f(y,x), & \text{if } x > y \\ 0, & \text{otherwise.} \end{cases}$$

\underbrace ⟨*argument*⟩
\overbrace ⟨*argument*⟩
\underline ⟨*argument*⟩
\overline ⟨*argument*⟩
\overleftarrow ⟨*argument*⟩
\overrightarrow ⟨*argument*⟩

These commands place extensible braces, lines, or arrows over or under the subformula given by ⟨*argument*⟩. TEX will make these constructs as wide as they need to be for the context. When TEX produces the extended braces, lines, or arrows, it considers only the dimensions of the box containing ⟨*argument*⟩. If you use more than one of these commands in a single formula, the braces, lines, or arrows they produce may not line up properly with each other. You can use the **\mathstrut** command (p. 168) to overcome this difficulty.

Example:
```
$$\displaylines{
\underbrace{x \circ y}\qquad \overbrace{x \circ y}\qquad
\underline{x \circ y}\qquad \overline{x \circ y}\qquad
\overleftarrow{x \circ y}\qquad
\overrightarrow{x \circ y}\cr
{\overline r + \overline t}\qquad
{\overline {r \mathstrut} + \overline {t \mathstrut}}\cr
}$$
```
produces:

$$\underbrace{x \circ y} \qquad \overbrace{x \circ y} \qquad \underline{x \circ y} \qquad \overline{x \circ y} \qquad \overleftarrow{x \circ y} \qquad \overrightarrow{x \circ y}$$

$$\overline{r} + \overline{t} \qquad \overline{r} + \overline{t}$$

\buildrel ⟨*formula*⟩ **\over** ⟨*relation*⟩

This command produces a box in which ⟨*formula*⟩ is placed on top of ⟨*relation*⟩. TEX treats the result as a relation for spacing purposes (see "class", p. 56).

Example:
```
$\buildrel \rm def \over \equiv$
```
produces:

$$\buildrel \rm def \over \equiv$$

■ *Dots*

☞ **\ldots**
\cdots

These commands produce three dots in a row. For **\ldots**, the dots are on the baseline; for **\cdots**, the dots are centered with respect to the axis (see the explanation of **\vcenter**, p. 213).

Example:
```
$t_1 + t_2 + \cdots + t_n \qquad x_1,x_2, \ldots\,, x_r$
```
produces:

$$t_1 + t_2 + \cdots + t_n \qquad x_1, x_2, \ldots, x_r$$

☞ **\vdots**

This command produces three vertical dots.

Example:
```
$$\eqalign{f(\alpha_1)& = f(\beta_1)\cr
    \noalign{\kern -4pt}%
    &\phantom{a}\vdots\cr % moves the dots right a bit
    f(\alpha_k)& = f(\beta_k)\cr}$$
```
produces:

$$f(\alpha_1) = f(\beta_1)$$
$$\vdots$$
$$f(\alpha_k) = f(\beta_k)$$

\ddots

This command produces three dots on a diagonal. Its most common use is to indicate repetition along the diagonal of a matrix.

Example:
```
$$\pmatrix{0&\ldots&0\cr
           \vdots&\ddots&\vdots\cr
           0&\ldots&0\cr}$$
```
produces:

$$\begin{pmatrix} 0 & \ldots & 0 \\ \vdots & \ddots & \vdots \\ 0 & \ldots & 0 \end{pmatrix}$$

See also: \dots (p. 99).

■ *Delimiters*

\lgroup
\rgroup
These commands produce large left and right parentheses that are defined as opening and closing delimiters. The smallest available size for these delimiters is \Big. If you use smaller sizes, you'll get weird characters.

Example:
```
$$\lgroup\dots\rgroup\qquad\bigg\lgroup\dots\bigg\rgroup$$
```
produces:

$$\Gamma\dots\Gamma\qquad\Bigg(\dots\Bigg)$$

☞ **\left**
\right
These commands must be used together in the pattern:

\left $\langle delim_1\rangle$ $\langle subformula\rangle$ **\right** $\langle delim_2\rangle$

This construct causes TEX to produce $\langle subformula\rangle$, enclosed in the delimiters $\langle delim_1\rangle$ and $\langle delim_2\rangle$. The vertical size of the delimiter is adjusted to fit the vertical size (height plus depth) of $\langle subformula\rangle$. $\langle delim_1\rangle$ and $\langle delim_2\rangle$ need not correspond. For instance, you could use ']' as a left delimiter and '(' as a right delimiter in a single use of \left and \right.

\left and \right have the important property that they define a group, i.e., they act like left and right braces. This grouping property is particularly useful when you put \over (p. 200) or a related command between \left and \right, since you don't need to put braces around the fraction constructed by \over.

If you want a left delimiter but not a right delimiter, you can use '.' in place of the delimiter you don't want and it will turn into empty space (of width \nulldelimiterspace).

Example:
```
$$\left\Vert\matrix{a&b\cr c&d\cr}\right\Vert
   \qquad \left\uparrow q_1\atop q_2\right.$$
```
produces:

$$\left\Vert\matrix{a&b\cr c&d}\right\Vert\qquad\left\uparrow{q_1\atop q_2}\right.$$

\delimiter $\langle number\rangle$
This command produces a delimiter whose characteristics are given by $\langle number\rangle$. $\langle number\rangle$ is normally written in hexadecimal notation. You

can use the `\delimiter` command instead of a character in any context where TeX expects a delimiter (although the command is rarely used outside of a macro definition). Suppose that $\langle number \rangle$ is the hexadecimal number $cs_1s_2s_3l_1l_2l_3$. Then TeX takes the delimiter to have class c, small variant $s_1s_2s_3$, and large variant $l_1l_2l_3$. Here $s_1s_2s_3$ indicates the math character found in position s_2s_3 of family s_1, and similarly for $l_1l_2l_3$. This is the same convention as the one used for `\mathcode` (p. 251).

Example:
```
\def\vert{\delimiter "026A30C} % As in plain TeX.
```

\delimiterfactor [$\langle number \rangle$ parameter]
\delimitershortfall [$\langle number \rangle$ parameter]
These parameters together tell TeX how the height of a delimiter should be related to the vertical size of the subformula with which the delimiter is associated. `\delimiterfactor` gives the minimum ratio of the delimiter size to the vertical size of the subformula, and `\delimitershortfall` gives the maximum by which the height of the delimiter will be reduced from that of the vertical size of the subformula.

Suppose that the box containing the subformula has height h and depth d, and let $y = 2 \max(h, d)$. Let the value of `\delimiterfactor` be f and the value of `\delimitershortfall` be δ. Then TeX takes the minimum delimiter size to be at least $y \cdot f/1000$ and at least $y - \delta$. In particular, if `\delimiterfactor` is exactly 1000 then TeX will try to make a delimiter at least as tall as the formula to which it is attached. See page 152 and page 446 (Rule 19) of *The TeXbook* for the exact details of how TeX uses these parameters. Plain TeX sets `\delimiterfactor` to 901 and `\delimitershortfall` to 5pt.

See also: `\delcode` (p. 251), `\vert`, `\Vert`, and `\backslash` (p. 188).

■ *Matrices*

\matrix $- \langle line \rangle$ **\cr** ... $\langle line \rangle$ **\cr** ″
\pmatrix $- \langle line \rangle$ **\cr** ... $\langle line \rangle$ **\cr** ″
\bordermatrix $- \langle line \rangle$ **\cr** ... $\langle line \rangle$ **\cr** ″
Each of these three commands produces a matrix. The elements of each row of the input matrix are separated by '&' and each row in turn is ended by `\cr`. (This is the same form that is used for an alignment.) The commands differ in the following ways:

- `\matrix` produces a matrix without any surrounding or inserted delimiters.

- \pmatrix produces a matrix surrounded by parentheses.
- \bordermatrix produces a matrix in which the first row and the first column are treated as labels. (The first element of the first row is usually left blank.) The rest of the matrix is enclosed in parentheses.

TEX can make the parentheses for \pmatrix and \bordermatrix as large as they need to be by inserting vertical extensions. If you want a matrix to be surrounded by delimiters other than parentheses, you should use \matrix in conjunction with \left and \right (p. 204).

Example:
```
$$\displaylines{
   \matrix{t_{11}&t_{12}&t_{13}\cr
          t_{21}&t_{22}&t_{23}\cr
          t_{31}&t_{32}&t_{33}\cr}\qquad
\left\{\matrix{t_{11}&t_{12}&t_{13}\cr
          t_{21}&t_{22}&t_{23}\cr
          t_{31}&t_{32}&t_{33}\cr}\right\}\cr
\pmatrix{t_{11}&t_{12}&t_{13}\cr
          t_{21}&t_{22}&t_{23}\cr
          t_{31}&t_{32}&t_{33}\cr}\qquad
\bordermatrix{&c_1&c_2&c_3\cr
          r_1&t_{11}&t_{12}&t_{13}\cr
          r_2&t_{21}&t_{22}&t_{23}\cr
          r_3&t_{31}&t_{32}&t_{33}\cr}\cr}$$
```
produces:

$$
\begin{matrix} t_{11} & t_{12} & t_{13} \\ t_{21} & t_{22} & t_{23} \\ t_{31} & t_{32} & t_{33} \end{matrix}
\qquad
\left\{ \begin{matrix} t_{11} & t_{12} & t_{13} \\ t_{21} & t_{22} & t_{23} \\ t_{31} & t_{32} & t_{33} \end{matrix} \right\}
$$

$$
\begin{pmatrix} t_{11} & t_{12} & t_{13} \\ t_{21} & t_{22} & t_{23} \\ t_{31} & t_{32} & t_{33} \end{pmatrix}
\qquad
\begin{matrix} & c_1 & c_2 & c_3 \\ r_1 & t_{11} & t_{12} & t_{13} \\ r_2 & t_{21} & t_{22} & t_{23} \\ r_3 & t_{31} & t_{32} & t_{33} \end{matrix}
$$

■ Roots and radicals

☞ **\sqrt** ⟨*argument*⟩

This command produces the notation for the square root of ⟨*argument*⟩.

Example:
```
$$x = {-b\pm\sqrt{b^2-4ac} \over 2a}$$
```
produces:
$$x = \frac{-b \pm \sqrt{b^2 - 4ac}}{2a}$$

☞ **\root** ⟨*argument₁*⟩ **\of** ⟨*argument₂*⟩

This command produces the notation for a root of ⟨*argument₂*⟩, where the root is given by ⟨*argument₁*⟩.

Example:
```
$\root \alpha \of {r \cos \theta}$
```
produces:
$$\sqrt[\alpha]{r \cos \theta}$$

\radical ⟨*number*⟩

This command produces a radical sign whose characteristics are given by ⟨*number*⟩. It uses the same representation as the delimiter code in the \delcode command (p. 251).

Example:
```
\def\sqrt{\radical "270370} % as in plain TeX
```

Equation numbers

☞ **\eqno**
\leqno

These commands attach an equation number to a displayed formula. \eqno puts the equation number on the right and \leqno puts it on the left. The commands must be given at the end of the formula. If you have a multiline display and you want to number more than one of the lines, use the \eqalignno or \leqalignno command (p. 208).

These commands are valid only in display math mode.

Example:
```
$$e^{i\theta} = \cos \theta + i \sin \theta\eqno{(11)}$$
```
produces:

$$e^{i\theta} = \cos \theta + i \sin \theta \eqno (11)$$

Example:
```
$$\cos^2 \theta + \sin^2 \theta = 1\leqno{(12)}$$
```
produces:

$$(12) \qquad\qquad \cos^2 \theta + \sin^2 \theta = 1$$

Multiline displays

\displaylines – ⟨*line*⟩ **\cr**...⟨*line*⟩ **\cr** ″
This command produces a multiline math display in which each line is centered independently of the other lines. You can use the **\noalign** command (p. 183) to change the amount of space between two lines of a multiline display.

If you want to attach equation numbers to some or all of the equations in a multiline math display, you should use **\eqalignno** or **\leqalignno**.

Example:
```
$$\displaylines{(x+a)^2 = x^2+2ax+a^2\cr
               (x+a)(x-a) = x^2-a^2\cr}$$
```
produces:

$$(x + a)^2 = x^2 + 2ax + a^2$$
$$(x + a)(x - a) = x^2 - a^2$$

\eqalign – ⟨*line*⟩ **\cr** ... ⟨*line*⟩ **\cr** ″
\eqalignno – ⟨*line*⟩ **\cr** ... ⟨*line*⟩ **\cr** ″
\leqalignno – ⟨*line*⟩ **\cr** ... ⟨*line*⟩ **\cr** ″
These commands produce a multiline math display in which certain corresponding parts of the lines are lined up vertically. The **\eqalignno** and **\leqalignno** commands also let you provide equation numbers for some or all of the lines. **\eqalignno** puts the equation numbers on the right and **\leqalignno** puts them on the left.

Each line in the display is ended by **\cr**. Each of the parts to be aligned (most often an equals sign) is preceded by '**&**'. An '**&**' also precedes each equation number, which comes at the end of a line. You can put more than one of these commands in a single display in order to produce several groups of equations. In this case, only the rightmost or leftmost group can be produced by **\eqalignno** or **\leqalignno**.

You can use the **\noalign** command (p. 183) to change the amount of space between two lines of a multiline display.

Example:
```
$$\left\{\eqalign{f_1(t) &= 2t\cr f_2(t) &= t^3\cr
         f_3(t) &= t^2-1\cr}\right\}
   \left\{\eqalign{g_1(t) &= t\cr g_2(t) &= 1}\right\}$$
```
produces:

$$\left\{ \begin{array}{l} f_1(t) = 2t \\ f_2(t) = t^3 \\ f_3(t) = t^2 - 1 \end{array} \right\} \left\{ \begin{array}{l} g_1(t) = t \\ g_2(t) = 1 \end{array} \right\}$$

Example:
```
$$\eqalignno{
\sigma^2&=E(x-\mu)^2&(12)\cr
    &={1 \over n}\sum_{i=0}^n (x_i - \mu)^2&\cr
    &=E(x^2)-\mu^2\cr}$$
```
produces:

$$\sigma^2 = E(x - \mu)^2 \qquad\qquad (12)$$
$$= \frac{1}{n}\sum_{i=0}^n (x_i - \mu)^2$$
$$= E(x^2) - \mu^2$$

Example:
```
$$\leqalignno{
\sigma^2&=E(x-\mu)^2&(6)\cr
    &=E(x^2)-\mu^2&(7)\cr}$$
```
produces:

$$(6) \qquad\qquad \sigma^2 = E(x - \mu)^2$$
$$(7) \qquad\qquad = E(x^2) - \mu^2$$

Example:
```
$$\eqalignno{
    &(x+a)^2 = x^2+2ax+a^2&(19)\cr
    &(x+a)(x-a) = x^2-a^2\cr}$$
% same effect as \displaylines but with an equation number
```
produces:

$$(x + a)^2 = x^2 + 2ax + a^2 \qquad\qquad (19)$$
$$(x + a)(x - a) = x^2 - a^2$$

Fonts in math formulas

☞ **\cal**   use calligraphic uppercase font
\mit   use math italic font
\oldstyle   use old style digit font

These commands cause TeX to typeset the following text in the specified font. You can only use them in math mode. The **\mit** command is useful for producing slanted capital Greek letters. You can also use the commands given in "Selecting fonts" (p. 102) to change fonts in math mode.

Example:
```
${\cal XYZ} \quad
{\mit AaBb\Gamma \Delta \Sigma} \quad
{\oldstyle 0123456789}$
```
produces:

$\mathcal{XYZ} \quad AaBb\Gamma\Delta\Sigma \quad 0123456789$

\itfam   family for italic type
\bffam   family for boldface type
\slfam   family for slanted type
\ttfam   family for typewriter type

These commands define type families for use in math mode. Their principal use is in defining the \it, \bf, \sl, and \tt commands so that they work in math mode.

\fam   [⟨*number*⟩ parameter]

When TeX is in math mode, it ordinarily typesets a character using the font family given in its mathcode. However, when TeX is in math mode and encounters a character whose class is 7 (Variable), it typesets that character using the font family given by the value of \fam, provided that the value of \fam is between 0 and 15. If the value of \fam isn't in that range, TeX uses the family in the character's mathcode as in the ordinary case. TeX sets \fam to −1 whenever it enters math mode. Outside of math mode, \fam has no effect.

By assigning a value to \fam you can change the way that TeX typesets ordinary characters such as variables. For instance, by setting \fam to \ttfam, you cause TeX to typeset variables using a typewriter font. Plain TeX defines \tt as a macro that, among other things, sets \fam to \ttfam.

Example:
```
\def\bf{\fam\bffam\tenbf} % As in plain TeX.
```

\textfont ⟨*family*⟩   [⟨*fontname*⟩ parameter]
\scriptfont ⟨*family*⟩   [⟨*fontname*⟩ parameter]
\scriptscriptfont ⟨*family*⟩   [⟨*fontname*⟩ parameter]

Each of these parameters specifies the font that TeX is to use for typesetting the indicated style in the indicated family. These choices have no effect outside of math mode.

Example:
```
\scriptfont2 = \sevensy % As in plain TeX.
```

See also: "Type styles" (p. 103).

Constructing math symbols

■ *Making delimiters bigger*

\big	\Big	\bigg	\Bigg
\bigl	\Bigl	\biggl	\Biggl
\bigm	\Bigm	\biggm	\Biggm
\bigr	\Bigr	\biggr	\Biggr

These commands make delimiters bigger than their normal size. The commands in the four columns produce successively larger sizes. The difference between \big, \bigl, \bigr, and bigm has to do with the class of the enlarged delimiter:

- \big produces an ordinary symbol.
- \bigl produces an opening symbol.
- \bigr produces a closing symbol.
- \bigm produces a relation symbol.

TeX uses the class of a symbol in order to decide how much space to put around that symbol.

These commands, unlike \left and \right, do *not* define a group.

Example:
```
$$(x) \quad \bigl(x\bigr) \quad \Bigl(x\Bigr) \quad
    \biggl(x\biggr) \quad \Biggl(x\Biggr)\qquad
[x] \quad \bigl[x\bigr] \quad \Bigl[x\Bigr] \quad
    \biggl[x\biggr] \quad \Biggl[x\Biggr]$$
```
produces:

$$(x) \quad \big(x\big) \quad \Big(x\Big) \quad \bigg(x\bigg) \quad \Bigg(x\Bigg) \qquad [x] \quad \big[x\big] \quad \Big[x\Big] \quad \bigg[x\bigg] \quad \Bigg[x\Bigg]$$

■ *Parts of large symbols*

\downbracefill
\upbracefill
These commands respectively produce upward-pointing and downward-pointing extensible horizontal braces. TeX will make the braces as wide

as necessary. These commands are used in the definitions of `\overbrace` and `\underbrace` (p. 202).

Example:
```
$$\hbox to 1in{\downbracefill} \quad
    \hbox to 1in{\upbracefill}$$
```
produces:

\arrowvert
\Arrowvert
\lmoustache
\rmoustache
\bracevert

These commands produce portions of certain large delimiters and can themselves be used as delimiters. They refer to characters in the `cmex10` math font.

Example:
```
$$\cdots \Big\arrowvert \cdots \Big\Arrowvert \cdots
    \Big\lmoustache \cdots \Big\rmoustache \cdots
    \Big\bracevert \cdots$$
```
produces:

$$\cdots \Big| \cdots \Big\| \cdots \int \cdots \Big\{ \cdots \Big| \cdots$$

Aligning parts of a formula

■ *Aligning accents*

\skew ⟨*number*⟩ ⟨*argument₁*⟩ ⟨*argument₂*⟩

This command shifts the accent ⟨*argument*$_1$⟩ by ⟨*number*⟩ mathematical units to the right of its normal position with respect to ⟨*argument*$_2$⟩. The most common use of this command is for modifying the position of an accent that's over another accent.

Example:
```
$$\skew 2\bar{\bar z}\quad\skew 3\tilde{\tilde y}\quad
    \skew 4\tilde{\hat x}$$
```
produces:

$$\bar{\bar z} \quad \tilde{\tilde y} \quad \tilde{\hat x}$$

\skewchar ⟨*font*⟩   [⟨*number*⟩ parameter]

The \skewchar of a font is the character in the font whose kerns, as defined in the font's metrics file, determine the positions of math accents. That is, suppose that TEX is applying a math accent to the character 'x'. TEX checks if the character pair 'x\skewchar' has a kern; if so, it moves the accent by the amount of that kern. The complete algorithm that TEX uses to position math accents (which involves many more things) is in Appendix G of *The TEXbook*.

If the value of \skewchar is not in the range 0–255, TEX takes the kern value to be zero.

Note that ⟨*font*⟩ is a control sequence that names a font, not a ⟨*font-name*⟩ that names font files. Beware: an assignment to \skewchar is *not* undone at the end of a group. If you want to change \skewchar locally, you'll need to save and restore its original value explicitly.

\defaultskewchar   [⟨*number*⟩ parameter]

When TEX reads the metrics file for a font in response to a \font command, it sets the font's \skewchar to \defaultskewchar. If the value of \defaultskewchar is not in the range 0–255, TEX does not assign any skew characters by default. Plain TEX sets \defaultskewchar to −1, and it's usually best to leave it there.

■ *Aligning material vertically*

\vcenter − ⟨*vertical mode material*⟩ ″
\vcenter to ⟨*dimen*⟩ − ⟨*vertical mode material*⟩ ″
\vcenter spread ⟨*dimen*⟩ − ⟨*vertical mode material*⟩ ″

Every math formula has an invisible "axis" that TEX treats as a kind of horizontal centering line for that formula. For instance, the axis of a formula consisting of a fraction is at the center of the fraction bar. The \vcenter command tells TEX to place the ⟨*vertical mode material*⟩ in a vbox and to center the vbox with respect to the axis of the formula it is currently constructing.

The first form of the command centers the material as given. The second and third forms expand or shrink the material vertically as in the \vbox command (p. 161).

Example:
```
$${n \choose k} \buildrel \rm def \over \equiv \>
\vcenter{\hsize 1.5 in \noindent the number of
combinations of $n$ things taken $k$ at a time}$$
```
produces:

$$\binom{n}{k} \overset{\mathrm{def}}{\equiv} \text{the number of combina-tions of } n \text{ things taken } k \text{ at a time}$$

Producing spaces

■ Fixed-width math spaces

```
\!
\,
\¿
\;
```

These commands produce various amounts of extra space in formulas. They are defined in terms of mathematical units, so TeX adjusts the amount of space according to the current style.

- \! produces a negative thin space, i.e., it reduces the space between its neighboring subformulas by the amount of a thin space.
- \, produces a thin space.
- \> produces a medium space.
- \; produces a thick space.

Example:
```
$$00\quad0\!0\quad0\,0\quad0\>0\quad0\;0\quad
{\scriptstyle 00\quad0\!0\quad0\,0\quad0\>0\quad0\;0}$$
```
produces:

$$00 \quad 00 \quad 00 \quad 0\,0 \quad 0\ 0 \qquad {\scriptstyle 00 \quad 00 \quad 00 \quad 00 \quad 00}$$

\thinmuskip	[⟨*muglue*⟩ parameter]
\medmuskip	[⟨*muglue*⟩ parameter]
\thickmuskip	[⟨*muglue*⟩ parameter]

These parameters define thin, medium, and thick spaces in math mode.

Example:
```
$00\quad0\mskip\thinmuskip0\quad0\mskip\medmuskip0
   \quad0\mskip\thickmuskip0$
```

produces:

    00 00 00 00

\jot   [⟨*dimen*⟩ parameter]

This parameter defines a distance that is equal to three points (unless you change it). The \jot is a convenient unit of measure for opening up math displays.

■ *Variable-width math spaces*

\mkern ⟨*mudimen*⟩

This command produces a kern, i.e., blank space, of width ⟨*mudimen*⟩. The kern is measured in mathematical units, which vary according to the style. Aside from its unit of measurement, this command behaves just like \kern (p. 157) does in horizontal mode.

Example:

    $0\mkern13mu 0 \qquad {\scriptscriptstyle 0 \mkern13mu 0}$

produces:

    0 0   ₀ ₀

\mskip ⟨*mudimen₁*⟩ **plus** ⟨*mudimen₂*⟩ **minus** ⟨*mudimen₃*⟩

This command produces horizontal glue that has natural width ⟨*mudimen₁*⟩, stretch ⟨*mudimen₂*⟩, and shrink ⟨*mudimen₃*⟩. The glue is measured in mathematical units, which vary according to the style. Aside from its units of measurement, this command behaves just like \hskip (p. 155).

Example:

    $0\mskip 13mu 0 \quad {\scriptscriptstyle 0 \mskip 13mu 0}$

produces:

    0 0   ₀ ₀

\nonscript

When TeX is currently typesetting in script or scriptscript style and encounters this command immediately in front of glue or a kern, it cancels the glue or kern. \nonscript has no effect in the other styles.

This command provides a way of "tightening up" the spacing in script and scriptscript styles, which generally are set in smaller type. It is of little use outside of macro definitions.

Example:
```
\def\ab{a\nonscript\; b}
$\ab^{\ab}$
```
produces:
  $a\ b^{ab}$

See also: \kern (p. 157), \hskip (p. 155).

■ *Spacing parameters for displays*

\displaywidth   [⟨*dimen*⟩ parameter]

This parameter specifies the maximum width that TeX allows for a math display. If TeX cannot fit the display into a space of this width, it sets an overfull hbox and complains. TeX sets the value of \displaywidth when it encounters the '$$' that starts the display. This initial value is \hsize (p. 114) unless it's overridden by changes to the paragraph shape. See pages 188–189 of *The TeXbook* for a more detailed explanation of this parameter.

\displayindent   [⟨*dimen*⟩ parameter]

This parameter specifies the space by which TeX indents a math display. TeX sets the value of \displayindent when it encounters the '$$' that starts the display. Usually this initial value is zero, but if the paragraph shape indicates that the display should be shifted by an amount s, TeX will set \displayindent to s. See pages 188–189 of *The TeXbook* for a more detailed explanation of this parameter.

\predisplaysize   [⟨*dimen*⟩ parameter]

TeX sets this parameter to the width of the line preceding a math display. TeX uses \predisplaysize to determine whether or not the display starts to the left of where the previous line ends, i.e., whether or not it visually overlaps the previous line. If there is overlap, it uses the \abovedisplayskip and \belowdisplayskip glue in setting the display; otherwise it uses the \abovedisplayshortskip and \belowdisplay-shortskip glue. See pages 188–189 of *The TeXbook* for a more detailed explanation of this parameter.

\abovedisplayskip   [⟨*glue*⟩ parameter]

This parameter specifies the amount of vertical glue that TEX inserts before a display when the display starts to the left of where the previous line ends, i.e., when it visually overlaps the previous line. Plain TEX sets \abovedisplayskip to `12pt plus3pt minus9pt`. See pages 188–189 of *The TEXbook* for a more detailed explanation of this parameter.

\belowdisplayskip   [⟨*glue*⟩ parameter]

This parameter specifies the amount of vertical glue that TEX inserts after a display when the display starts to the left of where the previous line ends, i.e., when it visually overlaps the previous line. Plain TEX sets \belowdisplayskip to `12pt plus3pt minus9pt`. See pages 188–189 of *The TEXbook* for a more detailed explanation of this parameter.

\abovedisplayshortskip   [⟨*glue*⟩ parameter]

This parameter specifies the amount of vertical glue that TEX inserts before a math display when the display starts to the right of where the previous line ends, i.e., when it does not visually overlap the previous line. Plain TEX sets \abovedisplayshortskip to `0pt plus3pt`. See pages 188–189 of *The TEXbook* for a more detailed explanation of this parameter.

\belowdisplayshortskip   [⟨*glue*⟩ parameter]

This parameter specifies the amount of vertical glue that TEX inserts after a display when the display starts to the right of where the previous line ends, i.e., when it does not visually overlap the previous line. Plain TEX sets \belowdisplayshortskip to `7pt plus3pt minus4pt`. See pages 188–189 of *The TEXbook* for a more detailed explanation of this parameter.

■ Other spacing parameters for math

\mathsurround   [⟨*dimen*⟩ parameter]

This parameter specifies the amount of space that TEX inserts before and after a math formula in text mode (i.e., a formula surrounded by single $'s). See page 162 of *The TEXbook* for further details about its behavior. Plain TEX leaves \mathsurround at `0pt`.

\nulldelimiterspace   [⟨*dimen*⟩ parameter]

This parameter specifies the width of the space produced by a null delimiter. Plain TEX sets \nulldelimiterspace to `1.2pt`.

\scriptspace   [⟨*dimen*⟩ parameter]

This parameter specifies the amount of space that TEX inserts before and after a subscript or superscript. The \nonscript command (p. 215) after a subscript or superscript cancels this space. Plain TEX sets \scriptspace to 0.5pt.

Categorizing math constructs

\mathord	\mathopen
\mathop	\mathclose
\mathbin	\mathpunct
\mathrel	

These commands tell TEX to treat the construct that follows as belonging to a particular class (see page 154 of *The TEXbook* for the definition of the classes). They are listed here in the order of the class numbers, from 0 to 6. Their primary effect is to adjust the spacing around the construct to be whatever it is for the specified class.

Example:
```
$\mathop{\rm minmax}\limits_{t \in A \cup B}\,t$
% By treating minmax as a math operator, we can get TeX to
% put something underneath it.
```
produces:

$$\operatorname*{minmax}_{t \in A \cup B} t$$

\mathinner

This command tells TEX to treat the construct that follows as an "inner formula", e.g., a fraction, for spacing purposes. It resembles the class commands given just above.

Special actions for math formulas

\everymath   [⟨*token list*⟩ parameter]
\everydisplay   [⟨*token list*⟩ parameter]

These parameters specify token lists that TEX inserts at the start of every text math or display math formula, respectively. You can take special actions at the start of each math formula by assigning those actions to

`\everymath` or `\everydisplay`. Don't forget that if you want both kinds of formulas to be affected, you need to set *both* parameters.

Example:
```
\everydisplay={\heartsuit\quad}
\everymath = {\clubsuit}
$3$ is greater than $2$ for large values of $3$.
$$4>3$$
```
produces:

♣3 is greater than ♣2 for large values of ♣3.

$$\heartsuit \quad 4 > 3$$

9 Commands for general operations

This section covers TEX's programming features and everything else that doesn't fit into the categories of commands in the previous chapters. For an explanation of the conventions used in this section, see "Descriptions of the commands" (p. 3).

Naming and modifying fonts

\font
\font ⟨*control sequence*⟩ = ⟨*fontname*⟩
\font ⟨*control sequence*⟩ = ⟨*fontname*⟩ **scaled** ⟨*number*⟩
\font ⟨*control sequence*⟩ = ⟨*fontname*⟩ **at** ⟨*dimen*⟩

Used alone, the `\font` control sequence designates the current font. `\font` isn't a true command when it's used alone, since it then can appear only as an argument to another command.

For the other three forms of `\font`, ⟨*fontname*⟩ names a set of files that define a font. These forms of `\font` are commands. Each of these forms has two effects:

(1) It defines ⟨*control sequence*⟩ as a name that selects the font ⟨*fontname*⟩, possibly magnified (see below).

(2) It causes TEX to load the font metrics file (`.tfm` file) for ⟨*fontname*⟩.

The name of a font file usually indicates its design size. For example, `cmr10` indicates Computer Modern roman with a design size of 10 points. The design size of a font is recorded in its metrics file.

If neither **scaled** ⟨*number*⟩ nor **at** ⟨*dimen*⟩ is present, the font is used at its design size—the size at which it usually looks best. Otherwise, a magnified version of the font is loaded:

- If `scaled` ⟨*number*⟩ is present, the font is magnified by a factor of ⟨*number*⟩/1000.
- If `at` ⟨*dimen*⟩ is present, the font is scaled to ⟨*dimen*⟩ by magnifying it by ⟨*dimen*⟩/*ds*, where *ds* is the design size of ⟨*fontname*⟩. ⟨*dimen*⟩ and *ds* are nearly always given in points.

Magnifications of less than 1 are possible; they reduce the size.

You usually need to provide a shape file (p. 65) for each magnification of a font that you load. However, some device drivers can utilize fonts that are resident in a printer. Such fonts don't need shape files.

See "font" (p. 64) and "magnification" (p. 78) for further information.

Example:
```
\font\tentt = cmtt10
\font\bigttfont = cmtt10 scaled \magstep2
\font\eleventtfont = cmtt10 at 11pt
First we use {\tentt regular CM typewriter}.
Then we use {\eleventtfont eleven-point CM typewriter}.
Finally we use {\bigttfont big CM typewriter}.
```
produces:

First we use `regular CM typewriter`. Then we use `eleven-point CM typewriter`. Finally we use `big CM typewriter`.

\fontdimen ⟨*number*⟩ ⟨*font*⟩   [⟨*dimen*⟩ parameter]

These parameters specify various dimensions associated with the font named by the control sequence ⟨*font*⟩ (as distinguished from the ⟨*fontname*⟩ that names the font files). Values of these parameters are specified in the metrics file for ⟨*font*⟩, but you can retrieve or change their values during a TeX run. The numbers and meanings of the parameters are:

Number	Meaning
1	slant per point
2	interword space
3	interword stretch
4	interword shrink
5	x-height (size of `1ex`)
6	quad width (size of `1em`)
7	extra space

TeX uses the slant per point for positioning accents. It uses the interword parameters for producing interword spaces (see `\spaceskip`, p. 107) and the extra space parameter for the additional space after a period (see `\xspaceskip`, p. 107). The values of these parameters for the plain TeX fonts are enumerated on page 433 of *The TeXbook*. Math symbol fonts have 15 additional parameters, which we won't discuss here.

Beware: assignments to these parameters are *not* undone at the end of a group. If you want to change these parameters locally, you'll need to save and restore their original settings explicitly.

Example:
```
Here's a line printed normally.\par
\fontdimen2\font = 3\fontdimen2\font
% Triple the interword spacing.
\noindent Here's a really spaced-out line.
```
produces:

Here's a line printed normally.
Here's   a   really   spaced-out   line.

\magnification = ⟨*number*⟩
\mag   [⟨*number*⟩ parameter]

An assignment to **\magnification** establishes the "scale factor" f that determines the magnification ratio of your document (see "magnification", p. 78). The assignment to **\magnification** must occur before the first page of your document has been shipped out.

The assignment sets f to ⟨*number*⟩ and also sets **\hsize** and **\vsize** respectively to **6.5true in** and **8.9true in**, the values appropriate for an $8\frac{1}{2}$-by-11-inch page. f must be between 0 and 32768. The magnification ratio of the document is $f/1000$. A scale factor of 1000 provides unit magnification, i.e., it leaves the size of your document unchanged. It's customary to use powers of 1.2 as scale factors, and most libraries of fonts are based on such factors. You can use the **\magstep** and **\magstephalf** commands to specify magnifications by these factors.

\magnification is not a parameter. You can't use it to *retrieve* the scale factor. If you write something like **\dimen0 = \magnification**, TeX will complain about it.

The **\mag** parameter contains the scale factor. Changing the value of **\mag** rescales the page dimensions, which is not usually what you want. Therefore it's usually better to change the magnification by assigning to **\magnification** rather than to **\mag**.

Example:
```
\magnification = \magstep2
% magnify fonts by 1.44 (=1.2x1.2)
```


\magstep ⟨*number*⟩

This command expands to the magnification ratio needed to magnify everything in your document (other than **true** dimensions) by 1.2^r, where r is the value of ⟨*number*⟩. ⟨*number*⟩ must be between 0 and 5.

Example:
```
\magnification = \magstep1 % Magnify by ratio of 1.2.
```

\magstephalf

This command expands to the magnification ratio needed to magnify everything in your document (other than **true** dimensions) by $\sqrt{1.2}$, i.e., halfway between 1 and 1.2.

Example:
```
\magnification = \magstephalf
```

Converting information to tokens

■ Numbers

\number ⟨*number*⟩

This command produces the representation of a number as a sequence of character tokens. The number can be either an explicit integer, a ⟨*number*⟩ parameter, or a ⟨*number*⟩ register.

Example:
```
\number 24 \quad \count13 = -10000 \number\count13
```
produces:
```
24   -10000
```

☞ \romannumeral ⟨*number*⟩

This command produces the roman numeral representation of a number as a sequence of character tokens. The number can be either an explicit integer, a ⟨*number*⟩ parameter, or a ⟨*number*⟩ register. If the number is zero or negative, \romannumeral produces no tokens.

Example:
```
\romannumeral 24 \quad (\romannumeral -16)\quad
\count13 = 6000 \romannumeral\count13
```
produces:
```
xxiv   ()   mmmmmm
```

■ Environmental information

\time   [⟨*number*⟩ parameter]

TEX sets this parameter to the number of minutes that have elapsed since midnight (of the current day). At noon, for instance, \time is 720. This command and the next three make use of the time and date as recorded in your computer. TEX retrieves them just once, at the beginning of your run, so `\time` at the end of the run always has the same value as `\time` at the beginning of the run (unless you've explicitly changed it).

\day   [⟨*number*⟩ parameter]

TEX sets this parameter to the current day of the month. It is a number between 1 and 31. `\day` is set at the beginning of your run (see the comments on `\time` above).

\month   [⟨*number*⟩ parameter]

TEX sets this parameter to the current month. It is a number between 1 and 12. `\month` is set at the beginning of your run (see the comments on `\time` above).

\year   [⟨*number*⟩ parameter]

TEX sets this parameter to the current year (A.D.). It is a number such as 1991. `\year` is set at the beginning of your run (see the comments on `\time` above).

\fmtname
\fmtversion

These commands produce the name and version number of the TEX format, e.g., plain TEX or LATEX, that you're using.

Example:

```
This book was produced with the \fmtname\ format,
version~\fmtversion.
```

produces:

This book was produced with the eplain format, version 1.0: 15 May 1990 (and plain 3.0).

\jobname

This command produces the base name of the file with which TEX was invoked. For example, if your main input file is `hatter.tex`, `\jobname` will expand to `hatter`. `\jobname` is most useful when you're creating an auxiliary file to be associated with a document.

Example:
```
\newwrite\indexfile  \openout\indexfile = \jobname.idx
% For input file 'hatter.tex', open index file 'hatter.idx'.
```

■ *Values of variables*

\meaning ⟨*token*⟩

This command produces the meaning of ⟨*token*⟩. It is useful for diagnostic output. You can use the `\the` command (p. 234) in a similar way to get information about the values of registers and other TeX entities.

Example:
```
[{\tt \meaning\eject}] [\meaning\tenrm] [\meaning Y]
```
produces:
```
[macro:->\par \break ] [select font cmr10] [the letter Y]
```

\string ⟨*control sequence*⟩

This command produces the characters that form the name of ⟨*control sequence*⟩, including the escape character. The escape character is represented by the current value of `\escapechar`. TeX gives the characters in the list a category code of 12 (other).

You can perform the reverse operation with the `\csname` command (p. 233), which turns a string into a control sequence.

Example:
```
the control sequence {\tt \string\bigbreak}
```
produces:
```
the control sequence \bigbreak
```

\escapechar   [⟨*number*⟩ parameter]

This parameter specifies the ASCII code of the character that TeX uses to represent the escape character when it's converting a control sequence name to a sequence of character tokens. This conversion occurs when you use the `\string` command and also when TeX is producing diagnostic messages. The default value of the escape character is 92, the ASCII character code for a backslash. If `\escapechar` is not in the range 0–255, TeX does not include an escape character in the result of the conversion.

Example:
```
  \escapechar = '!
  the control sequence {\tt \string\bigbreak}
```
produces:
  the control sequence `!bigbreak`

\fontname ⟨*font*⟩

This command produces the filename for ⟨*font*⟩. The filename is the ⟨*fontname*⟩ that was used to define ⟨*font*⟩.

Example:
```
  \font\myfive=cmr5 [\fontname\myfive]
```
produces:
  [cmr5]

Grouping

\begingroup
\endgroup

These two commands begin and end a group. A `\begingroup` does not match up with a right brace, nor an `\endgroup` with a left brace.

TeX treats `\begingroup` and `\endgroup` like any other control sequence when it's scanning its input. In particular, you can define a macro that contains a `\begingroup` but not an `\endgroup`, and conversely. This technique is often useful when you're defining paired macros, one of which establishes an environment and the other of which terminates that environment. You can't, however, use `\begingroup` and `\endgroup` as substitutes for braces other than the ones that surround a group.

Example:
```
  \def\a{One \begingroup \it two }
  \def\enda{\endgroup four}
  \a three \enda
```
produces:
  One *two three* four

\bgroup   \egroup

The left and right braces are commands that begin and end a group. The `\bgroup` and `\egroup` control sequences are equivalent to '`{`' and

'}', except that TEX treats \bgroup and \egroup like any other control sequence when it's scanning its input.

\bgroup and \egroup can be useful when you're defining paired macros, one of which starts a brace-delimited construct (not necessarily a group) and the other one of which ends that construct. You can't define such macros using ordinary braces—if you try, your macro definitions will contain unmatched braces and will therefore be unacceptable to TEX. Usually you should use these commands only when you can't use ordinary braces.

Example:
```
Braces define the {\it boundaries\/} of a group.
```
produces:
Braces define the *boundaries* of a group.

Example:
```
\def\a{One \vbox\bgroup}
% You couldn't use { instead of \bgroup  here because
% TeX would not recognize the end of the macro
\def\enda#1{{#1\egroup} two}
% This one is a little tricky, since the \egroup actually
% matches a left brace and the following right brace
% matches the \bgroup.  But it works!
\a \enda{\hrule width 1in}
```
produces:
One ＿＿＿＿＿＿＿ two

\global

This command makes the following definition or assignment global (see "global", p. 65) so that it becomes effective independent of group boundaries. You can apply a \global prefix to any kind of definition or assignment, including a macro definition or a register assignment.

Example:
```
{\global\let\la = \leftarrow}
$a \la b$
```
produces:
$a \leftarrow b$

\globaldefs   [⟨*number*⟩ parameter]

This parameter controls whether or not TEX takes definitions and other assignments to be global:

- If \globaldefs is zero (as it is by default), a definition is global if and only if it is preceded by \global either explicitly or implicitly. (The \gdef and \xdef commands (p. 231) have an implicit \global prefix).

- If \globaldefs is greater than zero, all assignments and definitions are implicitly prefixed by \global.
- If \globaldefs is less than zero, all \global prefixes are ignored.

\aftergroup ⟨*token*⟩

When TEX encounters this command during input, it saves ⟨*token*⟩. After the end of the current group, it inserts ⟨*token*⟩ back into the input and expands it. If a group contains several \aftergroups, the corresponding tokens are *all* inserted following the end of the group, in the order in which they originally appeared.

The example that follows shows how you can use \aftergroup to postpone processing a token that you generate within a conditional test.

Example:
```
\def\neg{negative} \def\pos{positive}
% These definitions are needed because \aftergroup applies
% to a single token, not to a sequence of tokens or even
% to a brace-delimited text.
\def\arith#1{Is $#1>0$? \begingroup
    \ifnum #1>-1 Yes\aftergroup\pos
    \else No\aftergroup\neg\fi
    , it's \endgroup. }
\arith 2
\arith {-1}
```
produces:

Is $2 > 0$? Yes, it's positive.   Is $-1 > 0$? No, it's negative.

\afterassignment ⟨*token*⟩

When TEX encounters this command it saves ⟨*token*⟩ in a special place. After it next performs an assignment, it inserts ⟨*token*⟩ into the input and expands it. If you call \afterassignment more than once before an assignment, only the last call has any effect. One use of \afterassignment is in writing macros for commands intended to be written in the form of assignments, as in the example below.

See page 279 of *The TEXbook* for a precise description of the behavior of \afterassignment.

Example:
```
\def\setme{\afterassignment\setmeA\count255}
\def\setmeA{$\number\count255\advance\count255 by 10
    +10=\number\count255$}
Some arithmetic: \setme = 27
% After expanding \setme, TeX sets \count255 to 27 and
% then calls \setmeA.
```
produces:
Some arithmetic: $27 + 10 = 37$

Macros

■ Defining macros

\def ⟨*control sequence*⟩ ⟨*parameter text*⟩ – ⟨*replacement text*⟩ ″
This command defines ⟨*control sequence*⟩ as a macro with the specified
⟨*parameter text*⟩ and ⟨*replacement text*⟩. See page 75 for a full explanation
of how to write a macro definition.

Example:
```
\def\add#1+#2=?{#1+#2&=
    \count255=#1 \advance\count255 by #2 \number\count255\cr}
$$\eqalign{
    \add 27+9=?
    \add -5+-8=?}$$
```
produces:
$$27 + 9 = 36$$
$$-5 + -8 = -13$$

\edef ⟨*control sequence*⟩ ⟨*parameter text*⟩ – ⟨*replacement text*⟩ ″
This command defines a macro in the same general way as \def. The
difference is that TeX expands the ⟨*replacement text*⟩ of an \edef immediately (but still without executing anything). Thus any definitions
within the ⟨*replacement text*⟩ are expanded, but assignments and commands that produce things such as boxes and glue are left as is. For
example, an \hbox command within the ⟨*replacement text*⟩ of an \edef
remains as a command and is not turned into a box as TeX is processing
the definition. It isn't always obvious what's expanded and what isn't, but
you'll find a complete list of expandable control sequences on pages 212–
215 of *The TeXbook*.

You can inhibit the expansion of a control sequence that would otherwise be expanded by using \noexpand (p. 234). You can postpone the expansion of a control sequence by using \expandafter (p. 233).

The \write, \message, \errmessage, \wlog, and \csname commands expand their token lists using the same rules that \edef uses to expand its replacement text.

Example:
```
\def\aa{xy} \count255 = 1
\edef\bb{w\ifnum \count255 > 0\aa\fi z}
% equivalent to \def\bb{wxyz}
\def\aa{} \count255 = 0 % leaves \bb unaffected
\bb
```
produces:
  wxyz

\gdef ⟨*control sequence*⟩ ⟨*parameter text*⟩ – ⟨*replacement text*⟩ ″
This command is equivalent to \global\def.

\xdef ⟨*control sequence*⟩ ⟨*parameter text*⟩ – ⟨*replacement text*⟩ ″
This command is equivalent to \global\edef.

\long

This command is used as a prefix to a macro definition. It tells TEX that the arguments to the macro are permitted to include \par tokens (p. 110), which normally indicate the end of a paragraph. If TEX tries to expand a macro defined without \long and any of the macro's arguments include a \par token, TEX will complain about a runaway argument. The purpose of this behavior is to provide you with some protection against unterminated macro arguments. \long gives you a way of bypassing the protection.

Example:
```
\long\def\aa#1{\par\hrule\smallskip#1\par\smallskip\hrule}
\aa{This is the first line.\par
This is the second line.}
% without \long, TeX would complain
```
produces:

This is the first line.
This is the second line.

\outer

This command is used as a prefix to a macro definition. It tells TEX that the macro is outer (p. 83) and cannot be used in certain contexts. If the macro is used in a forbidden context, TEX will complain.

Example:
```
\outer\def\chapterhead#1{%
    \eject\topglue 2in \centerline{\bf #1}\bigskip}
% Using \chapterhead in a forbidden context causes an
% error message.
```

\chardef ⟨*control sequence*⟩=⟨*charcode*⟩

This command defines ⟨*control sequence*⟩ to be ⟨*charcode*⟩. Although \chardef is most often used to define characters, you can also use it to give a name to a number in the range 0–255 even when you aren't using that number as a character code.

Example:
```
\chardef\percent = '\% 21\percent, {\it 19\percent}
% Get the percent character in roman and in italic
```
produces:
21%, *19%*

\mathchardef ⟨*control sequence*⟩=⟨*mathcode*⟩

This command defines ⟨*control sequence*⟩ as a math character with the given ⟨*mathcode*⟩. The control sequence will only be legal in math mode.

Example:
```
\mathchardef\alphachar = "010B % As in plain TeX.
$\alphachar$
```
produces:
α

■ *Other definitions*

\let ⟨*control sequence*⟩ = ⟨*token*⟩

This command causes ⟨*control sequence*⟩ to acquire the current meaning of ⟨*token*⟩. Even if you redefine ⟨*token*⟩ later, the meaning of ⟨*control sequence*⟩ will not change. Although ⟨*token*⟩ is most commonly a control sequence, it can also be a character token.

\futurelet ⟨*control sequence*⟩ ⟨*token*$_1$⟩ ⟨*token*$_2$⟩

This command tells TEX to make ⟨*token*$_2$⟩ the meaning of ⟨*control sequence*⟩ (as would be done with \let), and then to process ⟨*token*$_1$⟩ and

⟨*token₂*⟩ normally. \futurelet is useful at the end of macro definitions because it gives you a way of looking beyond the token that TEX is about to process before it processes it.

Example:
```
\def\predict#1{\toks0={#1}\futurelet\next\printer}
% \next will acquire the punctuation mark after the
% argument to \predict
\def\printer#1{A \punc\ lies ahead for \the\toks0. }
\def\punc{%
    \ifx\next;semicolon\else
        \ifx\next,comma\else
            ''\next''\fi\fi}
\predict{March}; \predict{April}, \predict{July}/
```
produces:

A semicolon lies ahead for March.   A comma lies ahead for April.   A "/" lies ahead for July.

\csname ⟨*token list*⟩ \endcsname

This command produces a control sequence from ⟨*token list*⟩. It provides a way of synthesizing control sequences, including ones that you can't normally write. ⟨*token list*⟩ can itself include control sequences; it is expanded in the same way as the replacement text of an \edef definition (p. 230). If the final expansion yields anything that isn't a character, TEX will complain. \csname goes from a list of tokens to a control sequence; you can go the other way with \string (p. 226).

Example:
```
\def\capTe{Te}
This book purports to be about \csname\capTe X\endcsname.
```
produces:

This book purports to be about TEX.

■ *Controlling expansion*

\expandafter ⟨*token₁*⟩ ⟨*token₂*⟩

This command tells TEX to expand ⟨*token₁*⟩ according to its rules for macro expansion *after* it has expanded ⟨*token₂*⟩ by one level. It's useful when ⟨*token₁*⟩ is something like '{' or \string that inhibits expansion of ⟨*token₂*⟩, but you want to expand ⟨*token₂*⟩ nevertheless.

Example:
```
\def\aa{xyz}
\tt % Use this font so '\' prints that way.
[\string\aa]  [\expandafter\string\aa]
[\expandafter\string\csname TeX\endcsname]
```
produces:
```
[\aa] [xyz] [\TeX]
```

\noexpand ⟨*token*⟩

This command tells TEX to suppress expansion of ⟨*token*⟩ if ⟨*token*⟩ is a control sequence that can be expanded. If ⟨*token*⟩ can't be expanded, e.g., it's a letter, TEX acts as though the \noexpand wasn't there and processes ⟨*token*⟩ normally. In other words the expansion of '\noexpand⟨*token*⟩' is simply ⟨*token*⟩ no matter what ⟨*token*⟩ happens to be.

Example:
```
\def\bunny{rabbit}
\edef\magic{Pull the \noexpand\bunny\ out of the hat! }
% Without \noexpand, \bunny would always be replaced
% by 'rabbit'
\let\oldbunny=\bunny \def\bunny{lagomorph} \magic
\let\bunny=\oldbunny \magic
```
produces:
Pull the lagomorph out of the hat! Pull the rabbit out of the hat!

\the ⟨*token*⟩

This command generally expands to a list of character tokens that represents ⟨*token*⟩. ⟨*token*⟩ can be any of the following:

- a TEX parameter, e.g., \parindent or \deadcycles
- a register, e.g., \count0
- a code associated with an input character, e.g., \catcode'(
- a font parameter, e.g., \fontdimen3\sevenbf
- the \hyphenchar or \skewchar of a font, e.g., \skewchar\teni
- \lastpenalty, \lastskip, or \lastkern (values derived from the last item on the current horizontal or vertical list)
- a control sequence defined by \chardef or \mathchardef

In addition, \the can expand to noncharacter tokens in the following two cases:

- \the ⟨*font*⟩, which expands to the most recently defined control sequence that selects the same font as the control sequence ⟨*font*⟩
- \the ⟨*token variable*⟩, which expands to a copy of the value of the variable, e.g., \the\everypar

See pages 214–215 of *The T_EXbook* for a more detailed description of what `\the` does in various cases.

Example:
```
The vertical size is currently \the\vsize.
The category code of '(' is \the\catcode '(.
```
produces:

The vertical size is currently 548.4975pt. The category code of '(' is 12.

See also: "Converting information to tokens" (p. 224), `\showthe` (p. 253).

■ Conditional tests

`\if` ⟨*token*₁⟩ ⟨*token*₂⟩

This command tests if ⟨*token*₁⟩ and ⟨*token*₂⟩ have the same character code, independent of their category codes. Before performing the test, T_EX expands tokens following the `\if` until it obtains two tokens that can't be expanded further. These two tokens become ⟨*token*₁⟩ and ⟨*token*₂⟩. The expansion includes replacing a control sequence `\let` equal to a character token by that character token. A control sequence that can't be further expanded is considered to have character code 256.

Example:
```
\def\first{abc}
\if\first true\else false\fi;
% ''c'' is left over from the expansion of \first.
% It lands in the unexecuted ''true'' part.
\if a\first\ true\else false\fi;
% Here ''bc'' is left over from the expansion of \first
\if \hbox\relax true\else false\fi
% Unexpandable control sequences test equal with ''if''
```
produces:

false; bc true; true

`\ifcat` ⟨*token*₁⟩ ⟨*token*₂⟩

This command tests if ⟨*token*₁⟩ and ⟨*token*₂⟩ have the same category code. Before performing the test, T_EX expands tokens following the `\ifcat` until it obtains two tokens that can't be expanded further. These two tokens become ⟨*token*₁⟩ and ⟨*token*₂⟩. The expansion includes replacing a control sequence `\let` equal to a character token by that character token. A control sequence that can't be further expanded is considered to have category code 16.

Example:

```
\ifcat axtrue\else false\fi;
\ifcat ]}true\else false\fi;
\ifcat \hbox\day true\else false\fi;
\def\first{12345}
\ifcat (\first true\else false\fi
% ''2345'' lands in the true branch of the test
```

produces:

true; false; true; 2345true

\ifx ⟨*token₁*⟩ ⟨*token₂*⟩

This command tests if ⟨*token₁*⟩ and ⟨*token₂*⟩ agree. Unlike \if and \ifcat, \ifx does *not* expand the tokens following \ifx, so ⟨*token₁*⟩ and ⟨*token₂*⟩ are the two tokens immediately after \ifx. There are three cases:

(1) If one token is a macro and the other one isn't, the tokens don't agree.

(2) If neither token is a macro, the tokens agree if:

    (a) both tokens are characters (or control sequences denoting characters) and their character codes and category codes agree, or

    (b) both tokens refer to the same TeX command, font, etc.

(3) If both tokens are macros, the tokens agree if:

    (a) their "first level" expansions, i.e., their replacement texts, are identical, and

    (b) they have the same status with respect to \long (p. 231) and \outer (p. 232).

      Note in particular that *any two undefined control sequences agree.*

This test is generally more useful than \if.

Example:

```
\ifx\alice\rabbit true\else false\fi;
% true since neither \rabbit nor \alice is defined
\def\a{a}%
\ifx a\a true\else false\fi;
% false since one token is a macro and the other isn't
\def\first{\a}\def\second{\aa}\def\aa{a}%
\ifx \first\second true\else false\fi;
% false since top level expansions aren't the same
\def\third#1:{(#1)}\def\fourth#1?{(#1)}%
\ifx\third\fourth true\else false\fi
% false since parameter texts differ
```

produces:
    true; false; false; false

\ifnum $\langle number_1 \rangle$ $\langle relation \rangle$ $\langle number_2 \rangle$

This command tests if $\langle number_1 \rangle$ and $\langle number_2 \rangle$ satisfy $\langle relation \rangle$, which must be either '<', '=', or '>'. The numbers can be constants such as 127, count registers such as \pageno or \count22, or numerical parameters such as \hbadness. Before performing the test, TeX expands tokens following the \ifnum until it obtains a sequence of tokens having the form $\langle number_1 \rangle$ $\langle relation \rangle$ $\langle number_2 \rangle$, followed by a token that can't be part of $\langle number_2 \rangle$.

Example:
    \count255 = 19 \ifnum \count255 > 12 true\else false\fi
produces:
    true

\ifodd $\langle number \rangle$

This command tests if $\langle number \rangle$ is odd. Before performing the test, TeX expands tokens following the \ifodd until it obtains a sequence of tokens having the form $\langle number \rangle$, followed by a token that can't be part of $\langle number \rangle$.

Example:
    \count255 = 19
    \ifodd 5 true\else false\fi
produces:
    true

\ifdim $\langle dimen_1 \rangle$ $\langle relation \rangle$ $\langle dimen_2 \rangle$

This command tests if $\langle dimen_1 \rangle$ and $\langle dimen_2 \rangle$ satisfy $\langle relation \rangle$, which must be either '<', '=', or '>'. The dimensions can be constants such as 1in, dimension registers such as \dimen6, or dimension parameters such as \parindent. Before performing the test, TeX expands tokens following the \ifdim until it obtains a sequence of tokens having the form $\langle dimen_1 \rangle$ $\langle relation \rangle$ $\langle dimen_2 \rangle$, followed by a token that can't be part of $\langle dimen_2 \rangle$.

Example:
    \dimen0 = 1000pt \ifdim \dimen0 > 3in true\else false\fi
produces:
    true

\ifhmode
\ifvmode
\ifmmode
\ifinner

These commands test what mode TEX is in:

- \ifhmode is true if TEX is in ordinary or restricted horizontal mode.
- \ifvmode is true if TEX is in ordinary or internal vertical mode.
- \ifmmode is true if TEX is in text math or display math mode.
- \ifinner is true if TEX is in an "internal" mode: restricted horizontal, internal vertical, or text math.

Example:
```
\def\modes{{\bf
  \ifhmode
      \ifinner IH\else H\fi
  \else\ifvmode
      \ifinner \hbox{IV}\else \hbox{V}\fi
  \else\ifmmode \hbox{M}\else
      error\fi\fi\fi}}
Formula $\modes$; then \modes,
  \hbox{next \modes\ and \vbox{\modes}}.
\par\modes
```
produces:
Formula **M**; then **H**, next **IH** and **IV**.
V

\ifhbox ⟨*register*⟩
\ifvbox ⟨*register*⟩
\ifvoid ⟨*register*⟩

These commands test the contents of the box register numbered ⟨*register*⟩. Let ⟨*register*⟩ be n. Then:

- \ifhbox is true if \box n is an hbox.
- \ifvbox is true if \box n is an vbox.
- \ifvoid is true if \box n is void, i.e, doesn't have a box in it.

Example:
```
\setbox0 = \vbox{} % empty but not void
\setbox1 = \hbox{a}
\setbox2 = \box1 % makes box1 void
\ifvbox0 true\else false\fi;
\ifhbox2 true\else false\fi;
\ifvoid1 true\else false\fi
```

produces:

  true; true; true

\ifeof ⟨*number*⟩

This command tests an input stream for end of file. It is true if input stream ⟨*number*⟩ has not been opened, or has been opened and the associated file has been entirely read in (or doesn't exist).

\ifcase ⟨*number*⟩⟨*case*$_0$ *text*⟩ \or ⟨*case*$_1$ *text*⟩ \or ... \or ⟨*case*$_n$ *text*⟩
\else ⟨*otherwise text*⟩ \fi

This command introduces a test with numbered multiple cases. If ⟨*number*⟩ has the value k, TEX will expand ⟨*case*$_k$ *text*⟩ if it exists, and ⟨*otherwise text*⟩ if it doesn't. You can omit the \else—in this case, TEX won't expand anything if none of the cases are satisfied.

Example:

```
\def\whichday#1{\ifcase #1<day 0>\or Sunday\or Monday%
    \or Tuesday\or Wednesday\or Thursday\or Friday%
    \or Saturday\else Nonday\fi
    \ is day \##1. }
\whichday2 \whichday3 \whichday9
```

produces:

  Monday is day #2. Tuesday is day #3. Nonday is day #9.

\iftrue
\iffalse

These commands are equivalent to tests that are always true or always false. The main use of these commands is in defining macros that keep track of the result of a test.

Example:

```
\def\isbigger{\let\bigger=\iftrue}
\def\isnotbigger{\let\bigger=\iffalse}
% These \let's MUST be buried in macros!  If they aren't,
% TeX erroneously tries to match them with \fi.
\def\test#1#2{\ifnum #1>#2 \isbigger\else\isnotbigger\fi}
\test{3}{6}
\bigger$3>6$\else$3\le6$\fi
```

produces:

  $3 \le 6$

\else

This command introduces the "false" alternative of a conditional test.

\fi

This command ends the text of a conditional test.

\newif \if⟨*test name*⟩

This command names a trio of control sequences with names \alphatrue, \alphafalse, and \ifalpha, where alpha is ⟨*test name*⟩. You can use them to define your own tests by creating a logical variable that records true/false information:

- \alphatrue sets the logical variable alpha true.
- \alphafalse sets the logical variable alpha false
- \ifalpha is a conditional test that is true if the logical variable alpha is true and false otherwise.

The logical variable alpha doesn't really exist, but TEX behaves as though it did. After \newif\ifalpha, the logical variable is initially false.

\newif is an outer command, so you can't use it inside a macro definition.

Example:
```
\newif\iflong  \longtrue
\iflong Rabbits have long ears.
\else Rabbits don't have long ears.\fi
```
produces:

Rabbits have long ears.

■ *Repeated actions*

\loop α **\if**Ω β **\repeat**
\repeat

These commands provide a looping construct for TEX. Here α and β are arbitrary sequences of commands and **\if**Ω is any of the conditional tests described in "Conditional tests" (p. 235). The \repeat replaces the \fi corresponding to the test, so you must not write an explicit \fi to terminate the test. Nor, unfortunately, can you associate an \else with the test. If you want to use the test in the opposite sense, you need to rearrange the test or define an auxiliary test with \newif (see above) and use that test in the sense you want (see the second example below).

TEX expands \loop as follows:

(1) α is expanded.

(2) \if$\Omega$ is performed. If the result is false, the loop is terminated.

(3) β is expanded.

(4) The cycle is repeated.

Example:
```
\count255 = 6
\loop
    \number\count255\
    \ifnum\count255 > 0
        \advance\count255 by -1
\repeat
```
produces:
 6 5 4 3 2 1 0

Example:
```
\newif\ifnotdone % \newif uses \count255 in its definition
\count255=6
\loop
    \number\count255\
    \ifnum\count255 < 1 \notdonefalse\else\notdonetrue\fi
    \ifnotdone
        \advance\count255 by -1
\repeat
```
produces:
 6 5 4 3 2 1 0

■ *Doing nothing*

\relax

This command tells TEX to do nothing. It's useful in a context where you need to provide a command but there's nothing that you want TEX to do.

Example:
```
\def\medspace{\hskip 12pt\relax}
% The \relax guards against the possibility that
% The next tokens are 'plus' or 'minus'.
```

\empty

This command expands to no tokens at all. It differs from \relax in that it disappears after macro expansion.

Registers

■ *Using registers*

\count ⟨*register*⟩ = ⟨*number*⟩	**\count** ⟨*register*⟩
\dimen ⟨*register*⟩ = ⟨*dimen*⟩	**\dimen** ⟨*register*⟩
\skip ⟨*register*⟩ = ⟨*glue*⟩	**\skip** ⟨*register*⟩
\muskip ⟨*register*⟩ = ⟨*muglue*⟩	**\muskip** ⟨*register*⟩
\toks ⟨*register*⟩ = ⟨*token variable*⟩	**\toks** ⟨*register*⟩
\toks ⟨*register*⟩ = – ⟨*token list*⟩ ˝	

The first six commands listed here assign something to a register. The ='s in the assignments are optional. The remaining five control sequences are not true commands because they can only appear as part of an argument. They yield the contents of the specified register. Although you can't use these control sequences by themselves as commands in text, you can use **\the** to convert them to text so that you can typeset their values.

You can name and reserve registers with the **\newcount** command and its relatives (p. 244). Using these commands is a safe way to obtain registers that are known not to have any conflicting usage.

A **\count** register contains an integer, which can be either positive or negative. Integers can be as large as you're ever likely to need them to be.[1] TEX uses count registers 0–9 to keep track of the page number (see page 119 of *The TEXbook*). **\count255** is the only count register available for use without a reservation.

Example:
```
\count255 = 17 \number\count255
```
produces:
```
17
```

A **\dimen** register contains a dimension. Registers **\dimen0** through **\dimen9** and **\dimen255** are available for scratch use.

Example:
```
\dimen0 = 2.5in
\hbox to \dimen0{$\Leftarrow$\hfil$\Rightarrow$}
```
produces:

⇐   ⇒

⌐ ' ' ' ┬ ' ' ' ┬ ' ' ' ┬ ' ' ' ┬ ' ' ' ┐ 3 in

---

[1] Here's the only exercise in this book: find out what's the largest integer that TEX will accept.

A `\skip` register contains the dimensions of glue. Unlike a `\dimen` register, it records an amount of shrink and stretch as well as a natural size. Registers `\skip0` through `\skip9` and `\skip255` are available for use without a reservation.

Example:
```
\skip2 = 2in
$\Rightarrow$\hskip \skip2 $\Leftarrow$
```
produces:

⇒   ⇐

2 in

A `\muskip` register is like a `\skip` register, but the glue in it is always measured in `mu` (see "mathematical unit", p. 81). The size of a `mu` depends on the current font. For example, it's usually a little smaller in a subscript than in ordinary text. Registers `\muskip0` through `\muskip9` and `\muskip255` are available for use without a reservation.

Example:
```
\muskip0 = 24mu % An em and a half, no stretch or shrink.
$\mathop{a \mskip\muskip0 b}\limits^{a \mskip\muskip0 b}$
% Note the difference in spacing.
```
produces:

$a \quad b$
$a \quad b$

You can assign either a token variable (a register or a parameter) or a token list to a `\toks` register. When you assign a token list to a token register, the tokens in the token list are *not* expanded.

Once the tokens in a token list have been inserted into text using `\the`, they are expanded just like tokens that were read in directly. They have the category codes that they received when TEX first saw them in the input.

Example:
```
\toks0 = {the \oystereaters\ were at the seashore}
% This assignment doesn't expand \oystereaters.
\def\oystereaters{Walrus and Carpenter}
\toks1 = \toks0
% the same tokens are now in \toks0 and \toks1
Alice inquired as to whether \the\toks1.
```
produces:

Alice inquired as to whether the Walrus and Carpenter were at the seashore.

\maxdimen

This control sequence yields a ⟨*dimen*⟩ that is the largest dimension acceptable to TEX (nearly 18 feet). It is not a true command because it can only appear as part of an argument to another command.

Example:
```
\maxdepth = \maxdimen % Remove restrictions on \maxdepth.
```

See also: \advance (p. 245), \multiply, \divide (p. 246), \setbox, \box (p. 164).

■ *Naming and reserving registers, etc.*

\newcount	**\newread**
\newdimen	**\newwrite**
\newskip	**\newfam**
\newmuskip	**\newinsert**
\newtoks	**\newlanguage**
\newbox	

These commands reserve and name an entity of the indicated type:

- \newcount, \newdimen, \newskip, \newmuskip, \newtoks, and \newbox each reserve a register of the indicated type.
- \newread and \newwrite reserve an input stream and an output stream respectively.
- \newfam reserves a family of math fonts.
- \newinsert reserves an insertion type. (Reserving an insertion type involves reserving several different registers.)
- \newlanguage reserves a set of hyphenation patterns.

You should use these commands whenever you need one of these entities, other than in a very local region, in order to avoid numbering conflicts.

There's an important difference among these commands:

- The control sequences defined by \newcount, \newdimen, \newskip, \newmuskip, and \newtoks each designate an entity of the appropriate type. For instance, after the command:

  ```
  \newdimen\listdimen
  ```

  the control sequence \listdimen can be used as a dimension.
- The control sequences defined by \newbox, \newread, \newwrite, \newfam, \newinsert, and \newlanguage each evaluate to the *number* of an entity of the appropriate type. For instance, after the command:

  ```
  \newbox\figbox
  ```

the control sequence \figbox must be used in conjunction with a
\box-like command, e.g.:

```
\setbox\figbox = \vbox{...}
```

\countdef ⟨*control sequence*⟩ = ⟨*register*⟩
\dimendef ⟨*control sequence*⟩ = ⟨*register*⟩
\skipdef ⟨*control sequence*⟩ = ⟨*register*⟩
\muskipdef ⟨*control sequence*⟩ = ⟨*register*⟩
\toksdef ⟨*control sequence*⟩ = ⟨*register*⟩

These commands define ⟨*control sequence*⟩ to refer to the register of the
indicated category whose number is ⟨*register*⟩. Normally you should use
the commands in the previous group (\newcount, etc.) in preference to
these commands in order to avoid numbering conflicts. The commands in
the previous group are defined in terms of the commands in this group.

Example:
```
\countdef\hatters = 19 % \hatters now refers to \count19
\toksdef\hares = 200 % \hares now refers to \toks200
```

See also: \newif (p. 240), \newhelp (p. 262).

■ *Doing arithmetic in registers*

\advance ⟨*count register*⟩ **by** ⟨*number*⟩
\advance ⟨*dimen register*⟩ **by** ⟨*dimen*⟩
\advance ⟨*skip register*⟩ **by** ⟨*glue*⟩
\advance ⟨*muskip register*⟩ **by** ⟨*muglue*⟩

This command adds a compatible quantity to a register. For ⟨*glue*⟩ or
⟨*muglue*⟩ all three components (natural value, stretch, and shrink) are
added. Any of the quantities can be negative. For purposes of these
calculations (and other assignments as well), ⟨*glue*⟩ can be converted
to a ⟨*dimen*⟩ by dropping the stretch and shrink, and a ⟨*dimen*⟩ can
be converted to a ⟨*number*⟩ by taking its value in scaled points (see
"dimension", p. 60). You can omit the word **by** in these commands—TEX
will understand them anyway.

Example:
```
\count0 = 18 \advance\count0 by -1 \number\count0\par
\skip0 = .5in \advance\skip0 by 0in plus 1in % add stretch
\hbox to 2in{a\hskip\skip0 b}
```
produces:

17

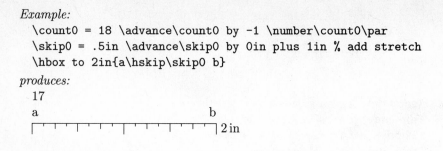

\multiply ⟨*register*⟩ **by** ⟨*number*⟩
\divide ⟨*register*⟩ **by** ⟨*number*⟩

These commands multiply and divide the value in ⟨*register*⟩ by ⟨*number*⟩ (which can be negative). The register can be a \count, \dimen, \skip, or \muskip register. For a \skip or \muskip register (p. 242), all three components of the glue in the register are modified. You can omit the word by in these commands—TEX will understand them anyway.

You can also obtain a multiple of a ⟨*dimen*⟩ by preceding it by a ⟨*number*⟩ or decimal constant, e.g., -2.5\dimen2. You can also use this notation for ⟨*glue*⟩, but watch out—the result is a ⟨*dimen*⟩, not ⟨*glue*⟩. Thus 2\baselineskip yields a ⟨*dimen*⟩ that is twice the natural size of \baselineskip, with no stretch or shrink.

Example:
```
\count0 = 9\multiply \count0 by 8 \number\count0 ;
\divide \count0 by 12 \number\count0 \par
\skip0 = 20pt plus 2pt minus 3pt \multiply \skip0 by 3
Multiplied value of skip0 is \the\skip0.\par
\dimen0 = .5in \multiply\dimen0 by 6
\hbox to \dimen0{a\hfil b}
```
produces:

72; 6
Multiplied value of skip0 is 60.0pt plus 6.0pt minus 9.0pt.

Ending the job

☞ **\bye**

This command tells TEX to fill out and produce the last page, print any held-over insertions, and end the job. It is the usual way to end your input file.

\end

This command tells TEX to produce the last page and end the job. It does not fill out the page, however, so it's usually better to use **\bye** rather than **\end**.

Input and output

■ *Operations on input files*

☞ **\input** ⟨*filename*⟩

This command tells TEX to read its input from file ⟨*filename*⟩. When that file is exhausted, TEX returns to reading from its previous input source. You can nest input files to any level you like (within reason).

When you're typesetting a large document, it's usually a good idea to structure your main file as a sequence of **\input** commands that refer to the subsidiary parts of the document. That way you can process the individual parts easily as you're working on drafts. It's also a good practice to put all of your macro definitions into a separate file and summon that file with an **\input** command as the first action in your main file.

TEX uses different rules for scanning file names than it does for scanning tokens in general (see p. 63). If your implementation expects file names to have extensions (usually indicated by a preceding dot), then TEX provides a default extension of **.tex**.

Example:
```
\input macros.tex
\input chap1 % equivalent to chap1.tex
```

\endinput

This command tells TEX to stop reading input from the current file when it next reaches the end of a line.

\inputlineno

This command yields a number (not a string) giving the line number of the current line, defined to be the number that would appear in an error message if an error occurred at this point.

\openin ⟨*number*⟩ = ⟨*filename*⟩

This command tells TEX to open the file named ⟨*filename*⟩ and make it available for reading via the input stream designated by ⟨*number*⟩.

⟨*number*⟩ must be between 0 and 15. Once you've opened a file and connected it to an input stream, you can read from the file using the \read command with the input stream's number.

You can associate more than one input stream with the same file. You can then read from several different positions within the file, one for each input stream.

You should allocate stream numbers for \openin using \newread (p. 244).

Example:
```
\newread\auxfile  \openin\auxfile = addenda.aux
% \auxfile now denotes the number of this opening
% of addenda.aux.
```

\closein ⟨*number*⟩

This command tells TEX to close the input stream numbered ⟨*number*⟩, i.e., end the association between the input stream and its file. The input stream with this number then becomes available for use with a different file. You should close an input stream once you're finished using its file.

Example:
```
\closein\auxfile
```

\read ⟨*number*⟩ **to** ⟨*control sequence*⟩

This command tells TEX to read a line from the file associated with the input stream designated by ⟨*number*⟩ and assign the tokens on that line to ⟨*control sequence*⟩. The control sequence then becomes a parameterless macro. No macro expansion takes place during the reading operation. If the line contains any unmatched left braces, TEX will read additional lines until the braces are all matched. If TEX reaches the end of the file without matching all the braces, it will complain.

If ⟨*number*⟩ is greater than 15 or hasn't been associated with a file using \openin, TEX prompts you with '⟨*control sequence*⟩ =' on your terminal and waits for you to type a line of input. It then assigns the input line to ⟨*control sequence*⟩. If ⟨*number*⟩ is less than zero, it reads a line of input from your terminal but omits the prompt.

Example:
```
\read\auxfile to \holder
% Expanding \holder will produce the line just read.
```

■ *Operations on output files*

\openout ⟨*number*⟩ = ⟨*filename*⟩

This command tells TEX to open the file named ⟨*filename*⟩ and make it available for writing via the output stream designated by ⟨*number*⟩. ⟨*number*⟩ must be between 0 and 15. Once you've opened a file and connected it to an output stream, you can write to the file using the \write command with the output stream's number.

An \openout generates a whatsit that becomes part of a box. The \openout does not take effect until TEX ships out that box to the .dvi file, unless you've preceded the \openout with \immediate.

TEX won't complain if you associate more than one output stream with the same file, but you'll get garbage in the file if you try it!

You should allocate stream numbers for \openout using \newwrite (p. 244).

Example:
```
\newwrite\auxfile  \openout\auxfile = addenda.aux
% \auxfile now denotes the number of this opening
% of addenda.aux.
```

\closeout ⟨*number*⟩

This command tells TEX to close the output stream numbered ⟨*number*⟩. i.e., end the association between the output stream and its file. The output stream with this number then becomes available for use with a different file. You should close an output stream once you're finished using its file.

A \closeout generates a whatsit that becomes part of a box. The \closeout does not take effect until TEX ships out that box to the .dvi file, unless you've preceded the \closeout with \immediate.

Example:
```
\closeout\auxfile
```

\write ⟨*number*⟩ − ⟨*token list*⟩ ″

This command tells TEX to write ⟨*token list*⟩ to the file associated with the output stream designated by ⟨*number*⟩. It generates a whatsit that becomes part of a box. The actual writing does not take place until TEX ships out that box to the .dvi file, unless you've preceded the \write with \immediate.

For a \write that is not immediate, TEX does not expand macros in ⟨*token list*⟩ until the token list is actually written to the file. The macro expansions follow the same rules as \edef (p. 230). In particular, any control sequence that is not the name of a macro is written as \escapechar followed by the control sequence name and a space. Any '#' tokens in ⟨*token list*⟩ are doubled, i.e., written as '##'.

If ⟨*number*⟩ is not in the range from 0 to 15, TEX writes ⟨*token list*⟩ to the log file. If ⟨*number*⟩ is greater than 15 or isn't associated with an output stream, TEX also writes ⟨*token list*⟩ to the terminal.

Example:
```
  \def\aa{a a}
  \write\auxfile{\hbox{$x#y$} \aa}
  % Writes the string '\hbox {$x##y$} a a' to \auxfile.
```

\immediate

This command should precede an \openout, \closeout, or \write. It tells TEX to perform the specified file operation without delay.

Example:
```
  \immediate\write 16{I'm stuck!}
  % has the same effect as \message
```

\special – ⟨*token list*⟩ ″

This command tells TEX to write ⟨*token list*⟩ directly to the .dvi file when it next ships out a page. A typical use of \special would be to tell the device driver to incorporate the contents of a named graphics file into the output page. The \special command produces a whatsit that associates ⟨*token list*⟩ with a particular position on the page, namely, the position that a zero-size box would have had if such a box had appeared instead of the \special command. Any use you might make of \special depends strictly on the device drivers that you have available.

Example:
```
  \special{graphic expic}
  % Display the graphics file 'expic' here.
```

\newlinechar   [⟨*number*⟩ parameter]

This parameter contains a character that indicates a new line on output. When TEX encounters this character while reading the argument of a \write, \message, or \errmessage command, it starts a new line. If \newlinechar is not in the range 0–255, there is no character that indicates a new line on output. Plain TEX sets \newlinechar to −1.

Example:
```
  \newlinechar = '\^^J
  \message{This message appears^^Jon two lines.}
```

produces in the log:
```
This message appears
on two lines.
```

See also: \newread, \newwrite (p. 244).

■ *Interpreting input characters*

\catcode ⟨*charcode*⟩   [⟨*number*⟩ table entry]

This table entry contains the category code of the character whose ASCII code is ⟨*charcode*⟩. The category codes are listed on page 53. By changing the category code of a character you can get TeX to treat that character differently.

Example:
```
\catcode '\[ = 1 \catcode '\] = 2
% Make [ and ] act like left and right braces.
```

\active

This command contains the category code for an active character, namely, the number 13.

Example:
```
\catcode '\@ = \active % Make @ an active character.
```

\mathcode ⟨*charcode*⟩   [⟨*number*⟩ table entry]

This table entry contains the mathcode of the character whose ASCII code is ⟨*charcode*⟩ (see "mathcode", p. 80). The mathcode specifies that character's interpretation in math mode.

Example:
```
\mathcode\> = "313E % as in plain TeX
% The > character has class 3 (relation), family 1 (math
% italic), and character code "3E
```

\delcode ⟨*charcode*⟩   [⟨*number*⟩ table entry]

This table entry specifies the delimiter code for the input character whose ASCII code is ⟨*charcode*⟩. The delimiter code tells TeX how to find the best output character to use for typesetting the indicated input character as a delimiter.

⟨*number*⟩ is normally written in hexadecimal notation. Suppose that ⟨*number*⟩ is the hexadecimal number $s_1s_2s_3\,l_1l_2l_3$. Then when the character is used as a delimiter, TeX takes the character to have small variant $s_1s_2s_3$ and large variant $l_1l_2l_3$. Here $s_1s_2s_3$ indicates the math character found in position s_2s_3 of family s_1, and similarly for $l_1l_2l_3$. This is the same convention as the one used for \mathcode (p. 251), except that \mathcode also specifies a class.

Example:
```
\delcode '( = "028300  % As in plain TeX.
```

\endlinechar   [⟨*number*⟩ parameter]

This parameter contains the character code for the character that TEX appends to the end of each input line. A value not in the range 0–255 indicates that no character should be appended. Plain TEX leaves \endlinechar at '\^^M (the ASCII code for ⟨return⟩).

\ignorespaces

This command tells TEX to read and expand tokens until it finds one that is not a space token, ignoring any space tokens that it finds on the way. \ignorespaces is often useful at the end of a macro as a way of making the macro insensitive to any spaces or ends of line that might follow calls on it. (An empty line after \ignorespaces still produces a \par token, however.)

Example:
```
\def\aa#1{yes #1\ignorespaces}
\aa{may}
be
```
produces:
```
yes maybe
```

Controlling interaction with TEX

\errorstopmode

This command tells TEX to stop for interaction whenever it finds an error. This is the normal mode of operation.

\scrollmode

This command tells TEX not to stop for most errors, but to continue displaying the error messages on your terminal. Typing 'S' or 's' in response to an error message puts you into scroll mode.

\nonstopmode

This command tells TEX not to stop for errors, even those pertaining to files that it can't find, but to continue displaying the error messages on your terminal. Typing 'R' or 'r' in response to an error message puts you into nonstop mode.

\batchmode

This command tells TEX not to stop for errors and to suppress all further output to your terminal. Typing 'Q' or 'q' in response to an error message puts you into batch mode.

\pausing   [⟨*number*⟩ parameter]

If this parameter is greater than zero, TEX will pause at each line of input to give you an opportunity to replace it with a different line. If you type in a replacement, TEX will use that line instead of the original one; if you respond with ⟨return⟩, TEX will use the original line.

Setting \pausing to 1 can be useful as a way of patching a document as TEX is processing it. For example, you can use this facility to insert \show commands (see below).

Diagnostic aids

■ *Displaying internal data*

\show ⟨*token*⟩
\showthe ⟨*argument*⟩
\showbox ⟨*number*⟩
\showlists

These commands record information in the log of your TEX run:

- \show records the meaning of ⟨*token*⟩.
- \showthe records whatever tokens would be produced by \the ⟨*argument*⟩ (see p. 234).
- \showbox records the contents of the box register numbered ⟨*number*⟩. The number of leading dots in the log indicates the number of levels of nesting of inner boxes.
- \showlists records the contents of each list that TEX is currently constructing. (These lists are nested one within another.) See pages 88–89 of *The TEXbook* for further information about interpreting the output of \showlists.

For \show and \showthe, TEX also displays the information at your terminal. For \showbox and \showlists, TEX displays the information at your terminal only if \tracingonline (p. 256) is greater than zero; if \tracingonline is zero or less (the default case), the information is not displayed.

Whenever TEX encounters a \show-type command it stops for interaction. The request for interaction does *not* indicate an error, but it does give you an opportunity to ask TEX to show you something else. If you don't want to see anything else, just press ⟨return⟩.

You can control the amount of output produced by \showbox by setting \showboxbreadth and \showboxdepth (p. 261). These parameters respectively have default values of 5 and 3, which is why just five items appear for each box described in the log output below. (The '..etc.' indicates additional items within the boxes that aren't displayed.)

Example:
```
\show a
\show \hbox
\show \medskip
\show &
```
produces in the log:
```
> the letter a.
> \hbox=\hbox.
> \medskip=macro:
->\vskip \medskipamount .
> alignment tab character &.
```

Example:
```
\showthe\medskipamount
\toks27={\hbox{Joe's\quad\ Diner}}
\showthe\toks27
```
produces in the log:
```
> 6.0pt plus 2.0pt minus 2.0pt.
> \hbox {Joe's\quad \ Diner}.
```

Example:
```
\setbox 3=\vbox{\hbox{A red dog.}\hrule A black cat.}
\showbox 3
```

produces in the log:

```
  > \box3=
 \vbox(16.23332+0.0)x53.05565
 .\hbox(6.94444+1.94444)x46.41675
 ..\tenrm A
 ..\glue 3.33333 plus 1.66498 minus 1.11221
 ..\tenrm r
 ..\tenrm e
 ..\tenrm d
 ..etc.
 .\rule(0.4+0.0)x*
 .\hbox(6.94444+0.0)x53.05565
 ..\tenrm A
 ..\glue 3.33333 plus 1.66498 minus 1.11221
 ..\tenrm b
 ..\tenrm l
 ..\tenrm a
 ..etc.
```

Example:
```
\vbox{A \hbox
    {formula
        $x \over y\showlists$}}
```
produces in the log:
```
### math mode entered at line 3
\mathord
.\fam1 y
this will be denominator of:
\fraction, thickness = default
\\mathord
\.\fam1 x
### restricted horizontal mode entered at line 2
\tenrm f
\tenrm o
\tenrm r
\tenrm m
\kern-0.27779
\tenrm u
\tenrm l
\tenrm a
\glue 3.33333 plus 1.66666 minus 1.11111
spacefactor 1000
### horizontal mode entered at line 1
\hbox(0.0+0.0)x20.0
\tenrm A
\glue 3.33333 plus 1.66498 minus 1.11221
spacefactor 999
### internal vertical mode entered at line 1
prevdepth ignored
### vertical mode entered at line 0
prevdepth ignored
```

See also: \showboxbreadth, \showboxdepth (p. 261).

■ *Specifying what is traced*

\tracingonline   [⟨*number*⟩ parameter]

If this parameter is greater than zero, TeX will display the results of tracing (including \showbox and \showlists) at your terminal in addition to recording them in the log file.

\tracingcommands   [⟨*number*⟩ parameter]

If this parameter is 1 or greater, TeX will record in the log file most commands that it executes. If \tracingonline is greater than zero, this information will also appear at your terminal. Typesetting the first character of a word counts as a command, but (for the purposes of the trace only) the actions of typesetting the subsequent characters and any punctuation following them do not count as commands. If \tracingcommands is 2 or greater, TeX will also record commands that are expanded rather than executed, e.g., conditional tests and their outcomes.

Example:
```
\tracingcommands = 1 If $x+y>0$ we quit.\par
On the other hand, \tracingcommands = 0
```
produces in the log:
```
{vertical mode: the letter I}
{horizontal mode: the letter I}
{blank space  }
{math shift character $}
{math mode: the letter x}
{the character +}
{the letter y}
{the character >}
{the character 0}
{math shift character $}
{horizontal mode: blank space  }
{the letter w}
{blank space  }
{the letter q}
{blank space  }
{\par}
{vertical mode: the letter O}
{horizontal mode: the letter O}
{blank space  }
{the letter t}
{blank space  }
{the letter o}
{blank space  }
{the letter h}
{blank space  }
{\tracingcommands}
```

\tracinglostchars   [⟨*number*⟩ parameter]

If this parameter is greater than zero, TeX will record an indication in the log file of each time that it drops an output character because that character does not exist in the current font. If \tracingonline is greater than zero, this information will also appear at your terminal. Plain TEX defaults it to 1 (unlike the others).

Example:
```
\tracinglostchars = 1
A {\nullfont few} characters.
```
produces in the log:
```
Missing character: There is no f in font nullfont!
Missing character: There is no e in font nullfont!
Missing character: There is no w in font nullfont!
```

\tracingmacros   [⟨*number*⟩ parameter]
If this parameter is 1 or greater, TEX will record in the log file the expansion and arguments of every macro that it executes. If \tracingmacros is 2 or greater, TEX will record, in addition, every expansion of a token list such as \output or \everycr. If \tracingonline is greater than zero, this information will also appear at your terminal.

Example:
```
\def\a{first \b, then \c}
\def\b{b} \def\c{c}
\tracingmacros = 2
Call \a once.
```
produces in the log:
```
\a ->first \b , then \c

\b ->b

\c ->c
```

\tracingoutput   [⟨*number*⟩ parameter]
If this parameter is greater than zero, TEX will record in the log file the contents of every box that it sends to the .dvi file. If \tracingonline is greater than zero, this information will also appear at your terminal. The number of leading dots in each line of the trace output indicates the nesting level of the box at that line. You can control the amount of tracing by setting \showboxbreadth and \showboxdepth (p. 261).

Setting \tracingoutput to 1 can be particularly helpful when you're trying to determine why you've gotten extra space on a page.

Example:
```
% This is the entire file.
\tracingoutput = 1 \nopagenumbers
One-line page. \bye
```

produces in the log:

```
Completed box being shipped out [1]
\vbox(667.20255+0.0)x469.75499
.\vbox(0.0+0.0)x469.75499, glue set 13.99998fil
..\glue -22.5
..\hbox(8.5+0.0)x469.75499, glue set 469.75499fil
...\vbox(8.5+0.0)x0.0
...\glue 0.0 plus 1.0fil
..\glue 0.0 plus 1.0fil minus 1.0fil
.\vbox(643.20255+0.0)x469.75499, glue set 631.2581fill
..\glue(\topskip) 3.05556
..\hbox(6.94444+1.94444)x469.75499, glue set 386.9771fil
...\hbox(0.0+0.0)x20.0
...\tenrm O
...\tenrm n
...\tenrm e
...\tenrm -
...etc.
..\glue 0.0 plus 1.0fil
..\glue 0.0 plus 1.0fill
.\glue(\baselineskip) 24.0
.\hbox(0.0+0.0)x469.75499, glue set 469.75499fil
..\glue 0.0 plus 1.0fil
```

\tracingpages   [⟨*number*⟩ parameter]

If this parameter is greater than zero, TEX will record in the log file its calculations of the cost of various page breaks that it tries. If \tracing-online is greater than zero, this information will also appear at your terminal. TEX produces a line of this output whenever it first places a box or insertion on the current page list, and also whenever it processes a potential break point for the page. Examining this output can be helpful when you're trying to determine the cause of a bad page break. See pages 112–114 of *The TEXbook* for an illustration and explanation of this output.

Some production forms of TEX ignore the value of \tracingpages so that they can run faster. If you need to use this parameter, be sure to use a form that responds to it.

\tracingparagraphs   [⟨*number*⟩ parameter]

If this parameter is greater than zero, TEX will record in the log file its calculations of the cost of various line breaks that it tries. If \tracingonline is greater than zero, this information will also appear at your terminal. TEX produces this output when it reaches the end of each paragraph. See pages 98–99 of *The TEXbook* for an illustration and explanation of this output.

Some production forms of TEX ignore the value of `\tracingparagraphs` so that they can run faster. If you need to use this parameter, be sure to use a form that responds to it.

\tracingrestores   [⟨*number*⟩ parameter]

If this parameter is greater than zero, TEX will record in the log file the values that it restores when it encounters the end of a group. If `\tracingonline` is greater than zero, this information will also appear at your terminal.

Some production forms of TEX ignore the value of `\tracingrestores` so that they can run faster. If you need to use this parameter, be sure to use a form that responds to it.

\tracingstats   [⟨*number*⟩ parameter]

If this parameter is 1 or greater, TEX will include a report on the resources that it used to run your job (see page 300 of *The TEXbook* for a list and explanation of these resources). Moreover, if `\tracingstats` is 2 or greater, TEX will report on its memory usage whenever it does a `\shipout` (p. 148) for a page. The report appears at the end of the log file. If `\tracingonline` is greater than zero, the information will also appear at your terminal. If you're having trouble with TEX exceeding one of its capacities, the information provided by `\tracingstats` may help you pinpoint the cause of the difficulty.

Some production forms of TEX ignore the value of `\tracingstats` so that they can run faster. If you need to use this parameter, be sure to use a form that responds to it.

The following example shows a sample of the tracing output you'd get on one implementation of TEX. It may be different on other implementations.

Example:

    \tracingstats=1

produces in the log:

    Here is how much of TeX's memory you used:
     4 strings out of 5540
     60 string characters out of 72328
     5956 words of memory out of 262141
     921 multiletter control sequences out of 9500
     14794 words of font info for 50 fonts, out of 72000 for 255
     14 hyphenation exceptions out of 607
     7i,4n,1p,68b,22s stack positions out of 300i,40n,60p,3000b,4000s

\tracingall

This command tells TEX to turn on every available form of tracing. It also sets \tracingonline to 1 so that the trace output will appear at your terminal.

\showboxbreadth [⟨*number*⟩ parameter]

This parameter specifies the maximum number of list items that TEX displays for one level of one box when it is producing the output for \showbox or \tracingoutput. Plain TEX sets \showboxbreadth to 5.

\showboxdepth [⟨*number*⟩ parameter]

This parameter specifies the level of the deepest list that TEX displays when it is producing the output for \showbox or \showlists. Plain TEX sets \showboxdepth is 3.

■ *Sending messages*

\message – ⟨*token list*⟩ ″
\errmessage – ⟨*token list*⟩ ″

These commands display the message given by ⟨*token list*⟩ on your terminal and also enter it into the log. Any macros in the message are expanded, but no commands are executed. This is the same rule that TEX uses for \edef (p. 230).

For \errmessage, TEX pauses in the same way that it does for one of its own error messages and displays the \errhelp tokens if you ask for help.

You can generate multiline messages by using the \newlinechar character (p. 250).

Example:
```
\message{Starting a new section.}
```

\wlog – ⟨*token list*⟩ ″

This command writes ⟨*token list*⟩ on the log file. TEX expands ⟨*token list*⟩ according to the same rules that it uses for \edef (p. 230).

Example:
```
\wlog{Take two aspirins and call me in the morning.}
```
produces in the log:
```
Take two aspirins and call me in the morning.
```

\errhelp [⟨*token list*⟩ parameter]

This parameter contains the token list that TEX displays when you ask for help in response to an \errmessage command. We recommend that when you're generating an error message with \errmessage, you set \errhelp to a string that describes the nature of the error and use \newhelp to produce that string. You can use the \newlinechar character to produce multiline messages.

\newhelp ⟨*control sequence*⟩ – ⟨*help text*⟩ ″
This command assigns the help message given by ⟨*help text*⟩ to ⟨*control sequence*⟩. It provides an efficient way of defining the help text that further explains an error message. Before issuing the error message with the \errmessage command, you should assign ⟨*control sequence*⟩ to \errhelp. The help text will then appear if the user types 'H' or 'h' in response to the error message.

Example:
```
\newhelp\pain{Your input includes a token that I find^^J
    to be offensive. Don't bother me again with this^^J
    document until you've removed it.}
\errhelp = \pain \newlinechar = '\^^J
% ^^J will start a new line
\errmessage{I do not appreciate receiving this token}
```
produces in the log:
```
! I do not appreciate receiving this token.
1.8 ...t appreciate receiving this token.}

? H
\Your input includes a token that I find
  to be offensive. Don't bother me again with this
  document until you've removed it.
```

\errorcontextlines   [⟨*number*⟩ parameter]
This parameter determines the number of pairs of context lines, not counting the top and bottom pairs, that TEX prints when it encounters an error. By setting it to 0 you can get rid of long error messages. You can still force out the full context by typing something like:

```
I\errorcontextlines=100\oops
```

in response to an error, since the undefined control sequence \oops will cause another error. Plain TEX sets \errorcontextlines to 5.

See also: \write (p. 249), \escapechar (p. 226).

Initializing TEX

\dump

This command, which must not appear inside a group, dumps the contents of TEX's memory to a format file (p. 65). By using `virtex`, a special "virgin" form of TEX, you can then reload the format file at high speed and continue in the same state that TEX was in at the time of the dump. `\dump` also ends the run. Since `\dump` can only be used in `initex`, not in production forms of TEX, it is only useful to people who are installing TEX.

\everyjob   [⟨*token list*⟩ parameter]

This parameter contains a token list that TEX expands at the start of every job. Because an assignment to `\everyjob` cannot affect the current run (by the time you've done the assignment it's already too late), it is only useful to people who are preparing format files.

10 | Tips and techniques

TeX is a complex program that occasionally works its will in mysterious ways. In this section we offer some tips on solving problems that you might encounter and explain some handy techniques.

Correcting bad page breaks

Sometimes TeX breaks a page right in the middle of material that you want to keep together—for example, a section heading and the text that follows it, or a short list of related items. There are two ways to correct the situation:

- You can force the material to be kept together.
- You can force a page break at a different place.

The simplest way to force TeX to keep material together on a page is to enclose the material in a vbox using the \vbox command (p. 161). A vbox is ordinarily better than an hbox for this purpose because most often the material to be kept together, e.g., a sequence of paragraphs, will be vertical mode material. You should precede and follow the vbox by an implicit or explicit paragraph command (either a blank line or \par); otherwise TeX may try to make the vbox part of an an adjacent paragraph. The vbox method has an important limitation: you can't apply it to portions of text smaller than a paragraph.

You can sometimes keep the lines of a single paragraph together by enclosing the paragraph in a group and assigning \interlinepenalty (p. 138) a value of 10000 at the start of the group (or elsewhere before the end of the paragraph). This method causes TeX to consider page breaks within that paragraph to be infinitely undesirable. However, if all the page breaks that TEX can find are infinitely undesirable, it may break the page within the paragraph anyway.

A \nobreak command (p. 136) after the end of a paragraph prevents TEX from breaking the page at the following item (unless that item happens to be a penalty of less than 10000). This is also the best way to prevent a page break after a heading, since a heading usually behaves like a paragraph. The \nobreak must follow the blank line or \par that ends the paragraph so that TEX won't treat the \nobreak as part of the paragraph. For the \nobreak to be effective, it must also come before any legal breakpoint at the end of the paragraph. The glue that TEX inserts before the next paragraph is such a breakpoint, and so is any vertical glue that you insert explicitly after a paragraph. Thus the \nobreak should usually be the very first thing after the end of the paragraph or heading.

You can use the \eject command (p. 137) to force TEX to break a page at a particular place. Within a paragraph, you can use the combination '\vadjust{\vfill\eject}' (p. 120) to force a break after the next complete output line. The reason for preceding \eject by \vfill (p. 157) is to get TEX to fill out the page with blank space. However, using \eject to fix page break problems has a major disadvantage: if the page boundaries in your document change, the page breaks that you've inserted may no longer be where you want them.

If you don't provide TEX with a \vfill command to fill out the page after an \eject, TEX redistributes the extra blank space as best it can and then usually complains that "an underfull \vbox (badness 10000) has occurred while \output is active." You may encounter a similar problem with any of the methods mentioned above for enclosing material that you want to keep together.

The \filbreak command (p. 137) provides a way of keeping the lines of one or more paragraphs (or other vertical mode material) together on a page. If you enclose a paragraph in \filbreaks, TEX will effectively ignore the \filbreaks if the paragraph fits on the current page and break the page before the first \filbreak if the paragraph doesn't fit. If you put \filbreaks around each paragraph in a sequence of paragraphs, like this:

```
\filbreak
⟨paragraph⟩
\filbreak
⟨paragraph⟩
\filbreak
   ⋮
⟨paragraph⟩
\filbreak
```

TeX will keep the lines of each paragraph together on a page. If TeX breaks a page at a `\filbreak`, it will fill the bottom of the page with blank space.

Sometimes you can get TeX to modify the length of a page by changing the `\looseness` parameter (p. 124) for one or more paragraphs. Setting `\looseness` negative within a paragraph causes TeX to try to squeeze the paragraph into fewer lines; setting it positive causes TeX to try to expand the paragraph into more lines. The disadvantage of changing `\looseness` is that the interword spacing in the affected region won't be optimal. You can get further information about TeX's attempted line breaks by setting `\tracingpages` (p. 259) to 1.

Preserving the end of a page

Sometimes you need to modify something on a single page and you want to avoid reprinting the entire document. If your modification doesn't change the page length too much, there's hope. You need to fix the end of the page so that it falls in the same place; the methods are similar to the ones for fixing a bad page break.

If the original end of page came between paragraphs, you can force a page break at the same place using any of the methods we've described above. Otherwise, you myst force *both* a line break and a page break at a particular place. If the new page is shorter than the old one, the sequence:

```
\vadjust{\vfill\eject}\break
```

should do the trick. But if the new page is longer, the problem is far more difficult because TeX has probably already squeezed the page as tightly as it can. Your only hopes in this case are to set `\looseness` (p. 124) to a negative value, to shorten some of the vertical skips on the page, to add some shrink to `\parskip` (p. 141) if it was nonzero, or, as a last resort, to decrease `\baselineskip` (p. 133) ever so slightly.

Leaving space at the top of a page

You can usually use the `\vskip` command (p. 155) to leave vertical space on a page. That doesn't work at the top of a page, however, since TeX discards glue, kerns, and penalties that occur just after a page break. Use the `\topglue` command (p. 156) instead; it produces glue that never disappears.

Correcting bad line breaks

If TeX breaks a line in the middle of material that you wanted to keep on a single line, there are several ways to correct the situation:

- You can force a break in a nearby place with the `\break` command (p. 120).
- You can insert a tie (˜) between two words (see p. 105) to prevent a break between them.
- You can tell TeX about hyphenations that it wouldn't otherwise consider by inserting one or more discretionary hyphens in various words (see `\-`, p. 126).
- You can enclose several words in an hbox using the `\hbox` command (p. 160).

The disadvantage of all of these methods, except for inserting discretionary hyphens, is that they may make it impossible for TeX to find a satisfactory set of line breaks. Should that happen, TeX will set one or more underfull or overfull boxes and complain about it. The hbox method has a further disadvantage: because TeX sets an hbox as a single unit without considering its context, the interword space within the hbox may not be consistent with the interword space in the rest of the line.

Correcting overfull or underfull boxes

If TeX complains about an overfull box, it means you've put more material into a box than that box has room for. Similarly, if TeX complains about an underfull box, it means you haven't put enough material into the box. You can encounter these complaints under many different circumstances, so let's look at the more common ones:

- An overfull hbox that's a line of a paragraph indicates that the line was too long and that TeX couldn't rearrange the paragraph to make the line shorter. If you set `\emergencystretch` (p. 124) to some nonzero value, that may cure the problem by allowing TeX to put more space between words. Another solution is to set `\tolerance` (p. 123) to 10000, but that's likely to yield lines with far too much space in them. Yet another solution is to insert a discretionary hyphen in a critical word that TEX didn't know how to hyphenate. If all else fails, you might try rewording the paragraph. A solution that is rarely satisfactory is increasing `\hfuzz` (p. 171), allowing TEX to construct lines that project beyond the right margin.

- An underfull hbox that's a line of a paragraph indicates that the line was too short and that TEX couldn't rearrange the paragraph to make the line longer. TEX will set such a line by stretching its interword spaces beyond their normal limits. Two of the cures for overfull lines mentioned above also apply to underfull lines: inserting discretionary hyphens and rewording the paragraph. Underfull lines won't trouble you if you're using ragged right formatting, which you can get with the `\raggedright` command (p. 116).

- The complaint:

  ```
  Underfull \vbox (badness 10000) has occurred
      while \output is active
  ```

  indicates that TEX didn't have enough material to fill up a page. The likely cause is that you've been using vboxes to keep material together and TEX has encountered a vbox near the bottom of a page that wouldn't fit on that page. It has put the vbox on the next page, but in doing so has left too much empty space in the current page. In this case you'll either have to insert some more space elsewhere on the current page or break up the vbox into smaller parts.

  Another possible cause of this complaint is having a long paragraph that occupies an entire page without a break. Since TEX won't ordinarily vary the spacing between lines, it may be unable to fill a gap at the bottom of the page amounting to a fraction of the line spacing. This can happen if `\vsize` (p. 140), the page length, is not an even multiple of `\baselineskip` (p. 133), the space between consecutive baselines.

  Yet another cause of this complaint, similar to the previous one, is setting `\parskip` (p. 141), the interparagraph glue, to a value that doesn't have any stretch or shrink. You can fix these last two problems by increasing `\vfuzz` (p. 171).

- The complaint

  ```
  Overfull \vbox (296.30745pt too high) has occurred
      while \output is active
  ```

  indicates that you constructed a vbox that was longer than the page. You'll just have to make it shorter.

- The only cures for an overfull hbox or vbox that you've constructed with the `\hbox` or `\vbox` commands (pp. 160, 161) are to take something out of the box, to insert some negative glue with `\hss` or `\vss` (p. 158), or to increase the size of the box.

- If you encounter an underfull hbox or vbox that you've constructed with \hbox or \vbox, you're usually best off to fill out the box with \hfil or \vfil (p. 157).

Recovering lost interword spaces

If you find that TeX has run two words together, the likely cause is a control sequence that's absorbed the spaces after it. Put a control space (\␣) after the control sequence.

Avoiding unwanted interword spaces

If you get a space in your document where you don't want and don't expect one, the most likely cause, in our experience, is an end of line or a space following a brace. (If you're doing fancy things with category codes, you've introduced lots of other likely causes.) TeX ordinarily translates an end-of-line into a space, and it considers a space after a right or left brace to be significant.

If the unwanted space is caused by a space after a brace within an input line, then remove that space. If the unwanted space is caused by a brace at the end of an input line, put a '%' immediately after the brace. The '%' starts a comment, but this comment needn't have any text.

A macro definition can also introduce unwanted spaces if you haven't written it carefully. If you're getting unwanted spaces when you call a macro, check its definition to be sure that you don't have an unintended space after a brace and that you haven't ended a line of the definition immediately after a brace. People often end lines of macro definitions after braces in order to make the definitions more readable. To be safe, put a '%' after any brace that ends a line of a macro definition. It may not be needed, but it won't do any harm.[1]

When you're having trouble locating the source of an unwanted space, try setting \tracingcommands (p. 257) to 2. You'll get a {blank space} command in the log file for each space that TeX sees.

It helps to know TeX's rules for spaces:

(1) Spaces are ignored at the beginnings of input lines.

(2) Spaces at the ends of input lines are ignored under *all* circumstances, although the end of line itself is treated like a space. (A completely blank line, however, generates a \par token.)

---

[1] Admittedly there are rare cases where you really do want an end of line after a brace.

(3) Multiple spaces are treated like a single space, but only if they appear together in your input. Thus a space following the arguments of a macro call is not combined with a final space produced by the macro call. Instead, you get two spaces.

(4) Spaces are ignored after control words.

(5) Spaces are in effect ignored after numbers, dimensions, and the '`plus`' and '`minus`' in glue specifications.[2]

If you've changed the category code of the space or the end-of-line character, all bets are off.

Avoiding excess space around a display

If you're getting too much space above a math display, it may be because you've left a blank line in your input above the display. The blank line starts a new paragraph and puts TEX into vertical mode. When TEX sees a '`$`' in vertical mode, it switches back to horizontal mode and inserts the interparagraph glue (`\parskip`) followed by the interline glue (`\baselineskip`). Then, when it starts the display itself, it inserts *more* glue (either `\abovedisplayskip` or `\abovedisplayshortskip`, depending on the length of the preceding line). This last glue is the only glue that you want. To avoid getting the interparagraph glue as well, don't leave a blank line above a math display or otherwise end a paragraph (with `\par`, say) just before a math display.

Similarly, if you're getting too much space below a math display, it may be because you've left a blank line in your input below the display. Just remove it.

Avoiding excess space after a paragraph

If you get too much vertical space after a paragraph that was produced by a macro, you may be getting the interparagraph glue produced by the macro, an empty paragraph, and then more interparagraph glue. You can get rid of the second paragraph skip by inserting:

```
\vskip -\parskip
\vskip -\baselineskip
```

---

[2] Actually, TEX ignores only a single space in these places. Since multiple spaces ordinarily reduce to a single space, however, the effect is that of ignoring any number of spaces.

just after the macro call. If you always get this problem with a certain macro, you can put these lines at the end of the macro definition instead. You may also be able to cure the problem by never leaving a blank line after the macro call—if you want a blank line just to make your input more readable, start it with a '%'.

Changing the paragraph shape

Several TeX parameters—\hangindent, \leftskip, etc.—affect the way that TeX shapes paragraphs and breaks them into lines. These parameters are used indirectly in plain TeX commands such as \narrower and \hang; you can also assign to them directly. If you've used one of these commands (or changed one of these parameters), but the command or parameter change does not seem to be having any effect on a paragraph, the problem may be that you've ended a group before you've ended the paragraph. For example:

```
{\narrower She very soon came to an open field, with
a wood on the other side of it: it looked much darker
than the last wood, and Alice felt a little timid
about going into it.}
```

This paragraph won't be set narrower because the right brace at the end terminates the \narrower group before TeX has had a chance to break the paragraph into lines. Instead, put a \par before the right brace; then you'll get the effect you want.

Putting paragraphs into a box

Suppose you have a few paragraphs of text that you want to put in a particular place on the page. The obvious way to do it is to enclose the paragraphs in an hbox of an appropriate size, and then place the hbox where you want it to be. Alas, the obvious way doesn't work because TeX won't do line breaking in restricted horizontal mode. If you try it, you'll get a misleading error message that suggests you're missing the end of a group. The way around this restriction is to write:

```
\vbox{\hsize = ⟨dimen⟩ ... ⟨paragraphs⟩ ...}
```

where ⟨*dimen*⟩ is the line length that you want for the paragraphs. This is what you need to do, in particular, when you want to enclose some paragraphs in a box (a box enclosed in ruled lines, not a TEX box).

Drawing lines

You can use the \hrule and \vrule commands (p. 172) to draw lines, i.e., rules. You'll need to know (a) where you can use each command and (b) how TEX determines the lengths of rules when you haven't given the lengths explicitly.

- You can only use \hrule when TEX is in a vertical mode and \vrule when TEX is in a horizontal mode. This requirement means that you can't put a horizontal rule into an hbox or a vertical rule into a vbox. You can, however, construct a horizontal rule that looks vertical by specifying all three dimensions and making it tall and skinny. Similarly, you can construct a vertical rule that looks horizontal by making it short and fat.
- A horizontal rule inside a vbox has the same width as does the vbox if you haven't given the width of the rule explicitly. Vertical rules inside hboxes behave analogously. If your rules are coming out too long or too short, check the dimensions of the enclosing box.

As an example, suppose we want to produce:

> Help! Let
> me out of
> here!

The following input will do it:

```
\hbox{\vrule
   \vbox{\hrule \vskip 3pt
      \hbox{\hskip 3pt
         \vbox{\hsize = .7in \raggedright
            \noindent Help! Let me out of here!}%
      \hskip 3pt}%
   \vskip 3pt \hrule}%
\vrule}
```

We need to put the text into a vbox in order to get TEX to process it as a paragraph. The four levels of boxing are really necessary—if you doubt it, try to run this example with fewer levels.

Creating multiline headers or footers

You can use the \headline and \footline commands (p. 143) to
produce headers and footers, but they don't work properly for headers
and footers having more than one line. However, you can get multiline
headers and footers by redefining some of the subsidiary macros in TEX's
output routine.

For a multiline header, you need to do three things:

(1) Redefine the \makeheadline macro that's called from TEX's output routine.

(2) Increase \voffset by the amount of vertical space consumed by
the extra lines.

(3) Decrease \vsize by the same amount.

The following example shows how you might do this:

```
\advance\voffset by 2\baselineskip
\advance\vsize by -2\baselineskip
\def\makeheadline{\vbox to 0pt{\vss\noindent
   Header line 1\hfil Page \folio\break
   Header line 2\hfil\break
   Header line 3\hfil}%
   \vskip\baselineskip}
```

You can usually follow the pattern of this definition quite closely, just
substituting your own header lines and choosing an appropriate multiple
of \baselineskip (one less than the number of lines in the header).

For a multiline footer, the method is similar:

(1) Redefine the \makefootline macro that's called from TEX's output routine.

(2) Decrease \vsize by the amount of vertical space consumed by the
extra lines.

The following example shows how you might do this:

```
\advance\vsize by -2\baselineskip
\def\makefootline{%
   \lineskip = 24pt
   \vbox{\raggedright\noindent
   Footer line 1\hfil\break
   Footer line 2\hfil\break
   Footer line 3\hfil}}
```

Again, you can usually follow the pattern of this definition quite closely.
The value of \lineskip determines the amount of space between the

baseline of the last line of the main text on the page and the baseline of the first line of the footer.

Finding mismatched braces

Most times when your TeX input suffers from mismatched braces, you'll get a diagnostic from TeX fairly near the place where you actually made the mistake. But one of the most frustrating errors you can get from a TeX run, just before TeX quits, is the following:

```
(\end occurred inside a group at level 1)
```

This indicates that there is an extra left brace or a missing right brace somewhere in your document, but it gives you no hint at all about where the problem might be. So how can you find it?

A debugging trick we've found useful is to insert the following line or its equivalent at five or six places equally spaced within the document (and not within a known group):

```
}% a fake ending
```

Let's assume the problem is an extra left brace. If the extra left brace is, say, between the third and fourth fake ending, you'll get error messages from the first three fake endings but not from the fourth one. The reason is that TeX will ignore the first three fake endings after complaining about them, but the fourth fake ending will match the extra left brace. Thus you know that the extra left brace is somewhere between the third and fourth fake ending. If the region of the error is still too large for you to find it, just remove the original set of fake endings and repeat the process within that region. If the problem is a missing right brace rather than an extra left brace, you should be able to track it down once you've found its mate.

This method doesn't work under all circumstances. In particular, it doesn't work if your document consists of several really large groups. But often you can find some variation on this method that will lead you to that elusive brace.

If all else fails, try shortening your input by removing the last half of the file (after stashing away the original version first!) or inserting a \bye command in the middle. If the error persists, you know it's in the first half; if it goes away, you know it's in the second half. By repeating this process you'll eventually find the error.

Setting dimensions

The simplest way to set a dimension is to specify it directly, e.g.:

```
\hsize = 6in
```

You can also specify a dimension in terms of other dimensions or as a mixture of different units, but it's a little more work. There are two ways to construct a dimension as such a combination:

(1) You can add a dimension to a dimension parameter or to a dimension register. For example:

```
\hsize = 6in \advance\hsize by 3pc % 6in + 3pc
```

(2) You can indicate a dimension as a multiple of a dimension or glue parameter or register. In this case, TeX converts glue to a dimension by throwing away the stretch and shrink. For example:

```
\parindent = .15\hsize
\advance\vsize by -2\parskip
```

Creating composite fonts

It's sometimes useful to create a "composite font", named by a control sequence $\mathcal{F}$, in which all the characters are taken from a font f_1 except for a few that are borrowed from another font f_2. You can then set text in the composite font by using $\mathcal{F}$ just as you'd use any other font identifier.

You can create such a composite font by defining $\mathcal{F}$ as a macro. In the definition of $\mathcal{F}$, you first select font f_1 and then define control sequences that produce the borrowed characters, set in f_2. For example, suppose that you want to create a composite font \britrm which has all the characters of cmr10 except for the dollar sign, for which you want to borrow the pound sterling symbol from font cmti10. The pound sterling symbol in cmti10 happens to be in the same font position as the dollar sign in cmr10. Here's how to do it:

```
\def\britrm{%
    \tenrm % \tenrm names the cmr10 font
    \def\${{\tenit\char '\$}}% \tenit names the cmti10 font.
}
```

Now whenever you start the font named \britrm, \$ will produce a pound sterling symbol.

You can also get the same effect by changing the category codes of the characters in question to make those characters active and then providing a definition for the character. For example:

```
\catcode '* = \active
\def*{{\tentt \char '\*}}
```

In this case the asterisk will be taken from the \tentt font. If you then type the input line:

```
Debbie was the * of the show.
```

it will be set as:

Debbie was the * of the show.

Reproducing text verbatim

Verbatim text is text that is reproduced in a typeset document just as it appeared in the input. The most common use of verbatim text is in typesetting computer input, including both computer programs and input to TeX itself. Computer input is not easy to produce verbatim for two reasons:

(1) Some characters (control symbols, escape characters, braces, etc.) have special meanings to TeX.
(2) Ends of line and multiple spaces are translated to single spaces.

In order to produce verbatim text, you have to cancel the special meanings and disable the translation. This is best done with macros.

To cancel the special meanings, you need to change the category codes of those characters that have special meanings. The following macro illustrates how you might do it:

```
\chardef \other = 12
\def\deactivate{%
    \catcode'\\ = \other      \catcode'\{ = \other
    \catcode'\} = \other      \catcode'\$ = \other
    \catcode'\& = \other      \catcode'\# = \other
    \catcode'\% = \other      \catcode'\~ = \other
    \catcode'\^ = \other      \catcode'\_ = \other
}
```

But beware! Once you've changed the category codes in this way, you've lost the ability to use control sequences since there's no longer an escape character. You need some way of getting back to the normal mode of operation. We'll explain how to do that in a moment, after considering the other problem: disabling the translation of spaces and ends of line.

Plain T_EX has two commands that together nearly solve the problem: \obeyspaces (p. 107) and \obeylines (p. 122). The two things that they don't do are to preserve spaces at the start of a line and to preserve blank lines. For that you need stronger measures—which are provided by the \obeywhitespace macro that we are about to define.

T_EX normally insists on collecting lines into paragraphs. One way to convince it to take line boundaries literally is to turn individual lines into paragraphs.[3] You can do this by redefining the end of line character to produce the \par control sequence. The following three macro definitions show how:

```
\def\makeactive#1{\catcode`#1 = \active \ignorespaces}
{% The group delimits the text over which ^^M is active.
    \makeactive\^^M %
    \gdef\obeywhitespace{%
    % Use \gdef so the definition survives the group.
        \makeactive\^^M %
        \let^^M = \newline %
        \aftergroup\removebox % Kill extra paragraph at end.
        \obeyspaces %
    }%
}
\def\newline{\par\indent}
\def\removebox{\setbox0=\lastbox}
```

A subtle point about the definition of \obeywhitespace is that ^^M must be made active both when \obeywhitespace is being *defined* and when it is being *used*.

In order to be able to get back to normal operation after verbatim text, you need to choose a character that appears rarely if at all in the verbatim text. This character serves as a temporary escape character. The vertical bar (|) is sometimes a good choice. With this choice, the macros:

```
\def\verbatim{\par\begingroup\deactivate\obeywhitespace
    \catcode `\| = 0 % Make | the new escape character.
}

\def\endverbatim{\endgroup\endpar}

\def\|{|}
```

will do the trick. Within the verbatim text, you can use a double vertical bar (||) to denote a single one, and you end the verbatim text with |endverbatim.

---

[3] Another way is to turn the end of line character into a \break command and provide infinite glue at the end of each line.

There are many variations on this technique:

- If a programming language has keywords, you can turn each keyword into a command that typesets that keyword in boldface. Each keyword in the input should then be preceded by the temporary escape character.

- If you have a character (again, let's assume it's the vertical bar) that *never* appears in the verbatim text, you can make it active and cause it to end the verbatim text. The macro definitions then go like this:

```
{\catcode '\| = \active
\gdef\verbatim{%
    \par\begingroup\deactivate\obeywhitespace
    \catcode '| = \active
    \def |{\endgroup\par}%
}}
```

The ideas presented here provide only a simple approach to typesetting computer programs. Verbatim reproduction is often not as revealing or easy to read as a version that uses typographical conventions to reflect the syntax and even the semantics of the program. If you'd like to pursue this subject further, we recommend the following book:

Baecker, Ronald M., and Marcus, Aaron, *Human Factors and Typography for More Readable Programs*. Reading, Mass.: Addison-Wesley, 1990.

Using outer macros

If TeX complains about a "forbidden control sequence", you've probably used an outer macro in a non-outer context (see "outer", p. 83). An outer macro is one whose definition is preceded by `\outer`. An outer macro can't be used in a macro argument, in a macro definition, in the preamble of an alignment, or in conditional text, i.e., text that will be expanded only when a conditional test has a particular outcome. Certain macros have been defined as outer because they aren't intended to be used in these contexts and such a use is probably an error. The only ways around this problem are to redefine the macro or to move its use to an acceptable context.

Using an outer macro in an improper context can also cause TeX to complain about a runaway situation or an incomplete conditional. The problem can be hard to diagnose because the error message gives no hint as to what it is. If you get such an error message, look around for a call on an outer macro. You may not always know that a particular macro is

outer, but the command '\show\a' (p. 253) will show you the definition
of \a and also tell you if \a is outer.

Changing category codes

Sometimes it's useful to make local changes to the category code of a
character in some part of your document. For instance, you might be
typesetting a computer program or something else that uses normally
active characters for special purposes. You'd then want to deacti-
vate those characters so that TEX will treat them as being like any
other character.

   If you make such a local change to the category code of a character,
you may sometimes be dismayed to find that TEX seems to be paying
no attention whatsoever to your change. Two aspects of TEX's behavior
are likely causes:

(1) TEX determines the category code of an input character and attaches
    it to the character when it reads in the character. Let's say you
    read in a tilde (~) and later change the category code of tildes,
    but make the change before TEX's stomach has actually processed
    that *particular* tilde (see "anatomy of TEX", p. 46). TEX will still
    respond to that tilde using the category code as it was before the
    change. This difficulty typically arises when the tilde is part of
    an argument to a macro and the macro itself changes the category
    code of tilde.

(2) When TEX is matching a call of a macro to the definition of that
    macro, it matches not just the characters in the parameter pattern
    but also their category codes. If the category code of a pattern
    character isn't equal to the category code of the same character in the
    call, TEX won't consider the characters as matching. This effect can
    produce mysterious results because it *looks* as though the pattern
    should match. For example, if you've defined a macro:

    \def\eurodate#1/#2/#3{#2.#1.#3}

    then the slash character must have the same category code when you
    call \eurodate as it had when you defined \eurodate.

   If the problem arises because the troublesome character is an argument
to a macro, then the usual cure is to redefine the macro as a pair of
macros \mstart and \mfinish, where \mstart is to be called before the
argument text and \mfinish is to be called after it. \mstart then sets
up the category codes and \mfinish undoes the change, perhaps just by
ending a group.

Making macro files more readable

You can make a file of macros more readable by setting the category codes of space to 9 (ignored character) and \endlinechar (p. 252) to −1 at the beginning of the file. Then you can use spaces and ends of line freely in the macro definitions without getting unwanted spaces when you call the macros. The ignored characters won't generate spaces, but they'll still act as terminators for control sequences. If you really do want a space, you can still get it with the \space command (p. 105).

Of course you'll need to restore the category codes of space and end of line to their normal values (10 and 5, respectively) at the end of the file. You can do this either by enclosing the entire file in a group or by restoring the values explicitly. If you choose to enclose the file in a group, then you should also set \globaldefs to 1 so that all the macro definitions will be global and thus visible outside of the group.

A miniature example of a macro file of this form is:

```
\catcode '\ = 9  \endlinechar = -1

\def \makeblankbox #1 #2 {
    \hbox{\lower \dp0 \vbox{\hidehrule {#1} {#2}
    \kern -#1 % overlap rules
    \hbox to \wd0{\hidevrule {#1} {#2}%
        \raise \ht0  \vbox to #1{} % vrule height
        \lower \dp0 \vtop to #1{}  % vrule depth
        \hfil \hidevrule {#2} {#1} }
    \kern -#1 \hidehrule {#2} {#1} } }

\def\hidehrule #1 #2 {
    \kern -#1 \hrule height#1 depth#2 \kern -#2 }
\def\hidevrule #1 #2 {
    \kern -#1 {\dimen0 = #1 \advance \dimen0 by #2
    \vrule width \dimen0 } \kern -#2 }

\catcode '\ = 10  \endlinechar = '\^^M
```

Without the changed category codes, these macros would have to be written much more compactly, using fewer spaces and more '%'s at the ends of lines.

11 Making sense of error messages

Interpreting TEX's error messages can sometimes be like going to your physician with a complaint that you're feeling fatigued and being handed, in response, a breakdown of your blood chemistry. The explanation of your distress is probably there, but it's not easy to figure out what it is. A few simple rules will go a long way in helping you to understand TEX's error messages and get the most benefit from them.

Your first goal should be to understand what you did that caused TEX to complain. Your second goal (if you're working interactively) should be to catch as many errors as you can in a single run.

Let's look at an example. Suppose that your input contains the line:

```
We skip \quid a little bit.
```

You meant to type '\quad', but you typed '\quid' instead. Here's what you'll get from TEX in response:

```
! Undefined control sequence.
l.291 We skip \quid
                    a little bit.
?
```

This message will appear both at your terminal and in your log file. The first line, which always starts with an exclamation point (!), tells you what the problem is. The last two lines before the '?' prompt (which in this case are also the next two lines) tell you how far TEX has gotten when it found the error. It found the error on line 291 of the current input file, and the break between the two message lines indicates TEX's precise position within line 291, namely, just after \quid. The current input file is the one just after the most recent unclosed left parenthesis in the terminal output of your run (see p. 9).

This particular error, an undefined control sequence, is one of the most common ones you can get. If you respond to the prompt with another '?', TEX will display the following message:

```
Type <return> to proceed, S to scroll future error messages,
R to run without stopping, Q to run quietly,
I to insert something, E to edit your file,
1 or ... or 9 to ignore the next 1 to 9 tokens of input,
H for help, X to quit.
```

Here's what these alternatives mean:

- If you type ⟨return⟩, TEX will continue processing your document. In this case it will just ignore the \quid.
- If you type 'S' (or 's'—uppercase and lowercase are equivalent here), TEX will process your document without stopping *except* if it encounters a missing file. Error messages will still appear at your terminal and in the log file.
- If you type 'R' or 'r', you'll get the same effect as 'S' except that TEX won't even stop for missing files.
- If you type 'Q' or 'q', TEX will continue processing your document but will neither stop for errors nor display them at your terminal. The errors will still show up in the log file.
- If you type 'X' or 'x', TEX will clean up as best it can, discard the page it's working on, and quit. You can still print or view the pages that TEX has already processed.
- If you type 'E' or 'e', TEX will clean up and terminate as it would for 'X' or 'x' and then enter your text editor, positioning you at the erroneous line. (Not all systems support this option.)
- If you type 'H' or 'h', you'll get a further explanation of the error displayed at your terminal and possibly some advice about what to do about it. This explanation will also appear in your log file. For the undefined control sequence above, you'll get:

  ```
  The control sequence at the end of the top line
  of your error message was never \def'ed. If you have
  misspelled it (e.g., '\hobx'), type 'I' and the correct
  spelling (e.g., 'I\hbox'). Otherwise just continue,
  and I'll forget about whatever was undefined.
  ```

- If you type '?', you'll get this same message again.

The other two alternatives, typing 'I' or a small integer, provide ways of getting TEX back on the track so that your error won't cause further errors later in your document:

- If you type 'I' or 'i' followed by some text, then TEX will insert that text as though it had occurred just after the point of the error, at the innermost level where TEX is working. In the case of the example above, that means at TEX's position in your original input, namely, just after '\quid'. Later you'll see an example that shows the difference between inserting something at the innermost level and inserting it into your original input. In the example above of the undefined control sequence, if you type:

```
I\quad
```

TEX will carry out the \quad command and produce a quad space where you intended to have one.

- If you type a positive integer less than 100 (not less than 10 as the message misleadingly suggests), TEX will delete that number of tokens from the innermost level where it is working. (If you type an integer greater than or equal to 100, TEX will delete 10 tokens!)

Here's an example of another common error:

```
Skip across \hskip 3cn by 3 centimeters.
```

The error message for this is:

```
! Illegal unit of measure (pt inserted).
<to be read again>
                     c
<to be read again>
                     n
l.340 Skip across \hskip 3cn
                             by 3 centimeters.
```

In this case TEX has observed that '3' is followed by something that isn't a proper unit of measure, and so it's assumed the unit of measure to be points. TEX will read the tokens of 'cn' again and insert them into your input, which is not what you want. In this case you can get a better result by first typing '2' to bypass the 'cn'. You'll get the message:

```
<recently read> n

l.340 Skip across \hskip 3cn
                             by 3 centimeters.
```

Now you can type 'I\hskip 3cm' to get the skip you wanted (in addition to the 3pt skip that you've already gotten).[1]

If you type something that's only valid in math mode, TEX will switch over to math mode for you whether or not that's what you really wanted. For example:

```
So \spadesuit s are trumps.
```

---

[1] By typing 'I\unskip\hskip 3cm' you can get rid of the 3pt skip.

Here's TeX's error message:

```
! Missing $ inserted.
<inserted text>
                    $
<to be read again>
                    \spadesuit
1.330 So \spadesuit
                s are trumps.
```

Since the \spadesuit symbol is only allowed in math mode, TeX has inserted a '$' in front of it. After TeX inserts a token, it's positioned in *front* of that token, in this case the '$', ready to read it. Typing '2' will cause TeX to skip both the '$' and the '\spadesuit' tokens, leaving it ready to process the 's' in 's are trumps.'. (If you just let TeX continue, it will typeset 's are trumps' in math mode.)

Here's an example where TeX's error diagnostic is downright wrong:

```
\hbox{One \vskip 1in two.}
```

The error message is:

```
! Missing } inserted.
<inserted text>
                    }
<to be read again>
                    \vskip
1.29 \hbox{One \vskip
                1in two.}
```

The problem is that you can't use \vskip when TeX is in restricted horizontal mode, i.e, constructing an hbox. But instead of rejecting the \vskip, TeX has inserted a right brace in front of it in an attempt to close out the hbox. If you accept TeX's correction, TeX will complain again when it gets to the correct right brace later on. It will also complain about anything before that right brace that isn't allowed in vertical mode. These additional complaints will be particularly confusing because the errors they indicate are bogus, a result of the propagated effects of the inappropriate insertion of the right brace. Your best bet is to type '5', skipping past all the tokens in '}\vskip 1in'.

Here's a similar example in which the error message is longer than any we've seen so far:

```
\leftline{Skip \smallskip a little further.} But no more.
```

The mistake here is that \smallskip only works in a vertical mode. The error message is something like:

```
! Missing } inserted.
<inserted text>
```

```
                          }
        <to be read again>
                             \vskip
        \smallskip ->\vskip
                             \smallskipamount
        <argument> Skip \smallskip
                                    a little further.
        \leftline #1->\line {#1
                                \hss }
        1.93 ...Skip \smallskip a little further.}
                                          But no more.
```

The error messages here give you a tour through the macros that are used in plain TEX's implementation of \leftline—macros that you probably don't care about. The first line tells you that TEX intends to cure the problem by inserting a right brace. TEX hasn't actually read the right brace yet, so you can delete it if you choose to. Each component of the message after the first line (the one with the '!') occupies a pair of lines. Here's what the successive pairs of lines mean:

(1) The first pair indicates that TEX has inserted, but not yet read, a right brace.

(2) The next pair indicates that after reading the right brace, TEX will again read a '\vskip' command (gotten from the macro definition of \smallskip).

(3) The third pair indicates that TEX was expanding the \smallskip macro when it found the error. The pair also displays the definition of \smallskip and indicates how far TEX has gotten in expanding and executing that definition. Specifically, it's just attempted unsuccessfully to execute the \vskip command. In general, a diagnostic line that starts with a control sequence followed by '->' indicates that TEX has been expanding and executing a macro by that name.

(4) The fourth pair indicates that TEX was processing a macro argument when it found the \smallskip and also indicates TEX's position in that argument, i.e., it's just processed the \smallskip (unsuccessfully). By looking ahead to the next pair of lines we can see that the argument was passed to \leftline.

(5) The fifth pair indicates that TEX was expanding the \leftline macro when it found the error. (In this example the error occurred while TEX was in the middle of interpreting several macro definitions at different levels of expansion.) Its position after #1 indicates that the last thing it saw was the first (and in this case the only) argument to \leftline.

(6) The last pair indicates where TEX is positioned in your input file. Note that this position is well beyond the position where it's inserting the right brace and reading '\vskip' again. That's because TEX has already read the entire argument to \leftline from your input file, even though it's only processed part of that argument. The dots at the beginning of the pair indicate a preceding part of the input line that isn't shown. This preceding part, in fact, includes the \leftline control sequence that made the \vskip illegal.

In a long message like this, you'll generally find only the first line and the last pair of lines to be useful; but it sometimes helps to know what the other lines are about. Any text that you insert or delete will be inserted or deleted at the innermost level. In this example the insertion or deletion would occur just before the inserted right brace. Note in particular that in this case TEX puts any text you might insert *not* into your input text but into a macro definition several levels down. (The original macro definition is of course not modified.)

You can use the \errorcontextlines command (p. 262) to limit the number of pairs of error context lines that TEX produces. If you're not interested in all the information that TEX is giving you, you can set \errorcontextlines to 0. That will give you just the first and last pairs of lines.

Finally, we'll mention two other indicators that can appear at the start of a pair of error message lines:

- <output> indicates that TEX was in the middle of its output routine when this error occurred.

- <write> indicates that TEX was in the middle of executing a \write command when this error occurred. TEX will detect such an error when it is actually doing the \write (during a \shipout), rather than when it first encounters the \write.

12 A compendium of useful macros

This section describes `eplain.tex`, a collection of macros and other definitions that extend plain TeX. The descriptions of the various macros explain their purposes, but usually do not explain how they work or provide explicit details on how to use them. That information is contained in the source files for `eplain.tex` and in the documentation that comes with it. See "Resources" (p. 18) for how to obtain `eplain.tex`.

Preliminaries

We start with some macros for changing category codes and convenient definitions for two of the commonly used ones.

```
\def\makeactive#1{\catcode`#1 = \active \ignorespaces}%
\chardef\letter = 11 \chardef\other = 12
\def\uncatcodespecials{%
   \def\do##1{\catcode`##1 = \other}%
   \dospecials}% Defined in plain.
```

In order to define '^^M' as an active character, you need to encase the definition in a group and invoke some extra machinery. The `\letreturn` macro lets you define '^^M' without that extra machinery (which you can see in the definition below).

```
{\makeactive\^^M \long\gdef\letreturn#1{\let^^M = #1}}%
```

These macros consume one, two, or three arguments.

```
\def\gobble#1{}\def\gobbletwo#1#2{}%
\def\gobblethree#1#2#3{}%
```

Now we establish some conventions for reading the rest of the file. Within the file we allow "private" control sequences that contain '@' in their names. These control sequences aren't accessible outside of this file (unless you change the category code of '@' again).

```
\catcode'@ = \letter    % Allow control sequences with @.
\let\@plainwlog = \wlog % Don't log register allocations.
\let\wlog = \gobble
\newlinechar = '^^J
```

The next two macros provide convenient forms of diagnostic output. \loggingall turns on all tracing, but causes the trace output to appear only in the log file and not at your terminal. \tracingboxes causes boxes to be displayed completely when they're traced. (TeX normally shows only three levels of boxing and five items within each box.)

```
\def\loggingall{\tracingcommands\tw@\tracingstats\tw@
    \tracingpages\@ne\tracingoutput\@ne
    \tracinglostchars\@ne\tracingmacros\tw@
    \tracingparagraphs\@ne\tracingrestores\@ne
    \showboxbreadth\maxdimen\showboxdepth\maxdimen}%
\def\tracingboxes{\showboxbreadth = \maxdimen
    \showboxdepth = \maxdimen}%
```

The default thickness of rules is 0.4 pt. You can produce rules of any default thickness you choose by redefining \vruledefaultwidth, \hruledefaultheight, and \hruledefaultdepth and then using \ehrule and \evrule instead of \hrule and \vrule. (The 'e' stands for "eplain".) If you give an explicit dimension (e.g., \ehrule height 16pt), TeX will use it.

```
\newdimen\hruledefaultheight  \hruledefaultheight = 0.4pt
\newdimen\hruledefaultdepth   \hruledefaultdepth = 0.0pt
\newdimen\vruledefaultwidth   \vruledefaultwidth = 0.4pt
\def\ehrule{\hrule height\hruledefaultheight
    depth\hruledefaultdepth}%
\def\evrule{\vrule width\vruledefaultwidth}%
```

The \% convention for writing a '%' character doesn't work when you want to include that character in the token list of \write. You can use \percentchar to achieve this. We also redefine ^^L to be nonouter so that you can use it in a macro definition or argument.

```
{\catcode'\% = \other \gdef\percentchar{%}}%
 \def^^L{\par
}%
```

\tokstostring converts its argument into a list of character tokens. It uses only expansions that are handled in TeX's gullet. This property is necessary for it to work with \edef. It is used by the cross-referencing macros (p. 302).

In order to split the argument up at spaces, we have to use two subsidiary macros. \@ttsA finds the spaces, and \@ttsB handles a token sequence without any spaces. Each space is replaced by the expansion of \spacesub.

```
\def\tokstostring#1{\@ttsA#1 \ttsmarkA}%
\def\@ttsA#1 #2\ttsmarkA{\ifempty{#1}\else
    \@ttsB #1\@ttsmarkB
    \ifempty{#2}\else
        \spacesub\@ttsA#2\ttsmarkA\fi\fi}%
\def\@ttsB#1{\ifx #1\@ttsmarkB\else
    \string #1%
    \expandafter\@ttsB\fi}%
\def\@ttsmarkB{\@ttsmarkB}% should never be expanded
\def\spacesub{+}%
```

\ifempty tests if its argument is empty.

```
\def\ifempty#1{\@ifempty #1\@emptymarkA\@emptymarkB}%
\def\@ifempty#1#2\@emptymarkB{\ifx #1\@emptymarkA}%
\def\@emptymarkA{\@emptymarkA}%
```

The \for macro implements a TEX version of the for loop in traditional programming languages. These macros come directly from LATEX.

```
\def\for#1:=#2\do#3{\edef\@fortmp{#2}%
    \ifx\@fortmp\empty \else
        \expandafter\@forloop#2,\@nil,\@nil\@@#1{#3}\fi}%
\def\@nnil{\@nil}%
\def\@fornoop#1\@@#2#3{}%
\def\@forloop#1,#2,#3\@@#4#5{\def#4{#1}\ifx #4\@nnil
    \else #5\def#4{#2} ifx #4\@nnil \else
        #5\@iforloop #3\@@#4{#5}\fi\fi}%
\def\@iforloop#1,#2\@@#3#4{\def#3{#1}\ifx #3\@nnil
    \let\@nextwhile=\@fornoop \else #4\relax
        \let\@nextwhile=\@iforloop\fi
            \@nextwhile#2\@@#3{#4}}%
```

\obeywhitespace is useful for reproducing line breaks, blank lines, and spaces in your input. It combines the effects of \obeylines and \obeyspaces, and also causes spaces at the start of a line to be printed. Tab characters are not affected by this; they still produce normal glue.

```
\def\alwaysspace{\hglue\fontdimen2\the\font \relax}%
{\makeactive\^^M \makeactive\ %
\gdef\obeywhitespace{%
\makeactive\^^M\def^^M{\par\indent}%
```

```
\aftergroup\@removebox% Kill extra paragraph at end.
\makeactive\ \let =\alwaysspace}}%
\def\@removebox{\setbox0=\lastbox}
```

\frac is a good way to print fractions in text when you don't want to use \over and "1/2" just doesn't look right. This macro is the answer to Exercise 11.6 of *The TEXbook*.

```
\def\frac#1/#2{\leavevmode
    \kern.1em \raise .5ex \hbox{\the\scriptfont0 #1}%
    \kern-.1em $/$%
    \kern-.15em \lower .25ex \hbox{\the\scriptfont0 #2}}%
```

The following macros produce logos that are useful in the TEX world. The $\mathcal{AMS}$-TEX logo is from page 420 of *The TEXbook*. The LATEX logo is slightly modified from the one in `latex.tex` (we use a different font for the 'A'); similarly, the BIBTEX logo uses \sevenrm instead of a true caps-and-small-caps font. The `.mf` source file for the METAFONT logo is given in the METAFONT manual:

Knuth, Donald E., *The METAFONTbook*. Reading, Mass.: Addison-Wesley, 1986.

```
\def\LaTeX{L\kern-.26em \raise.6ex\hbox{\fiverm A}%
    \kern-.15em TeX}%
\def\AMSTeX{$\cal A\kern-.1667em \lower.5ex\hbox{$\cal M$}%
    \kern-.125em S$-\TeX}%
\def\BibTeX{{\rm B\kern-.05em {\sevenrm I\kern-.025em B}%
    \kern-.08em T\kern-.1667em \lower.7ex\hbox{E}%
    \kern-.125emX}}%
\font\mflogo = logo10
\def\MF{{\mflogo META}{\tenrm \-}{\mflogo FONT}}%
```

The next two macros produce boxes. \blackbox produces a "square bullet", used in the list macros (p. 298). \makeblankbox (from page 311 of *The TEXbook*) produces an unfilled rectangle, with the thickness of the border rules given by the arguments.

```
\def\blackbox{\vrule height .8ex width .6ex depth -.2ex}%
\def\makeblankbox#1#2{%
    \hbox{\lower\dp0\vbox{\hidehrule{#1}{#2}%
        \kern -#1% overlap rules
        \hbox to \wd0{\hidevrule{#1}{#2}%
            \raise\ht0\vbox to #1{}% vrule height
            \lower\dp0\vtop to #1{}% vrule depth
            \hfil\hidevrule{#2}{#1}}%
        \kern-#1\hidehrule{#2}{#1}}}}%
\def\hidehrule#1#2{\kern-#1\hrule height#1 depth#2
    \kern-#2}%
```

```
\def\hidevrule#1#2{\kern-#1{\dimen0 = #1
    \advance\dimen0 by #2 \vrule width\dimen0}\kern-#2}%
```

`\numbername` produces the written-out form of a number. (If the number is greater than ten, the macro just reproduces the numerals of its argument.)

```
\def\numbername#1{\ifcase#1%
    zero\or one\or two\or three\or four\or five%
    \or six\or seven\or eight\or nine\or ten\or #1\fi}%
```

`\testfileexistence` determines whether a file `\jobname.#1` is non-empty and sets `\iffileexists` appropriately. The file name in the argument need not end in a space token since the macro provides the space token.

```
\newif\iffileexists
\def\testfileexistence#1{\begingroup
    \immediate\openin0 = \jobname.#1\space
    \ifeof 0\global\fileexistsfalse
    \else \global\fileexiststrue\fi
    \immediate\closein0
\endgroup}%
```

Displays

By default, TEX centers displayed material (the material between `$$`'s). `\leftdisplays` causes displays to be left-justified by default. You can return to centered displays with `\centereddisplays`.

The macros here are more general than they need to be just for doing left-justified displays. For every display, `\ifeqno` will be true if an `\eqno` occurred in the display. `\ifleqno` will be true if an `\leqno` occurred. If either kind of equation number occurred, `\eqn` produces the text of the equation number. `\eq` always produces the text of the equation itself.

These macros are based on the code on page 376 of *The TEXbook*.

```
\newif\ifeqno \newif\ifleqno
\newtoks\@eqtoks \newtoks\@eqnotoks
\def\eq{\the\@eqtoks}\def\eqn{\the\@eqnotoks}%
\def\displaysetup#1$$%
    \@displaytest#1\eqno\eqno\@displaytest}%
\def\@displaytest#1\eqno#2\eqno#3\@displaytest{%
    \if #3% No \eqno, check for \leqno:
        \@ldisplaytest#1\leqno\leqno\@ldisplaytest
```

```
    \else
        \eqnotrue \leqnofalse % Have \eqno, not \leqno.
        \@eqnotoks = {#2}\@eqtoks = {#1}%
    \fi
    \generaldisplay$$}%
  \def\@ldisplaytest#1\leqno#2\leqno#3\@ldisplaytest{%
    \@eqtoks = {#1}%
    \if #3%
        \eqnofalse % No \leqno; we're done.
    \else
        \eqnotrue \leqnotrue % Have \leqno.
        \@eqnotoks = {#2}%
    \fi}%
```

You can format displays differently by defining your own macro,
analogous to \leftdisplays. The macro definition must place a call on
\displaysetup in \everydisplay so as to ensure that \displaysetup
is called at the start of every display. The macro definition must also
include a definition of \generaldisplay.

```
\newtoks\previouseverydisplay
\def\leftdisplays{%
    \previouseverydisplay = \everydisplay
    \everydisplay =
        {\the\previouseverydisplay \displaysetup}%
    \def\generaldisplay{%
        \leftline{%
            \strut \indent \hskip\leftskip
            \dimen0 = \parindent
            \advance\dimen0 by \leftskip
            \advance\displaywidth by -\dimen0
            \@redefinealignmentdisplays
            \ifeqno \ifleqno
                \kern-\dimen0
                \rlap{$\displaystyle\eqn$}%
                \kern\dimen0
            \fi\fi
            $\displaystyle{\eq}$%
            \ifeqno \ifleqno\else
                \hfill $\displaystyle{\eqn}$%
            \fi\fi}}}%
\def\centereddisplays{\let\displaysetup = \relax}%
```

\leftdisplays must go to some pains to make sure that \display-lines, \eqalignno, and \leqalignno still work properly. \eq is typeset in math mode, and \halign is illegal in math mode. We use \vcenter to change the context so that \halign becomes legal again. We also remove the \hfil commands at the left of the template to obtain the flush left formatting. Other than those changes, the macros are the same as in plain.tex.

```
\def\@redefinealignmentdisplays{%
   \def\displaylines##1{\displ@y
      \vcenter{\halign{\hbox to\displaywidth{$\@lign
            \displaystyle####\hfil$}\crcr##1\crcr}}%
   \def\eqalignno##1{\displ@y
      \vcenter{\halign to\displaywidth{%
            $\@lign\displaystyle{####}$\tabskip\z@skip
         &$\@lign\displaystyle{{}####}$
            \hfil\tabskip\centering
         &\llap{$\@lign####$}\tabskip\z@skip\crcr
            ##1\crcr}}%
   \def\leqalignno##1{\displ@y
      \vcenter{\halign to\displaywidth{%
            $\@lign\displaystyle{####}$\tabskip\z@skip
         &$\@lign\displaystyle{{}####}
            $\hfil\tabskip\centering
         &\kern-\displaywidth
            \rlap{\kern-\parindent\kern-\leftskip$
               \@lign####$}%
            \tabskip\displaywidth\crcr
            ##1\crcr}}}%
```

Time of day

When TeX starts up, it sets the values of the \time, \day, \month, and \year parameters. \monthname produces the name of the month, abbreviated to three letters. \timestring produces the current time, as in "1:14 p.m.". \timestamp produces the text of the complete date, as in "23 Apr 1964   1:14 p.m.".

```
\def\monthname{%
   \ifcase\month
      \or Jan\or Feb\or Mar\or Apr\or May\or Jun%
      \or Jul\or Aug\or Sep\or Oct\or Nov\or Dec%
   \fi}%
```

```
\def\timestring{\begingroup
   \count0 = \time \divide\count0 by 60
   \count2 = \count0    % The hour.
   \count4 = \time \multiply\count0 by 60
   \advance\count4 by -\count0    % The minute.
   \ifnum\count4<10 \toks1 = {0}% Get a leading zero.
   \else            \toks1 = {}%
   \fi
   \ifnum\count2<12 \toks0 = {a.m.}%
   \else            \toks0 = {p.m.}%
      \advance\count2 by -12
   \fi
   \ifnum\count2=0 \count2 = 12 \fi % Make midnight '12'.
   \number\count2:\the\toks1 \number\count4
   \thinspace \the\toks0
\endgroup}%
\def\timestamp{\number\day\space\monthname\space
   \number\year\quad\timestring}%
```

Lists

`\numberedlist` produces numbered lists; `\endnumberedlist` ends them.
`\unnumberedlist` is analogous. For either of these, items inside the
lists begin with `\li` ("list item"). You can put `\listcompact` at the
beginning of a list if you don't want any additional space between the
items of that list. Lists can be nested arbitrarily.

You can control the spacing between the items more generally by
assigning values to the registers listed below. If the items in your lists
tend to be long, you might want to make `\interitemskip` nonzero.
The left indentation of each list item is given by `\parindent` plus
`\listleftindent`; the right indentation of each list item is given by
`\listrightindent`.

```
\newskip\abovelistskip  \abovelistskip = .5\baselineskip
\newskip\interitemskip  \interitemskip = 0pt
\newskip\belowlistskip  \belowlistskip = .5\baselineskip
\newdimen\listleftindent  \listleftindent = \parindent
\newdimen\listrightindent \listrightindent = 0pt
\def\listcompact{\interitemskip = 0pt \relax}%
```

Both numbered and unnumbered lists use the macros that follow. We
don't change `\parindent`, since many existing macros, e.g., `\footnote`,
depend on `\parindent`. We must account for the possibility that items

are more than one paragraph long. In this case, all paragraphs after the first will be indented. We use `\leftskip` and `\rightskip` to indent the list items. Indentation of displays is accounted for by changes to `\everydisplay`.

```
\newdimen\@listindent
\def\beginlist{%
   \@listindent = \parindent
   \advance\@listindent by \listleftindent
   \everydisplay = \expandafter{\the\everydisplay
      % Don't lose user's \everydisplay:
      \advance\displayindent by \@listindent
      \advance\displaywidth by -\@listindent
      \advance\displaywidth by -\listrightindent}%
   \nobreak\vskip\abovelistskip
   \parskip = 0pt
   % \leftskip shifts nested lists to the right on the page.
   \advance\leftskip by \@listindent
   \advance\rightskip by \listrightindent}%
\def\printitem{\par\noindent
   \llap{\hskip-\listleftindent \marker \enspace}}%
\def\endlist{\vskip\belowlistskip}%
```

You can change the way the item labels are typeset by redefining the `\numberedmarker` macro.

```
\newcount\numberedlistdepth \newcount\itemnumber
\newcount\itemletter
\def\numberedmarker{%
   \ifcase\numberedlistdepth
        (impossible)%
   \or \itemnumberout)%
   \or \itemletterout)%
   \else *%
   \fi}%
```

Here are the definitions of `\numberedlist` and `\unnumberedlist`. Both definitions have the same structure.

```
\def\numberedlist{\environment{@numbered-list}%
   \advance\numberedlistdepth by 1
   \itemnumber = 1 \itemletter = `a
   \beginlist \let\marker = \numberedmarker
   \def\li{%
      \ifnum\itemnumber=1\else \vskip\interitemskip \fi
      \printitem
      \advance\itemnumber by 1 \advance\itemletter by 1
   }}%
```

```
\def\itemnumberout{\number\itemnumber}%
\def\itemletterout{\char\itemletter}%
\def\endnumberedlist{\par
    \endenvironment{@numbered-list}\endlist}%


\newcount\unorderedlistdepth
\def\unorderedmarker{%
    \ifcase\unorderedlistdepth
        (impossible)%
    \or \blackbox
    \or ---%
    \else *%
    \fi}%
\def\unorderedlist{\environment{@unordered-list}%
    \advance\unorderedlistdepth by 1
    \beginlist \itemnumber = 1
    \let\marker = \unorderedmarker
    \def\li{%
        \ifnum\itemnumber=1\else \vskip\interitemskip \fi
        \printitem \advance\itemnumber by 1
    }}%
\def\endunorderedlist{\par
    \endenvironment{@unordered-list}\endlist}%
```

Verbatim listing

The `\listing` macro produces a verbatim listing of a specified file in
the `\tt` font. It is based on the code on page 380 of *The TEXbook*.
Tabs produce a fixed amount of space, and form feeds produce a page
break. Other control characters produce whatever happens to be at that
font position, which is generally not very useful. By redefining `\setup-
listinghook`, you can take additional actions that are appropriate for
your particular fonts and/or environment before the file is read in.

```
\def\listing#1{%
    \par \begingroup \@setuplisting \setuplistinghook
    \input #1 \endgroup}%
\let\setuplistinghook = \empty
\def\@setuplisting{%
    \uncatcodespecials
    \obeywhitespace \makeactive\` \makeactive\^^I
    \def^^L{\vfill\eject}\tt}%
```

```
{\makeactive\` \gdef`{\relax\lq}}% Defeat ligatures.
{\makeactive\^^I\gdef^^I{\hskip8\fontdimen2\tt \relax}}%
```

Tables of contents

The macro `\writetocentry` writes a macro call to the file `\jobname.toc`.
The first argument of `\writetocentry`, e.g., "chapter", is used to compose
the name of the called macro. The second argument is the text to appear
in the table of contents entry. `\writetocentry` appends the page number
to the macro call. For example:

```
\writetocentry{chapter}{Introduction}
```

will produce the line:

```
\tocchapterentry{Introduction}{2}
```

in the `.toc` file, indicating that 'Introduction' started on page 2.

You can use `\writenumberedtocentry` to provide a third parameter,
such as a chapter number. For example:

```
\writenumberedtocentry{chapter}{The second chapter}{2}
```

will write a line:

```
\tocchapterentry{The second chapter}{2}{14}
```

You can also `\write` to `\tocfile` yourself.

```
\newwrite\tocfile \newif\iftocfileopened
\def\opentocfile{\iftocfileopened\else
        \tocfileopenedtrue
        \immediate\openout\tocfile = \jobname.toc
\fi}%
\def\writenumberedtocentry#1#2#3{\ifrewritetocfile
    \opentocfile
    \write\tocfile{%
        \expandafter\noexpand \csname toc#1entry\endcsname
        {#2}{#3}{\folio}}%
\ignorespaces\fi}%
\def\writenumberedtocentry#1#2#3{\ifrewritetocfile
    \opentocfile
    \write\tocfile{%
        \expandafter\noexpand \csname toc#1entry\endcsname
        {#2}{#3}{\folio}}%
\ignorespaces\fi}%
```

To produce a table of contents, read the `.toc` file with `\readtocfile`.
You should call `\readtocfile` before the first `\writetocentry`. When

you're processing the table of contents without regenerating it, you should not rewrite the .toc file—if you do, its contents will be lost. The command \rewritetocfilefalse will prevent the rewrite.

```
\newif\ifrewritetocfile \rewritetocfiletrue
\def\readtocfile{\testfileexistence{toc}%
    \iffileexists
        \input \jobname.toc
        \ifrewritetocfile \opentocfile \fi
    \fi}%
```

Here are some definitions of possible \toc...entry macros. These definitions are meant only as examples—running leaders across the line is usually not the best way to typeset a table of contents.

```
\def\tocchapterentry#1#2{\line{\bf #1 \dotfill\ #2}}%
\def\tocsectionentry#1#2{%
    \line{\quad\sl #1 \dotfill\ \rm #2}}%
\def\tocsubsectionentry#1#2{%
    \line{\qquad\rm #1 \dotfill\ #2}}%
```

Cross-references

The macros that follow provide symbolic cross-referencing, so that you can refer to something in another part of a document by name instead of by its actual page number. \xrdef{foo} defines a label **foo** to be the current page number, and \xrefn{foo} produces that page number, e.g., 77. More often you'll want to say something like "see p. 77", so \xref{foo} produces "p. 77". If **foo** is not defined, a warning message will be given. \xrefwarningfalse suppresses the warning.

These macros provide no protection against duplicate definitions. You can check for duplicate definitions by sorting the cross-reference file and checking, either mechanically or by eye, for adjacent definitions of the same symbol.

```
\newif\ifxrefwarning \xrefwarningtrue
\def\xrdef#1{\begingroup
    \xrlabel{#1}%
    \edef\@wr{\@writexrdef{\the\@xrlabeltoks}}%
    \@wr
    \endgroup \ignorespaces}%
\def\@writexrdef#1{\write\reffile{%
        \string\gdef
            \expandafter\string\csname#1\endcsname
```

```
                {\noexpand\folio}\percentchar}}%
\def\xrefnumber#1{%
  \xrlabel{#1}%
  % \@xrlabeltoks now has the control sequence name.
  \toks0 =
      \expandafter{\csname\the\@xrlabeltoks\endcsname}%
  \expandafter \ifx\the\toks0\relax
      \ifxrefwarning \message{Undefined label
          '\tokstostring{#1}'.}\fi
      {\let\spacesub = \space
       \expandafter\xdef\the\toks0
          {'{\tt \tokstostring{#1}}'}}\fi
  \the\toks0}%
\def\xref#1{p.\thinspace\xrefnumber{#1}}%
\def\xrefn#1{\xrefnumber{#1}}%
```

This macro turns a label into a list of character tokens in the token register `\labeltoks`. A label can include blanks and control sequences in it as well as normal characters, but it can't include braces.

```
\newtoks\@xrlabeltoks
\def\xrlabel#1{\begingroup
      \escapechar = '\_ \edef\tts{\tokstostring{#1_}}%
      \global\@xrlabeltoks = \expandafter{\tts}%
  \endgroup}%
```

It takes two passes to get the cross-references right, since the definitions are written out to the auxiliary file `\jobname.aux`. `\readreffile` reads them back in. If you don't issue this command before the first definition, you'll lose all the definitions from the previous run.

```
\newwrite\reffile \newif\ifreffileopened
\def\openreffile{\ifreffileopened\else
      \reffileopenedtrue
      \immediate\openout\reffile = \jobname.aux
  \fi}%
\def\readreffile{%
  \testfileexistence{aux}%
  \iffileexists
    \begingroup
      \@setletters
      \input \jobname.aux
    \endgroup
  \else
    \message{No cross-reference file; I won't give you
        warnings about undefined labels.}%
    \xrefwarningfalse
```

```
    \fi
    \openreffile}%
\def\@setletters{%
    \catcode'_ = \letter \catcode'+ = \letter
    \catcode'- = \letter \catcode'@ = \letter
    \catcode'0 = \letter \catcode'1 = \letter
    \catcode'2 = \letter \catcode'3 = \letter
    \catcode'4 = \letter \catcode'5 = \letter
    \catcode'6 = \letter \catcode'7 = \letter
    \catcode'8 = \letter \catcode'9 = \letter
    \catcode'( = \letter \catcode') = \letter}%
```

You can give symbolic names to equations in a similar way, using
\eqdef and \eqref. \eqdef inserts its own \eqno command, so it must
be invoked in a place where \eqno is legal.

```
\newcount\eqnumber
\def\eqdef#1{\global\advance\eqnumber by 1
    \expandafter\xdef
        \csname#1eqref\endcsname{\the\eqnumber}%
    \immediate\write\reffile{\string\def
        \expandafter\string\csname#1eqref\endcsname
            {\the\eqnumber}}%
    \eqno
    \eqprint{\the\eqnumber}}%
```

\eqref produces "(equation number)". You can handle fancier formatting by redefining \eqprint. For example, you could redefine it so that
the equation numbers include the chapter number.

```
\def\eqref#1{%
    \expandafter \ifx \csname#1eqref\endcsname \relax
        \ifxrefwarning \message{Undefined equation label
            '#1'.}\fi
        \expandafter\def\csname#1eqref\endcsname{00}%
    \else \eqprint{\csname#1eqref\endcsname}%
    \fi}%
\def\eqprint#1{(#1)}%
```

Environments

These macros let you define your own named groups (environments) for
parts of your manuscript. Like TEX groups, these groups can be nested,
and in fact their nesting can be intertwined with the nesting of TEX

groups. If the names at the beginning and end of an environment don't match, you'll get an error message. The macros are designed so that the message you get when such an error occurs will give you a good chance of localizing the cause of the error easily.

You begin an environment with `\environment {foo}` and end it with `\endenvironment{foo}`, where foo is the name of the environment. Our macros slightly improve on the answer to Exercise 5.7 of *The TEXbook*, by doing some checks on `\begingroup` and `\endgroup` pairs, as well as making sure `\environment` and `\endenvironment` pairs match.

```
\def\environment#1{\ifx\@groupname\undefined\else
      \errhelp = \@unnamedendgrouphelp
      \errmessage{'\@groupname' was not closed by
         \string\endenvironment}\fi
   \def\@groupname{#1}%
   \begingroup
      \let\@groupname = \undefined \ignorespaces}%
\def\endenvironment#1{\endgroup
   \def\@thearg{#1}%
   \ifx\@groupname\@thearg
   \else
      \ifx\@groupname\undefined
         \errhelp = \@isolatedendenvironmenthelp
         \errmessage{Isolated
            \string\endenvironment\space for '#1'}%
      \else
         \errhelp = \@mismatchedenvironmenthelp
         \errmessage{Environment '#1' ended,
            but '\@groupname' started}%
         \endgroup % Probably a typo in the names.
      \fi
   \fi
   \let\@groupname = \undefined \ignorespaces}%
```

We also define help messages for each of the errors above.

```
\newhelp\@unnamedendgrouphelp{%
   Most likely, you just forgot an^^J%
   \string\endenvironment.
   Maybe you should try inserting another^^J%
   \string\endgroup to recover.}%
\newhelp\@isolatedendenvironmenthelp{%
   You ended an environment X, but^^J%
   no \string\environment\space to start it
   is anywhere in sight.^^J%
   You might also be at an
```

```
    \string\endenvironment\space that would match^^J%
    a \string\begingroup, i.e., you forgot an
    \string\endgroup.}%
\newhelp\@mismatchedenvironmenthelp{%
    You started an environment X, but^^J%
    you ended it with Y.  Maybe you made a typo
    in one or the other^^J%
    of the names.}%
```

Some environments should not be allowed to occur within another environment. Let's call these environments "outer environments". \checkenv checks that no outer environment is currently in effect and complains if one is. To use \checkenv, you must issue the command \environment-true at the beginning of every outer environment.

```
\newif\ifenvironment
\def\checkenv{%
    \ifenvironment
        \errhelp = \@interwovenenvhelp
        \errmessage{Interwoven environments}%
        \endgroup
    \fi}%
\newhelp\@interwovenenvhelp{%
    Perhaps you forgot to end the previous^^J%
    environment? I'm finishing off the current group,^^J%
    hoping that will fix it.}%
```

Justification

The three macros \flushleft, \flushright, and \center justify the text on the following lines in the indicated way. The command should appear on a line by itself. Both the command and the text should be enclosed in a group—the end of the group indicates the end of the text. The entire group is set as a single paragraph, with lines filled out on one side or another as appropriate. Blank lines are reproduced.

```
\begingroup
    \catcode '\^^M = \active
    \globaldefs = 1 %
    \def\flushleft{\beforejustify %
        \aftergroup\@endflushleft %
        \def^^M{\null\hfil\break}%
        \def\@eateol^^M{}\@eateol}%
    \def\flushright{\beforejustify %
```

```
      \aftergroup\@endflushright %
      \def^^M{\break\null\hfil}%
      \def\@eateol^^M{\hfil\null}\@eateol}%
   \def\center {\beforejustify %
      \aftergroup\@endcenter %
      \def^^M{\hfil\break\null\hfil}%
      \def\@eateol^^M{\hfil\null}\@eateol}%
\endgroup
```

The following commands are called as a result of the \aftergroup in the definitions of \flushleft, \flushright, and \center. They perform the necessary cleanup operations.

```
\def\@endflushleft{\unpenalty
   {\parfillskip = 0pt plus 1 fil\par}%
   \ignorespaces}%
\def\@endflushright{%
   % Remove the \hfil\null\break we just put on.
   \unskip \setbox0=\lastbox \unpenalty
   % We have fil glue at the left of the line;
   % \parfillskip shouldn't affect that.
   {\parfillskip = 0pt \par}\ignorespaces}%
\def\@endcenter{%
   % Remove the \hfil\null\break we just put on.
   \unskip \setbox0=\lastbox \unpenalty
   % We have fil glue at the left of the line;
   % \parfillskip must balance it.
   {\parfillskip = 0pt plus 1fil \par}\ignorespaces}%
\def\beforejustify{%
   \par\noindent
   \catcode'\^^M = \active
   \checkenv \environmenttrue}%
```

Tables

The \makecolumns macro enables you to give all the entries in a table without having to worry about where the columns break. For example, if you're typing a long alphabetical list that will be formatted in several columns, you usually won't know in advance where one column ends and the next begins. Moreover, if another item gets added, the column breaks will change.

\makecolumns takes two (delimited) arguments: the total number of entries in the table and the number of columns in the table. For example,

'\makecolumns 37/3:' specifies a three-column table whose entries are the next 37 lines. You can adjust the positioning of the table on the page by changing \parindent, which determines the space to the left, and \hsize, which determines the space from the left margin of the page to the right of the block. You can allow a page break above the \valign by changing \abovecolumnspenalty.

```
\newcount\abovecolumnspenalty
\abovecolumnspenalty = 10000
\newcount\@linestogo        % Lines remaining to process.
\newcount\@linestogoincolumn % Lines remaining in column.
\newcount\@columndepth      % Number of lines in a column.
\newdimen\@columnwidth      % Width of each column.
\newtoks\crtok  \crtok = {\cr}%
\def\makecolumns#1/#2: {\par \begingroup
   \@columndepth = #1 \advance\@columndepth by #2
   \advance\@columndepth by -1
   \divide \@columndepth by #2
   \@linestogoincolumn = \@columndepth \@linestogo = #1
   \def\@endcolumnactions{%
      \ifnum \@linestogo<2
         \the\crtok \egroup \endgroup \par
            % End \valign and \makecolumns.
      \else
         \global\advance\@linestogo by -1
         \ifnum\@linestogoincolumn<2
            \global\@linestogoincolumn = \@columndepth
            \the\crtok
         \else &\global\advance\@linestogoincolumn by -1
         \fi
      \fi}%
\makeactive\^^M\letreturn\@endcolumnactions
\@columnwidth = \hsize
\advance\@columnwidth by -\parindent
\divide\@columnwidth by #2
\penalty\abovecolumnspenalty
\noindent % It's not a paragraph (usually).
\valign\bgroup
   &\hbox to \@columnwidth{\strut ##\hfil}\cr
}% The next end-of-line starts everything going.
```

Footnotes

Footnotes are most commonly typeset by using a raised number as the reference mark. We define the `\numberedfootnote` macro to do this. It also redefines `\vfootnote` to allow slightly more general formatting of footnotes than plain TeX does. The dimension register `\footnote-markseparation` controls the space between the footnote mark (e.g., the number) and the beginning of the text. The `\everyfootnote` tokens are inserted before producing the footnote.

The plain TeX definitions of `\footnote` and `\vfootnote` are preserved in `\@plainfootnote` and `\@plainvfootnote` in case you should need them.

```
\newcount\footnotenumber \newtoks\everyfootnote
\newdimen\footnotemarkseparation
\footnotemarkseparation = .5em
\let\@plainfootnote = \footnote
\let\@plainvfootnote = \vfootnote
\def\vfootnote#1{\insert\footins\bgroup
  \interlinepenalty\interfootnotelinepenalty
  \splittopskip\ht\strutbox \splitmaxdepth\dp\strutbox
  \floatingpenalty\@MM
  \leftskip\z@skip \rightskip\z@skip \spaceskip\z@skip
  \xspaceskip\z@skip
  \everypar = {}%
  \the\everyfootnote
  \indent\llap{#1\kern\footnotemarkseparation}\footstrut
  \futurelet\next\fo@t}%
\def\numberedfootnote{\global\advance\footnotenumber by 1
  \@plainfootnote{$^{\number\footnotenumber}$}}%
```

Double columns

The `\doublecolumns` command begins double-column output, while the `\singlecolumn` command restores single-column output. You can switch back and forth between them on a single page. The glue specified by `\abovedoublecolumnskip` and `\belowdoublecolumnskip` is inserted before and after the double-column material.

The approach is derived from page 417 of *The TeXbook*.

```
\newskip\abovedoublecolumnskip
```

```
\newskip\belowdoublecolumnskip
\abovedoublecolumnskip = \bigskipamount
\belowdoublecolumnskip = \bigskipamount
\newdimen\gutter                  \gutter = 2pc
\newdimen\doublecolumnhsize \doublecolumnhsize = \hsize
\newbox\@partialpage              \newdimen\singlecolumnhsize
\newdimen\singlecolumnvsize \newtoks\previousoutput
\def\doublecolumns{\par % Don't start in horizontal mode.
   \previousoutput = \expandafter{\the\output}
   \advance\doublecolumnhsize by -\gutter
   \divide\doublecolumnhsize by 2
   \output = {\global\setbox\@partialpage =
        \vbox{\unvbox255\vskip\abovedoublecolumnskip}}%
   \pagegoal = \pagetotal \break % Expands \output above.
   \output = {\doublecolumnoutput}%
   \singlecolumnhsize = \hsize
   \singlecolumnvsize = \vsize
   \hsize = \doublecolumnhsize \vsize = 2\vsize}%
```

The `\@doublecolumnsplit` macro does the actual splitting. Insertions
are assumed to be single-column material. If you don't want this to be
the case, you'll have to modify the output routine. After `\@double-`
`columnsplit` has done its work, `\box255` will have the double-column
material. The double-column material will be preceded by any single-
column material that was typeset before `\doublecolumns` was invoked.
`\box4` will have the material that didn't fit on the page.

```
\def\@doublecolumnsplit{%
   \splittopskip = \topskip \splitmaxdepth = \maxdepth
   \dimen0 = \singlecolumnvsize
      \advance\dimen0 by -\ht\@partialpage
      \advance\dimen0 by -\ht\footins
      \advance\dimen0 by -\skip\footins
      \advance\dimen0 by -\ht\topins
   \begingroup
      \vbadness = 10000
      \global\setbox1=\vsplit255 to \dimen0 \wd1=\hsize
      \global\setbox3=\vsplit255 to \dimen0 \wd3=\hsize
   \endgroup
   \global\setbox4=\vbox{\unvbox255
      \penalty\outputpenalty}%
   \global\setbox255=\vbox{\unvbox\@partialpage
      \hbox to \singlecolumnhsize{\box1\hfil\box3}%
      \vfill}}%
```

\doublecolumnoutput is the real output routine. We call the old \output to do the work of actually shipping out the box.

```
\def\doublecolumnoutput{\@doublecolumnsplit
    \hsize = \singlecolumnhsize \vsize = \singlecolumnvsize
    \previousoutput \unvbox4}%
```

\singlecolumn resumes typesetting in one column. It assumes that \doublecolumns has been called.

```
\def\singlecolumn{\par % Don't start in horizontal mode.
    \output = {\global\setbox1 =
        \vbox{\unvbox255\vskip\abovedoublecolumnskip}}%
    \pagegoal = \pagetotal \break \setbox255 = \box1
    {\singlecolumnvsize = \ht255
        \divide\singlecolumnvsize by 2
        \advance\singlecolumnvsize by +\ht\@partialpage
        \advance\singlecolumnvsize by +\ht\footins
        \advance\singlecolumnvsize by +\skip\footins
        \advance\singlecolumnvsize by +\ht\topins
    \@doublecolumnsplit}%
    \hsize = \singlecolumnhsize
    \vsize = \singlecolumnvsize
    \output = \expandafter{\the\previousoutput}%
    \unvbox255}%
```

Finishing up

We now must undo the changes that we made when we started (see p. 292). We also give a version identification, which is subsequently available in \fmtname and \fmtversion.

```
\let\wlog = \@plainwlog \catcode`\@ = \other
\def\fmtname{eplain}%
{\edef\plainversion{\fmtversion}%
 \xdef\fmtversion{1.0: 15 May 1990
    (and plain \plainversion)}%
}%
```

13 ∎ Capsule summary of commands

This section contains one-line descriptions of the primitive TEX commands and the TEX commands defined in plain TEX. These include both control sequences and special characters. We've omitted those commands that are only intended for internal use in the plain TEX definition (Appendix B of *The TEXbook*). Note that ordinary characters such as 'a' or '6' are also commands, and indeed the most common ones (see "character", p. 55).

To keep the descriptions brief, we've adopted certain conventions:

- An asterisk in front of a command indicates that the command is primitive, i.e., built into the TEX computer program (see "primitive", p. 88).
- The words "music", "punctuation", "function", "symbol", "relation", "delimiter", or "operator" in a command description imply that the command is only legal in math modes.
- The verb "display" applies to information that TEX sends to the log file, unless otherwise indicated. If \tracingonline is positive, TEX also sends that output to the terminal. We use the noun "display" to refer to math displays (see p. 61), i.e., material between $$'s.
- The phrase "produce x" indicates that the command will typeset x and put the result in a box. We sometimes omit "produce" when the omission is unlikely to cause confusion. For example, we describe \alpha as "math Greek letter α", not "produce the math Greek letter α".

*\␣ interword space (p. 104)
 \! negative thin space for math (p. 214)
 \" umlaut accent for text, as in ö (p. 100)

\#   introduce a macro parameter, or indicate where the text of an entry goes in an alignment preamble (p. 75, p. 45)

\\#   produce # character from current font (p. 98)

\$ begin or end a math formula (p. 16)

\\$ produce \$ character from current font (p. 98)

* %   begin a comment (p. 13)

\\%   produce % character from current font (p. 98)

\&   separate templates and entries in an alignment (p. 44)

\\&   produce & character from current font (p. 98)

'   prime symbol for math, as in p' (p. 188)

\'   acute accent for text, as in é (p. 100)

*   multiplication symbol that allows a line break (p. 190)

\+   begin tabbed line (p. 176)

\,   thin space for math (p. 214)

*\-   specify a legal hyphenation point (p. 126)

\.   dot accent for text, as in ṅ (p. 100)

*\/   italic correction for the previous character (p. 106)

\;   thick space for math (p. 214)

\=   macron accent for text, as in r̄ (p. 100)

* \   begin a control sequence (p. 10)

\>   medium space for math (p. 214)

^   produce a specified subformula as a superscript (p. 197)

\^   circumflex accent for text, as in ô (p. 100)

^^L   equivalent to the \par primitive (p. 110)

*^^M   an end-of-line (p. 105)

_   produce a specified subformula as a subscript (p. 197)

_   underscore: _ (p. 98)

\`   grave accent for text, as in è (p. 100)

\{   start a group (p. 227)

\\{   left brace delimiter for math: { (p. 191)

\\| parallel lines for math: ‖ (p. 188)

}   end a group (p. 227)

\\}   right brace delimiter for math: } (p. 191)

~   interword space at which a line will not break (p. 105)

\~   tilde accent for text, as in ã (p. 100)

\aa   Scandinavian letter: å (p. 97)

\AA   Scandinavian letter: Å (p. 97)

*\above   produce a fraction with a bar of specified thickness (p. 200)

*\abovedisplayshortskip   glue TEX inserts before a display when the previous line fits in the display's indentation, by default 0 pt plus 3 pt (p. 217)

*`\abovedisplayskip` glue TEX inserts before a display when the previous line doesn't fit in the display's indentation, by default 12 pt plus 3 pt minus 9 pt (p. 217)

*`\abovewithdelims` produce a fraction with a bar of specified thickness and surrounded by specified delimiters (p. 201)

*`\accent` put specified accent over the next character (p. 100)

`\active` category code for active characters, viz., the number 13 (p. 251)

`\acute` acute accent for math, as in $\acute{x}$ (p. 199)

*`\adjdemerits` additional demerits for a line break which would result in adjacent lines with incompatible word spacing, by default 10000 (p. 125)

*`\advance` add a number to a `\count` register (p. 245)

`\advancepageno` if `\pageno` is positive, add one; if it's negative, subtract one (p. 142)

`\ae` æ ligature (p. 97)

`\AE` Æ ligature (p. 97)

*`\afterassignment` wait to expand the following token until the next assignment is done (p. 229)

*`\aftergroup` wait to expand the following token until the end of the current group (p. 229)

`\aleph` only Hebrew letter for math: ℵ (p. 188)

`\allowbreak` do `\penalty0`, i.e., allow a line or page break where one could not ordinarily occur (p. 121, p. 136)

`\alpha` math Greek letter α (p. 187)

`\amalg` amalgamation operator: ⨿ (p. 189)

`\angle` angle symbol: ∠ (p. 188)

`\approx` approximation relation: ≈ (p. 190)

`\arccos` arc cosine function: arccos (p. 193)

`\arcsin` arc sine function: arcsin (p. 193)

`\arctan` arc tangent function: arctan (p. 193)

`\arg` argument (phase) function: arg (p. 193)

`\arrowvert` vertical portion of an extensible double arrow (p. 212)

`\Arrowvert` vertical portion of an extensible single arrow (p. 212)

`\ast` asterisk operator: ∗ (p. 189)

`\asymp` asymptote relation: ≍ (p. 190)

*`\atop` produce a fraction without a fraction bar (p. 200)

*`\atopwithdelims` produce a fraction without a fraction bar and surrounded by specified delimiters (p. 201)

`\b` bar-under accent for math, as in x̲ (p. 199)

`\backslash` backslash symbol: \ (p. 188)

*`\badness` the badness of the glue setting in the last box made (p. 170)

`\bar`   bar accent for math, as in $\bar{x}$ (p. 199)

*`\baselineskip`   glue for the normal vertical distance from one baseline to the next, by default 12 pt (p. 133)

*`\batchmode`   don't stop at errors and don't output to terminal (p. 253)

*`\begingroup`   start a group to be ended by `\endgroup` (p. 227)

`\beginsection`   begin a major subdivision of a document (p. 129)

*`\belowdisplayshortskip`   glue TeX inserts after a display when the previous line fits in the display's indentation, by default 7 pt plus 0.3 pt minus 4 pt (p. 217)

*`\belowdisplayskip`   glue TeX inserts after a display when the previous line doesn't fit in the display's indentation, by default 12 pt plus 3 pt minus 9 pt (p. 217)

`\beta`   math Greek letter β (p. 187)

`\bf`   use boldface, i.e., do `\tenbf\fam=\bffam` (p. 103)

`\bffam`   boldface family for math (p. 210)

`\bgroup`   implicit beginning-of-group character (p. 227)

`\big`   make the specified delimiter larger than an ordinary one, but still small enough for text (p. 211)

`\Big`   make the specified delimiter about 11.5 pt tall (p. 211)

`\bigbreak`   indicate desirable page break with `\penalty-200` and produce `\bigskipamount` glue (p. 137)

`\bigcap`   large cap operator (no, it doesn't produce a large capital letter!): $\bigcap$ (p. 194)

`\bigcirc`   large circle operator: $\bigcirc$ (p. 189)

`\bigcup`   large cup operator: $\bigcup$ (p. 194)

`\bigg`   make the specified delimiter about 14.5 pt tall (p. 211)

`\Bigg`   make specified delimiter about 17.5 pt tall (p. 211)

`\biggl`   sized like `\bigg`, but spaced as an opening (p. 211)

`\Biggl`   sized like `\Bigg`, but spaced as an opening (p. 211)

`\biggm`   sized like `\bigg`, but spaced as a relation (p. 211)

`\Biggm`   sized like `\Bigg`, but spaced as a relation (p. 211)

`\biggr`   sized like `\bigg`, but spaced as a closing (p. 211)

`\Biggr`   sized like `\Bigg`, but spaced as a closing (p. 211)

`\bigl`   sized like `\big`, but spaced as an opening (p. 211)

`\Bigl`   sized like `\Big`, but spaced as an opening (p. 211)

`\bigm`   sized like `\big`, but spaced as a relation (p. 211)

`\Bigm`   sized like `\Big`, but spaced as a relation (p. 211)

`\bigodot`   large circled dot operator: $\bigodot$ (p. 194)

`\bigoplus`   large circled plus operator: $\bigoplus$ (p. 194)

`\bigotimes`   large circled times operator: $\bigotimes$ (p. 194)

`\bigr`   sized like `\big`, but spaced as a closing (p. 211)

`\Bigr`   sized like `\Big`, but spaced as a closing (p. 211)

\bigskip   produce \bigskipamount glue (p. 154)

\bigskipamount   glue for a big vertical skip, by default 12 pt plus 4 pt minus 4 pt (p. 155)

\bigsqcup   large square cup operator: $\bigsqcup$ (p. 194)

\bigtriangledown   triangle operator pointing downward: $\bigtriangledown$ (p. 189)

\bigtriangleup   triangle operator pointing upward: $\triangle$ (p. 189)

\biguplus   large cupped plus operator: $\biguplus$ (p. 194)

\bigvee   large logical "or" operator: $\bigvee$ (p. 194)

\bigwedge   large logical "and" operator: $\bigwedge$ (p. 194)

*\binoppenalty   additional penalty for breaking after a binary math operator, by default 700 (p. 126)

\bmod   modulus operator, as in $n \bmod 2$ (p. 193)

\bordermatrix   produce matrix with labelled rows and columns (p. 205)

\bot   lattice bottom symbol: $\bot$ (p. 188)

*\botmark   the last mark item on the page just boxed (p. 144)

\bowtie   bowtie relation: $\bowtie$ (p. 190)

*\box   append the box in a specified box register to the current list, and void the register (p. 164)

*\boxmaxdepth   maximum depth of vboxes, by default \maxdimen (p. 163)

\brace $n\brace k$ produces braced notation: $\left\{ {n \atop k} \right\}$ (p. 200)

\bracevert   vertical portion of extensible large brace (p. 212)

\brack $n\brack k$ produces bracketed notation: $\left[{n \atop k} \right]$ (p. 200)

\break   do \penalty-10000, i.e., force a line or page break (p. 120, p. 136)

\breve   breve accent for math, as in $\breve{x}$ (p. 199)

*\brokenpenalty   penalty for line break at a discretionary item, by default 100 (p. 139)

\buildrel   produce specified formula over the specified relation (p. 202)

\bullet   bullet operation: $\bullet$ (p. 189)

\bye   \vfill the last page with blank space, \supereject it, and \end the job (p. 246)

\c   cedilla accent for text, as in ç (p. 100)

\cal   use calligraphic font for uppercase letters in math, as in $\mathcal{XYZ}$ (p. 209)

\cap   cap operator: $\cap$ (p. 189)

\cases   produce cases for math, as in $\left\{ {\vdots} \right.$ (p. 201)

*\catcode   the category code of a specified character (p. 251)

\cdot   centered dot operator: $\cdot$ (p. 189)

\cdotp   centered dot punctuation: $\cdot$ (p. 196)

\cdots   centered dots for math: $\cdots$ (p. 203)

\centerline   produce line with its text centered (p. 108)

*\char   produce the character from the current font with the specified code (p. 99)

*\chardef   define a specified control sequence to be a character's code, a number between 0 and 255 (p. 232)

\check   check accent for math, as in $\check{x}$ (p. 199)

\chi   math Greek letter χ (p. 187)

\choose $n\choose k$ produces combinatorial notation: $\binom{n}{k}$ (p. 200)

\circ   circle operation: $\circ$ (p. 189)

*\cleaders   produce leaders with half of leftover space before the first box, and half after the last (p. 174)

\cleartabs   clear all the tabs for tabbing alignments (p. 177)

*\closein   close a specified input stream (p. 248)

*\closeout   close a specified output stream (p. 249)

*\clubpenalty   additional penalty for a single line remaining before a page break, by default 150 (p. 138)

\clubsuit   club suit symbol: $\clubsuit$ (p. 188)

\colon   colon punctuation symbol for math: : (p. 196)

\cong   congruence relation: $\cong$ (p. 190)

\coprod   coproduct operator: $\coprod$ (p. 194)

*\copy   like \box, but don't void the register (p. 164)

\copyright   copyright mark: © (p. 98)

\cos   cosine function: cos (p. 193)

\cosh   hyperbolic cosine function: cosh (p. 193)

\cot   cotangent function : cot (p. 193)

\coth   hyperbolic cotangent function: coth (p. 193)

*\count   the specified integer register (p. 242)

*\countdef   define a specified control sequence to be a number corresponding to a \count register (p. 245)

*\cr   end a row (or column) within an alignment (p. 180)

*\crcr   does nothing if the last command was \cr or \noalign; otherwise, equivalent to \cr (p. 180)

\csc   cosecant function: csc (p. 193)

*\csname   start a control sequence name to be ended by \endcsname (p. 233)

\cup   cup operator: $\cup$ (p. 189)

\d   underdot accent for text, as in $\d{r}$ (p. 100)

\dag   dagger symbol for text: † (p. 98)

\dagger   dagger operator for math: $\dagger$ (p. 189)

\dashv   right turnstile relation: $\dashv$ (p. 190)

*\day   current day of the month, as a number (p. 225)

\ddag   double dagger symbol for text: ‡ (p. 98)

\ddagger   double dagger operator for math: $\ddagger$ (p. 189)

\ddot   double dot accent for math: $\ddot{x}$ (p. 199)

\ddots   diagonal dots for math: $\ddots$ (p. 203)

*\deadcycles   number of \output initiations since the last \shipout (p. 148)

*\def   define a control sequence to be a macro (p. 230)

*\defaulthyphenchar   default hyphenation character code (p. 129)

*\defaultskewchar   default accent skewing character code (p. 213)

\deg   degree function: deg (p. 193)

*\delcode   the delimiter code of a specified character (p. 251)

*\delimiter   produce a specified delimiter (p. 204)

*\delimiterfactor   1000 times the ratio of the minimum size of a delimiter to the size that would completely cover the formula, by default 901 (p. 205)

*\delimitershortfall   minimum difference between formula height and delimiter height, by default 5 pt (p. 205)

\delta   math Greek letter δ (p. 187)

\Delta   math Greek letter Δ (p. 187)

\det   determinant function: det (p. 193)

\diamond   diamond operator: $\diamond$ (p. 189)

\diamondsuit   diamond suit symbol: $\diamondsuit$ (p. 188)

\dim   dimension function: dim (p. 193)

*\dimen   the specified dimension register (p. 242)

*\dimendef   define a specified control sequence to be a number corresponding to a \dimen register (p. 245)

*\discretionary   specify three texts, the first two for before and after a line break, the third for no line break (p. 127)

*\displayindent   TeX sets this to the indentation of a display (p. 216)

*\displaylimits   place limits above and below operators only in display styles (p. 195)

\displaylines   produce specified multiline display with each line centered (p. 208)

*\displaystyle   use displaystyle size in a formula (p. 198)

*\displaywidowpenalty   penalty for a single line beginning a page just before a display, by default 50 (p. 138)

*\displaywidth   TeX sets this to the width of a display (p. 216)

\div   division operator: $\div$ (p. 189)

*\divide   divide a specified \count register by a specified integer (p. 246)

\dot   dot accent for math, as in $\dot{x}$ (p. 199)

\doteq   dotted equality relation: $\doteq$ (p. 190)

\dotfill   fill enclosing horizontal space with dots (p. 175)

\dots   ellipsis for sequences: $x_1, \ldots, x_n$ (p. 99)

*\doublehyphendemerits   demerits for two consecutive lines ending with hyphens, by default 10000 (p. 125)

\downarrow   relation: ↓ (p. 192)

\Downarrow   relation: ⇓ (p. 192)

\downbracefill   fill enclosing hbox with a downwards facing brace: ⏜ (p. 211)

*\dp   the depth of the box in a specified box register (p. 167)

*\dump   end the job and produce a format file (p. 263)

*\edef   define a control sequence to be a macro, immediately expanding the replacement text (p. 230)

\egroup   implicit end-of-group character (p. 227)

\eject   end current paragraph and force a page break, stretching out current page (p. 137)

\ell   script letter for math: ℓ (p. 188)

*\else   false or default case alternative for a conditional (p. 239)

*\emergencystretch   additional stretch added to every line if \tolerance is not satisfied (p. 124)

\empty   macro that expands to nothing (p. 241)

\emptyset   empty set symbol: $\emptyset$ (p. 188)

*\end   \output the last page and end the job (p. 247)

*\endcsname   end a control sequence name started by \csname (p. 233)

\endgraf   equivalent to the \par primitive (p. 111)

*\endgroup   end a group started by \begingroup (p. 227)

*\endinput   terminate input from the current file (p. 247)

\endinsert   end insertion (p. 147)

\endline   equivalent to the \cr primitive (p. 180)

*\endlinechar   character TeX inserts at the end of each input line, by default ^^M (p. 252)

\enskip   horizontal glue with width $1/2$ em (p. 154)

\enspace   kern $1/2$ em (p. 154)

\epsilon   math Greek letter ϵ (p. 187)

\eqalign   produce specified multiline display whose indicated parts are vertically aligned (p. 208)

\eqalignno   produce specified multiline display with equation numbers whose indicated parts are vertically aligned (p. 208)

*\eqno   put a specified equation number on the right of a display (p. 207)

\equiv   equivalence relation: $\equiv$ (p. 190)

*\errhelp   token list whose expansion TeX displays when the user asks for help in response to an \errmessage (p. 261)

*\errmessage   give specified error message (p. 261)

*\errorcontextlines   the number of lines of context TeX displays at an error, by default 5 (p. 262)

*\errorstopmode stop for interaction at error messages (p. 252)

*\escapechar character with which TEX precedes control sequence names that are displayed (p. 226)

\eta math Greek letter η (p. 187)

*\everycr token list TEX expands after a \cr, or a \crcr not following \cr or \noalign (p. 185)

*\everydisplay token list TEX expands when a math display begins (p. 218)

*\everyhbox token list TEX expands when an hbox begins (p. 164)

*\everyjob token list TEX expands when a job begins (p. 263)

*\everymath token list TEX expands when text math mode begins (p. 218)

*\everypar token list TEX expands when a paragraph begins (p. 113)

*\everyvbox token list TEX expands when a vbox begins (p. 164)

*\exhyphenpenalty additional penalty for a line break after an explicit hyphen, by default 50 (p. 125)

\exists "there exists" symbol: $\exists$ (p. 188)

\exp exponential function: exp (p. 193)

*\expandafter expand the next token only after expanding the token following it (p. 233)

*\fam font family TEX uses for characters with class seven (i.e., variables) in math (p. 210)

*\fi end a conditional (p. 240)

\filbreak force a page break unless the text up to another \filbreak also fits on the page (p. 137)

*\finalhyphendemerits penalty for the second to last line breaking at a hyphen, by default 5000 (p. 126)

*\firstmark first mark item on the page just boxed (p. 144)

\fivebf use 5-point bold font, cmbx5 (p. 102)

\fivei use 5-point math italic font, cmmi5 (p. 102)

\fiverm use 5-point roman font, cmr5 (p. 102)

\fivesy use 5-point symbol font, cmsy5 (p. 102)

\flat flat symbol for music: $\flat$ (p. 188)

*\floatingpenalty penalty for insertions that are split across pages, by default 0 (p. 139)

\fmtname name of the current format (p. 225)

\fmtversion version number of the current format (p. 225)

\folio produce \pageno as characters; in roman numerals if it's negative (p. 143)

*\font define a specified control sequence to select a font (p. 221)

*\fontdimen a specified parameter of a specified font (p. 222)

*\fontname produce the filename of a specified font as characters (p. 227)

\footline   token list that produces line at the bottom of each page
   (p. 143)

\footnote   produce a specified footnote with a specified reference mark
   (p. 145)

\forall   "for all" symbol: ∀ (p. 188)

\frenchspacing   make interword spacing independent of punctuation
   (p. 106)

\frown   frown relation: ⌢ (p. 190)

*\futurelet   assign the third following token to a specified control
   sequence, then expand the second following token (p. 232)

\gamma   math Greek letter γ (p. 187)

\Gamma   math Greek letter Γ (p. 187)

\gcd   greatest common denominator function: gcd (p. 193)

*\gdef   equivalent to \global\def, i.e., globally define a macro (p. 231)

\ge   greater than or equal relation: ≥ (p. 190)

\geq   equivalent to \ge (p. 190)

\gets   gets relation: ← (p. 192)

\gg   much greater than relation: ≫ (p. 190)

*\global   make the following definition global (p. 228)

*\globaldefs   overrides \global prefixes on assignments (p. 228)

\goodbreak   indicate desirable page break with \penalty-500 (p. 137)

\grave   grave accent for math, as in $\grave{x}$ (p. 199)

\H   Hungarian umlaut accent for text, as in ő (p. 100)

*\halign   align text in columns (p. 178)

\hang   indent the current paragraph by \parindent (p. 117)

*\hangafter   starting line number for hanging indentation (p. 117)

*\hangindent   space for hanging indentation (p. 117)

\hat   hat accent for math, as in $\hat{x}$ (p. 199)

*\hbadness   badness threshold for reporting underfull or overfull hboxes,
   by default 1000 (p. 170)

\hbar   math symbol: ℏ (p. 188)

*\hbox   produce a specified hbox (p. 160)

\headline   token list that produces the line at the top of every page
   (p. 143)

\heartsuit   heart suit symbol: ♡ (p. 188)

*\hfil   produce infinitely stretchable horizontal glue (p. 157)

*\hfill   produce horizontal glue even more infinitely stretchable than
   that produced by \hfil (p. 157)

*\hfilneg   produce infinitely negative stretchable horizontal glue (p. 159)

*\hfuzz   space threshold for reporting overfull hboxes, by default 0.1 pt
   (p. 171)

`\hglue`   produce horizontal glue that doesn't disappear at line breaks (p. 156)

`\hidewidth`   ignore width of an entry in an alignment, so that it extends out from its box in the direction of the `\hidewidth` (p. 184)

*`\hoffset`   page offset relative to one inch from the paper's left edge (p. 140)

*`\holdinginserts`   if positive, do not remove insertions from the current page (p. 149)

`\hom`   homology function: hom (p. 193)

`\hookleftarrow`   relation: ↩ (p. 192)

`\hookrightarrow`   relation: ↪ (p. 192)

`\hphantom`   produce an invisible formula with zero height and depth but natural width (p. 169)

*`\hrule`   produce a horizontal rule; legal only in vertical modes (p. 172)

`\hrulefill`   fill enclosing space with a horizontal rule (p. 175)

*`\hsize`   line length, by default 6.5 in (p. 114)

*`\hskip`   produce specified horizontal glue (p. 155)

*`\hss`   produce horizontal glue that is infinitely stretchable and infinitely shrinkable (p. 158)

*`\ht`   the height of the box in a specified box register (p. 167)

*`\hyphenation`   add specified words to the hyphenation exception dictionary (p. 127)

*`\hyphenchar`   the hyphenation character in a specified font (p. 129)

*`\hyphenpenalty`   additional penalty for a line break at a hyphen, by default 50 (p. 125)

`\i`   dotless letter 'ı' for use with accents (p. 100)

`\ialign`   start an `\halign` with the `\tabskip` glue zero and `\everycr` empty (p. 180)

*`\if`   test if two specified tokens have the same character code (p. 235)

*`\ifcase`   expand case n for specified value n (p. 239)

*`\ifcat`   test if two specified tokens have the same category code (p. 235)

*`\ifdim`   test for a specified relationship between two specified dimensions (p. 237)

*`\ifeof`   test for being at the end of a specified file (p. 239)

`\iff`   if and only if relation: ⟺ (p. 192)

*`\iffalse`   test that is always false (p. 239)

*`\ifhbox`   test if a specified box register contains an hbox (p. 238)

*`\ifhmode`   test if TEX is in a horizontal mode (p. 238)

*`\ifinner`   test if TEX is in an internal mode (p. 238)

*`\ifmmode`   test if TEX is in a math mode (p. 238)

*`\ifnum`   test for a specified relationship between two specified numbers (p. 237)

*\ifodd   test if a specified number is odd (p. 237)

*\iftrue   test that is always true (p. 239)

*\ifvbox   test if a specified box register contains a vbox (p. 238)

*\ifvmode   test if TeX is in a vertical mode (p. 238)

*\ifvoid   test if a specified box register is void (p. 238)

*\ifx   test if two tokens are the same, or if two macros have the same top-level definition (p. 236)

*\ignorespaces   ignore any following space tokens (p. 252)

\Im   complex imaginary part symbol: $\Im$ (p. 188)

\imath   dotless letter '$\imath$' for use with math accents (p. 188)

*\immediate   perform the specified file operation without delay (p. 250)

\in   containment relation: $\in$ (p. 190)

*\indent   produce an empty box of width \parindent and enter horizontal mode (p. 111)

\inf   inferior function: inf (p. 193)

\infty   infinity symbol: ∞ (p. 188)

*\input   begin to read from a specified file (p. 247)

*\inputlineno   the current line number of the current input file (p. 247)

*\insert   produce an insertion of a specified class (p. 147)

*\insertpenalties   sum of penalties due to insertions (p. 139)

\int   integral symbol: $\int$ (p. 194)

*\interlinepenalty   additional penalty for a page break between lines of a paragraph, by default 0 (p. 138)

\iota   math Greek letter ι (p. 187)

\it   use italics, i.e., do \tenit\fam=\itfam (p. 103)

\item   begin a paragraph with hanging indentation of \parindent and preceded by a specified label (p. 130)

\itemitem   like \item, but with indentation of 2\parindent (p. 130)

\itfam   italic family for math (p. 210)

\j   dotless letter 'ȷ', for use with accents (p. 100)

\jmath   dotless letter '$\jmath$' for use with math accents (p. 188)

*\jobname   base name of the file with which TeX was invoked (p. 225)

\jot   unit of measure for opening up displays (p. 215)

\kappa   math Greek letter κ (p. 187)

\ker   kernel function: ker (p. 193)

*\kern   produce a specified amount of space at which a break is not allowed (p. 157)

\l   Polish letter: ł (p. 97)

\L   Polish letter: Ł (p. 97)

\lambda   math Greek letter λ (p. 187)

\Lambda   math Greek letter Λ (p. 187)

\land   logical "and" operator: ∧ (p. 189)

\langle   left angle delimiter: ⟨ (p. 191)

*\language   the current set of hyphenation patterns (p. 128)

*\lastbox   retrieve and remove the last item from the current list, if it's a box (p. 171)

*\lastkern   retrieve the last item from the current list, if it's a kern (p. 171)

*\lastpenalty   retrieve the last item from the current list, if it's a penalty (p. 171)

*\lastskip   retrieve the last item from the current list, if it's glue (p. 171)

\lbrace   left brace delimiter: { (p. 191)

\lbrack   left bracket delimiter: [(p. 191)

*\lccode   the character code for the lowercase form of a letter (p. 103)

\lceil   left ceiling delimiter: ⌈ (p. 191)

\ldotp   dot on baseline as punctuation: . (p. 196)

\ldots   dots on baseline for math: ... (p. 203)

\le   less than or equal relation: ≤ (p. 190)

*\leaders   fill a specified horizontal or vertical space by repeating a specified box or rule (p. 174)

*\left   produce the specified delimiter, sizing it to cover the following subformula ended by \right (p. 204)

\leftarrow   relation: ← (p. 192)

\Leftarrow   relation: ⇐ (p. 192)

\leftarrowfill   fill enclosing hbox with a \leftarrow: ⟵ (p. 175)

\leftharpoondown   relation: ↽ (p. 192)

\leftharpoonup   relation: ↼ (p. 192)

*\lefthyphenmin   size of the smallest word fragment TEX allows before a hyphen at the beginning of a word, by default 2 (p. 128)

\leftline   produce line with its text pushed to left margin (p. 108)

\leftrightarrow   relation: ↔ (p. 192)

\Leftrightarrow   relation: ⇔ (p. 192)

*\leftskip   glue TEX inserts at the left of each line (p. 115)

\leq   equivalent to \le (p. 190)

\leqalignno   produce specified multiline display with equation numbers on the left whose indicated parts are vertically aligned (p. 208)

*\leqno   put a specified equation number on the left of a display (p. 207)

*\let   define a control sequence to be the next token (p. 232)

\lfloor   left floor delimiter: ⌊ (p. 191)

\lg   logarithm function: lg (p. 193)

\lgroup   left group delimiter (the smallest size is shown here): ((p. 204)

\lim   limit function: lim (p. 193)

\liminf   inferior limit function: lim inf (p. 193)

*\limits   place superscript above and subscript below a large operator (p. 195)

\limsup   superior limit function: lim sup (p. 193)

\line   produce a justified line of type (p. 109)

*\linepenalty   penalty for line breaking added to each line, by default 10 (p. 125)

*\lineskip   vertical glue from one baseline to the next if the lines are closer together than \lineskiplimit, by default 1 pt (p. 133)

*\lineskiplimit   threshold for using \lineskip instead of \baseline-skip, by default 0 pt (p. 133)

\ll   much less than relation: ≪ (p. 190)

\llap   produce text (with no width) extending to the left of the current position (p. 109)

\lmoustache   top half of a large brace: ∫ (p. 212)

\ln   natural logarithm function: ln (p. 193)

\lnot   logical "not" symbol: ¬ (p. 188)

\log   logarithm function: log (p. 193)

*\long   allow \par tokens in the argument(s) of the following definition (p. 231)

\longleftarrow   relation: ⟵ (p. 192)

\Longleftarrow   relation: ⟸ (p. 192)

\longleftrightarrow   relation: ⟷ (p. 192)

\Longleftrightarrow   relation: ⟺ (p. 192)

\longmapsto   relation: ⟼ (p. 192)

\longrightarrow   relation: ⟶ (p. 192)

\Longrightarrow   relation: ⟹ (p. 192)

\loop   start a loop to be ended by \repeat (p. 240)

*\looseness   difference between the number of lines you want a paragraph to be relative to the optimal number (p. 124)

\lor   logical "or" operator: ∨ (p. 189)

*\lower   lower a specified box by a specified amount (p. 166)

*\lowercase   convert uppercase letters in the specified text to lowercase (p. 104)

\lq   left quote character for text: ' (p. 98)

*\mag   1000 times the ratio for enlarging all dimensions (p. 223)

\magnification   like \mag, but don't enlarge the page size (p. 223)

\magstep $1000 \cdot 1.2^n$ for a specified n (p. 223)

\magstephalf $1000 \cdot \sqrt{1.2}$ (p. 224)

\mapsto   relation: $\mapsto$ (p. 192)

*\mark   produce a mark item with a specified text (p. 144)

*\mathaccent   put specified math accent over the next character (p. 199)

*\mathbin   space a specified subformula as a binary operator (p. 218)

*\mathchar   produce the math character with the specified mathcode (p. 99)

*\mathchardef   define a specified control sequence to be a mathcode, a number between 0 and $2^{15} - 1$ (p. 232)

*\mathchoice   select one of four specified math subformulas depending on the current style (p. 198)

*\mathclose   space a specified subformula as a closing delimiter (p. 218)

*\mathcode   the mathcode of a specified character (p. 251)

*\mathinner   space a specified subformula as an inner formula, e.g., a fraction (p. 218)

*\mathop   space a specified subformula as a large math operator (p. 218)

*\mathopen   space a specified subformula as an opening delimiter (p. 218)

*\mathord   space a specified subformula as an ordinary character (p. 218)

\mathpalette   produce a \mathchoice which expands a specified control sequence depending on the current style (p. 198)

*\mathpunct   space a specified subformula as punctuation (p. 218)

*\mathrel   space a specified subformula as a relation (p. 218)

\mathstrut   produce an invisible box with the height and depth of a left parenthesis and no width (p. 168)

*\mathsurround   space TeX kerns before and after math in text (p. 217)

\matrix   produce a specified matrix (p. 205)

\max   maximum function: max (p. 193)

*\maxdeadcycles   value of \deadcycles at which TeX complains, and then uses its own output routine, by default 25 (p. 148)

*\maxdepth   maximum depth of the bottom box on a page, by default 4 pt (p. 141)

\maxdimen   largest dimension acceptable to TeX (p. 244)

*\meaning   produce the human-understandable meaning of a specified token as characters (p. 226)

\medbreak   indicate desirable page break with \penalty-100 and produce \medskipamount glue (p. 137)

*\medmuskip   glue for a medium math space, by default 4 mu plus 2 mu minus 4 mu (p. 214)

\medskip   produce \medskipamount glue (p. 154)

\medskipamount   glue for a medium vertical skip, by default 6 pt plus 2 pt minus 2 pt (p. 155)

*\message   show expansion of the specified text on the terminal (p. 261)

\mid   middle relation: | (p. 190)

\midinsert   produce the specified text at the current position if possible, otherwise at the top of the next page (p. 146)

\min   minimum function: min (p. 193)

\mit   use math italics, i.e., do \fam=1 (p. 209)

*\mkern   produce a specified kern in units of mu for math (p. 215)

\models   models relation: ⊨ (p. 190)

*\month   current month, as a number (p. 225)

*\moveleft   move a specified box left by a specified space; legal only in vertical modes (p. 166)

*\moveright   move a specified box right by a specified space; legal only in vertical modes (p. 166)

\mp   minus and plus operator: ∓ (p. 189)

*\mskip   produce specified glue in units of mu for math (p. 215)

\mu   math Greek letter μ (p. 187)

*\multiply   multiply a specified \count register by a specified integer (p. 246)

\multispan   make next alignment entry span a specified number of columns (or rows) (p. 182)

*\muskip   the specified muglue register (p. 242)

*\muskipdef   define a specified control sequence to be a number corresponding to a \muskip register (p. 245)

\nabla   backwards difference symbol: ∇ (p. 188)

\narrower   make both left and right margins narrower by \parindent (p. 114)

\natural   natural symbol for music: ♮ (p. 188)

\nearrow   northeast arrow relation: ↗ (p. 192)

\ne   not equal relation: ≠ (p. 190)

\neg   logical "not" symbol: ¬ (p. 188)

\negthinspace   kern $-\frac{1}{6}$ em (p. 153)

\neq   not equal relation: ≠ (p. 190)

\newbox   reserve and name a \box register (p. 244)

\newcount   reserve and name a \count register (p. 244)

\newdimen   reserve and name a \dimen register (p. 244)

\newfam   reserve and name a math family (p. 244)

\newhelp   name a specified help message (p. 262)

\newif   define a new conditional with the specified name (p. 240)

\newinsert   name an insertion class, and reserve a corresponding \box, \count, \dimen, and \skip registers (p. 244)

\newlanguage   reserve and name a \language (p. 244)

*\newlinechar   end-of-line character for \write, etc. (p. 250)

\newmuskip   reserve and name a \muskip register (p. 244)

\newread   reserve and name an input stream (p. 244)

`\newskip` reserve and name a `\skip` register (p. 244)

`\newtoks` reserve and name a `\toks` register (p. 244)

`\newwrite` reserve and name an output stream (p. 244)

`\ni` "reverse in" relation: $\ni$ (p. 190)

*`\noalign` insert material between rows (or columns) of an alignment (p. 183)

*`\noboundary` inhibit ligatures or kerns involving the current font's `boundarychar` (p. 101)

`\nobreak` do `\penalty10000`, i.e., inhibit a line or page break (p. 121, p. 136)

*`\noexpand` suppress expansion of the next token (p. 234)

*`\noindent` enter horizontal mode without indenting the paragraph (p. 112)

`\nointerlineskip` inhibit interline glue before the next line (p. 135)

*`\nolimits` place superscript and subscript after large operators (p. 195)

`\nonfrenchspacing` make interword spacing depend on punctuation (p. 106)

*`\nonscript` inhibit any following glue or kern when in script and scriptscript styles (p. 215)

*`\nonstopmode` don't stop at errors, even those about missing files (p. 253)

`\nopagenumbers` inhibit printing of page numbers, i.e., do `\footline` = `\hfil` (p. 142)

`\normalbaselines` set `\baselineskip`, `\lineskip`, and `\lineskiplimit` to the normal values for the current type size (p. 134)

`\normalbaselineskip` value of `\baselineskip` for the current type size (p. 134)

`\normalbottom` make the bottom margin be the same from page to page (p. 137)

`\normallineskip` value of `\lineskip` for the current type size (p. 134)

`\normallineskiplimit` value of `\lineskiplimit` for the current type size (p. 134)

`\not` a slash with zero width for constructing negations of math relations, as in $\neq$ (p. 191)

`\notin` noninclusion relation: $\notin$ (p. 190)

`\nu` math Greek letter ν (p. 187)

`\null` expands to an empty hbox (p. 169)

*`\nulldelimiterspace` space produced by a null delimiter, by default 1.2 pt (p. 217)

*`\nullfont` primitive font with no characters in it (p. 102)

*`\number` produce a specified number as characters (p. 224)

`\nwarrow` northwest arrow relation: $\nwarrow$ (p. 192)

\o   Danish letter: ø (p. 97)

\O   Danish letter: Ø (p. 97)

\obeylines   make each end-of-line in the input file equivalent to \par (p. 122)

\obeyspaces   produce space in the output for each space character in the input (p. 107)

\odot   centered dot operation: ⊙ (p. 189)

\oe   œ ligature (p. 97)

\OE   Œ ligature (p. 97)

\offinterlineskip   inhibit interline glue from now on (p. 135)

\oint   contour integral operator: $\oint$ (p. 194)

\oldstyle   use old style digits: 1234567890 (p. 209)

\omega   math Greek letter ω (p. 187)

\Omega   math Greek letter Ω (p. 187)

\ominus   circled minus operator: ⊖ (p. 189)

*\omit   skip a column's (or row's) template in an alignment (p. 181)

*\openin   prepare a specified input stream to read from a file (p. 247)

*\openout   prepare a specified output stream to write to a file (p. 249)

\openup   increase \baselineskip, \lineskip, and \lineskiplimit by a specified amount (p. 135)

\oplus   circled plus operator: ⊕ (p. 189)

*\or   separate the cases of an \ifcase (p. 239)

\oslash   circled slash operator: ⊘ (p. 189)

\otimes   circled times operator: ⊗ (p. 189)

*\outer   make the following macro definition illegal in contexts in which tokens are absorbed at high speed (p. 232)

*\output   token list TeX expands when it finds a page break (p. 148)

*\outputpenalty   if the page break occurred at a penalty, the value of that penalty; otherwise zero (p. 149)

*\over   produce a fraction with a bar of default thickness (p. 200)

\overbrace   produce a brace covering the top of a formula, as in $\overbrace{h+w}$ (p. 202)

*\overfullrule   width of the rule appended to an overfull box (p. 170)

\overleftarrow   produce a left arrow covering the top of a formula, as in $\overleftarrow{r+a}$ (p. 202)

*\overline   produce a line covering the top of a formula, as in $\overline{2b}$ (p. 202)

\overrightarrow   produce a right arrow covering the top of a formula, as in $\overrightarrow{i+t}$ (p. 202)

*\overwithdelims   produce a fraction with a bar of the default thickness and surrounded by specified delimiters (p. 201)

\owns   owns relation: ∋ (p. 190)

\P   paragraph character for text: ¶ (p. 98)

*\pagedepth   TeX sets this to the current depth of the current page
(p. 139)

*\pagefilllstretch   TeX sets this to the amount of `filll` stretch on
the current page (p. 140)

*\pagefillstretch   TeX sets this to the amount of `fill` stretch on the
current page (p. 140)

*\pagefilstretch   TeX sets this to the amount of `fil` stretch on the
current page (p. 140)

*\pagegoal   TeX sets this to the desired height for the current page
(i.e., \vsize when the first box is put on the page) (p. 139)

\pageinsert   produce the specified text on the following page, and use
up the full page (p. 146)

\pageno   the register \count0, which contains the (possibly negative)
page number (p. 142)

*\pageshrink   TeX sets this to the total amount of shrinkability on the
current page (p. 140)

*\pagestretch   TeX sets this to the total amount of stretchability on
the current page (p. 140)

*\pagetotal   TeX sets this to the natural height of the current page
(p. 139)

*\par   finish paragraph and terminate horizontal mode (p. 110)

\parallel   parallel relation: ‖ (p. 190)

*\parfillskip   horizontal glue TeX inserts at the end of a paragraph
(p. 111)

*\parindent   horizontal space TeX inserts at the start of a paragraph
(p. 113)

*\parshape   specify the width and length of each line in the next
paragraph (p. 118)

*\parskip   vertical glue TeX inserts before a paragraph (p. 141)

\partial   partial derivative symbol: ∂ (p. 188)

*\pausing   if positive, stop after reading each line of input for a possible
replacement (p. 253)

*\penalty   produce penalty (or bonus, if negative) for breaking line or
page here (p. 121, p. 136)

\perp   perpendicular relation: ⊥ (p. 190)

\phantom   produce an invisible formula with the dimensions of a
specified subformula (p. 168)

\phi   math Greek letter ϕ (p. 187)

\Phi   math Greek letter Φ (p. 187)

\pi   math Greek letter π (p. 187)

\Pi   math Greek letter Π (p. 187)

\plainoutput   plain TeX's \output routine (p. 148)

\pm   plus and minus operator: $\pm$ (p. 189)

\pmatrix   produce a parenthesized matrix (p. 205)

\pmod   parenthesized modulus notation to put at the end of a formula, as in $x \equiv y + 1 \pmod 2$ (p. 194)

***\postdisplaypenalty**   additional penalty for a line break just after a display, by default 0 (p. 138)

\Pr   probability function: Pr (p. 193)

\prec   precedes relation: $\prec$ (p. 190)

\preceq   precedes or equals relation: $\preceq$ (p. 190)

***\predisplaypenalty**   additional penalty for a line break just before a display, by default 0 (p. 138)

***\predisplaysize**   T$_{\!E}$X sets this to the width of the line preceding a display (p. 216)

***\pretolerance**   badness tolerance for line breaks without hyphenation, by default 100 (p. 123)

***\prevdepth**   depth of the last nonrule box on the current vertical list (p. 134)

***\prevgraf**   T$_{\!E}$X sets this to the number of lines in the paragraph so far (in horizontal mode) or in the previous paragraph (in vertical mode) (p. 120)

\prime   prime math symbol, as in r' (p. 188)

\proclaim   begin a theorem, lemma, hypothesis, ... (p. 131)

\prod   large product operator: $\prod$ (p. 194)

\propto   proportional to relation: $\propto$ (p. 190)

\psi   math Greek letter ψ (p. 187)

\Psi   math Greek letter Ψ (p. 187)

\qquad   produce horizontal glue with width 2 em (p. 154)

\quad   produce horizontal glue with width 1 em (p. 154)

***\radical**   produce a specified radical symbol (p. 207)

\raggedbottom   allow the bottom margin to vary from page to page (p. 137)

\raggedright   allow the right margin to vary from line to line (p. 116)

***\raise**   raise a specified box by a specified amount (p. 166)

\rangle   right angle delimiter: $\rangle$ (p. 191)

\rbrace   right brace delimiter: $\}$ (p. 191)

\rbrack   right bracket delimiter: $]$ (p. 191)

\rceil   right ceiling delimiter: $\rceil$ (p. 191)

\Re   complex real part symbol: $\Re$ (p. 188)

***\read**   read a line from a specified input stream (p. 248)

***\relax**   do nothing (p. 241)

***\relpenalty**   additional penalty for breaking after a relation, by default 500 (p. 126)

`\repeat`   end a loop started with `\loop` (p. 240)

`\rfloor`   right floor delimiter: $\rfloor$ (p. 191)

`\rgroup`   right group delimiter (the smallest size is shown here): $\Big)$
(p. 204)

`\rho`   math Greek letter ρ (p. 187)

*`\right`   produce the specified delimiter at the right end of a subformula
started with `\left` (p. 204)

`\rightarrow`   relation: $\rightarrow$ (p. 192)

`\Rightarrow`   relation: $\Rightarrow$ (p. 192)

`\rightarrowfill`   fill enclosing hbox with a `\rightarrow`: $\longrightarrow$
(p. 175)

`\rightharpoondown`   relation: $\rightharpoondown$ (p. 192)

`\rightharpoonup`   relation: $\rightharpoonup$ (p. 192)

`\rightleftharpoons`   relation: $\rightleftharpoons$ (p. 192)

`\rightline`   produce line with its text pushed to right margin (p. 108)

*`\rightskip`   glue TEX inserts at the right of each line (p. 115)

*`\righthyphenmin`   size of the smallest word fragment TEX allows after
a hyphen at the end of a word, by default 3 (p. 128)

`\rlap`   produce text (with no width) extending to the right of the
current position (p. 109)

`\rm`   use roman type, i.e., do `\tenrm\fam=0` (p. 103)

`\rmoustache`   bottom half of a large brace: $\big\rmoustache$ (p. 212)

`\romannumeral`   produce the lowercase roman numeral representation
of a specified number as characters (p. 224)

`\root`   produce a specified root of a specified subformula, as in $\sqrt[3]{2}$
(p. 207)

`\rq`   right quote character for text: ' (p. 98)

`\S`   section character for text: § (p. 98)

`\sb`   implicit subscript character (p. 197)

*`\scriptfont`   the script style font in a specified math family (p. 210)

*`\scriptscriptfont`   the scriptscript style font in a specified math
family (p. 210)

*`\scriptscriptstyle`   use scriptscriptstyle size in a formula (p. 198)

*`\scriptspace`   additional space TEX kerns after a subscript or
superscript, by default 0.5 pt (p. 218)

*`\scriptstyle`   use scriptstyle size in a formula (p. 198)

*`\scrollmode`   don't stop at most errors, but do stop at errors about
missing files (p. 252)

`\searrow`   southeast arrow relation: $\searrow$ (p. 192)

`\sec`   secant function: sec (p. 193)

*`\setbox`   define a specified box register to be a box (p. 164)

*\setlanguage   change to a specified set of hyphenation rules, but don't change \language (p. 128)

\setminus   set difference operator: \ (p. 189)

\settabs   define the tabs for a tabbing alignment (p. 176)

\sevenbf   use 7-point bold font, cmbx7 (p. 102)

\seveni   use 7-point math italic font, cmmi5 (p. 102)

\sevenrm   use 7-point roman font, cmr7 (p. 102)

\sevensy   use 7-point symbol font, cmsy7 (p. 102)

*\sfcode   the space factor code of a specified character (p. 107)

\sharp   sharp symbol for music: ♯ (p. 188)

*\shipout   output a box to the .dvi file (p. 148)

*\show   show, in the log and on the terminal, the meaning of a specified token (p. 253)

*\showbox   display the contents of a specified box register (p. 253)

*\showboxbreadth   maximum number of items shown on each nesting level, by default 5 (p. 261)

*\showboxdepth   maximum nesting level shown, by default 3 (p. 261)

\showhyphens   show, in the log and on the terminal, hyphenations in the specified text (p. 128)

*\showlists   display all lists being worked on (p. 253)

*\showthe   show, in the log and on the terminal, what \the would produce (p. 253)

\sigma   math Greek letter σ (p. 187)

\Sigma   math Greek letter Σ (p. 187)

\sim   similarity relation: $\sim$ (p. 190)

\simeq   similar or equal relation: $\simeq$ (p. 190)

\sin   sine function: sin (p. 193)

\sinh   hyperbolic sine function: sinh (p. 193)

\skew   shift a specified accent by a specified amount on a specified accented character (p. 212)

*\skewchar   character in a specified font used for positioning accents (p. 213)

*\skip   the specified glue register (p. 242)

*\skipdef   define a specified control sequence to be a number corresponding to a \skip register (p. 245)

\sl   use slanted type, i.e., do \tensl\fam=\slfam (p. 103)

\slash   / character that allows a line break (p. 122)

\slfam   slanted family for math (p. 210)

\smallbreak   indicate somewhat desirable page break with \penalty-50 and produce \smallskipamount glue (p. 137)

\smallint   small integral symbol: $\smallint$ (p. 194)

\smallskip   produce \smallskipamount glue (p. 154)

`\smallskipamount` glue for a small vertical skip, by default 3 pt plus 1 pt minus 1 pt (p. 155)

`\smash` produce formula with zero height and depth (p. 169)

`\smile` smile relation: $\smile$ (p. 190)

`\sp` implicit superscript character (p. 197)

`\space` produce normal interword glue (p. 105)

*`\spacefactor` modifies stretch and shrink of interword glue if not 1000 (p. 107)

*`\spaceskip` if nonzero and `\spacefactor` < 2000, overrides the normal interword glue (p. 107)

`\spadesuit` spade suit symbol: ♠ (p. 188)

*`\span` either combine entries in an alignment body or expand tokens in a preamble (p. 181)

*`\special` write tokens to the `.dvi` file to be interpreted by a DVI-reading program (p. 250)

*`\splitbotmark` last mark item in a box resulting from `\vsplit` (p. 144)

*`\splitfirstmark` first mark item in a box resulting from `\vsplit` (p. 144)

*`\splitmaxdepth` maximum depth of a box resulting from `\vsplit` (p. 150)

*`\splittopskip` glue TeX inserts at the top of a box resulting from `\vsplit` (p. 150)

`\sqcap` square cap operator: $\sqcap$ (p. 189)

`\sqcup` square cup operator: $\sqcup$ (p. 189)

`\sqrt` produce square root of a subformula, as in $\sqrt{2}$ (p. 206)

`\sqsubseteq` square subset or equal relation: $\sqsubseteq$ (p. 190)

`\sqsupseteq` square superset or equal relation: $\sqsupseteq$ (p. 190)

`\ss` German letter: ß (p. 97)

`\star` star operator: $\star$ (p. 189)

*`\string` produce a specified token, most commonly a control sequence, as characters (p. 226)

`\strut` box with zero width, but height and depth of a standard line, from baseline to baseline, in the current font (p. 167)

`\subset` subset relation: $\subset$ (p. 190)

`\subseteq` subset or equal relation: $\subseteq$ (p. 190)

`\succ` successor relation: $\succ$ (p. 190)

`\succeq` successor or equal relation: $\succeq$ (p. 190)

`\sum` large summation operator: $\sum$ (p. 194)

`\sup` superior function: sup (p. 193)

`\supereject` force a page break, and output all insertions (p. 137)

`\supset` superset relation: $\supset$ (p. 190)

`\supseteq` superset or equal relation: $\supseteq$ (p. 190)

\surd   surd symbol: $\surd$ (p. 188)

\swarrow   southwest arrow relation: $\swarrow$ (p. 192)

\t   tie-after accent for text, as in u͡u (p. 100)

\tabalign   equivalent to \+, except it's not \outer (p. 176)

*\tabskip   glue between columns (or rows) of an alignment (p. 184)

\tan   tangent function: tan (p. 193)

\tanh   hyperbolic tangent function: tanh (p. 193)

\tau   math Greek letter τ (p. 187)

\tenbf   use 10-point bold font, cmbx10 (p. 102)

\tenex   use 10-point math extension font, cmex10 (p. 102)

\teni   use 10-point math italic font, cmmi10 (p. 102)

\tenit   use 10-point text italic font, cmti10 (p. 102)

\tenrm   use 10-point roman text font, cmr10 (p. 102)

\tensl   use 10-point slanted roman font, cmsl10 (p. 102)

\tensy   use 10-point math symbol font, cmsy10 (p. 102)

\tentt   use 10-point typewriter font, cmtt10 (p. 102)

\TeX   produce the TeX logo (p. 98)

*\textfont   the text style font in a specified math family (p. 210)

\textindent   like \item, but doesn't do hanging indentation (p. 112)

*\textstyle   use textstyle size in a formula (p. 198)

*\the   give the value of a specified token (p. 234)

\theta   math Greek letter θ (p. 187)

\Theta   math Greek letter Θ (p. 187)

*\thickmuskip   glue for a thick math space, by default 5 mu plus 5 mu (p. 214)

*\thinmuskip   glue for a thin math space, by default 3 mu (p. 214)

\thinspace   kern $1/6$ em (p. 153)

\tilde   tilde accent for math, as in $\tilde{x}$ (p. 199)

*\time   the time of day, in minutes since midnight (p. 224)

\times   times operator: $\times$ (p. 189)

*\toks   the specified token register (p. 242)

*\toksdef   define a specified control sequence to be a number corresponding to a \toks register (p. 245)

*\tolerance   badness tolerance for line breaks with hyphenation (p. 123)

\to   mapping relation: $\to$ (p. 192)

\top   lattice top symbol: $\top$ (p. 188)

\topglue   produce specified vertical glue at the top of a page (p. 156)

\topinsert   produce the specified text at top of a page (p. 146)

*\topmark   \botmark before the current page was boxed (p. 144)

*\topskip   glue between the headline and the first line of text on a page, by default 10 pt (p. 141)

`\tracingall`   turn on maximal tracing (p. 261)

*`\tracingcommands`   display execution of commands (p. 257)

*`\tracinglostchars`   display characters that are asked for, but not defined (p. 257)

*`\tracingmacros`   display macro expansions (p. 258)

*`\tracingonline`   show diagnostic output on the terminal as well as in the log file (p. 256)

*`\tracingoutput`   display contents of shipped-out boxes (p. 258)

*`\tracingpages`   display page break calculations (p. 259)

*`\tracingparagraphs`   display line break calculations (p. 259)

*`\tracingrestores`   display values restored at the end of a group (p. 260)

*`\tracingstats`   display memory usage statistics (p. 260)

`\triangle`   triangle symbol: $\triangle$ (p. 188)

`\triangleleft`   left triangle operator: $\triangleleft$ (p. 189)

`\triangleright`   right triangle operator: $\triangleright$ (p. 189)

`\tt`   use typewriter type, i.e., do `\tentt\fam=\ttfam` (p. 103)

`\ttfam`   typewriter family for math (p. 210)

`\ttraggedright`   use typewriter type and allow right margins of paragraphs to vary from line to line (p. 116)

`\u`   breve accent for text, as in ř (p. 100)

*`\uccode`   the character code for the uppercase form of a letter (p. 103)

*`\uchyph`   if positive, consider hyphenating words that start with a capital letter (p. 128)

`\underbar`   underline the specified text without avoiding any descenders, as in <u>fog</u> (p. 163)

`\underbrace`   produce a brace covering the bottom of a formula, as in $\underbrace{x+x}$ (p. 202)

*`\underline`   underline a math formula below the descenders, as in $\underline{x+y}$ (p. 202)

*`\unhbox`   append the contents of the box in a specified box register to the current list, and void the register; legal only in horizontal modes (p. 165)

*`\unhcopy`   like `\unhbox`, but doesn't void the register (p. 165)

*`\unkern`   if the last item on the current list is a kern, remove it (p. 172)

*`\unpenalty`   if the last item on the current list is a penalty, remove it (p. 172)

*`\unskip`   if the last item on the current list is glue, remove it (p. 172)

*`\unvbox`   append the contents of the box in a specified box register to the current list, and void the register; legal only in vertical modes (p. 165)

*`\unvcopy`   like `\unvbox`, but doesn't void the register (p. 165)

\uparrow   relation: ↑ (p. 192)

\Uparrow   relation: ⇑ (p. 192)

\upbracefill   fill enclosing hbox with an upwards facing brace: ⏜ (p. 211)

\updownarrow   relation: ↕ (p. 192)

\Updownarrow   relation: ⇕ (p. 192)

\uplus   cupped plus operator: ⊎ (p. 189)

*\uppercase   convert lowercase letters in the specified text to uppercase (p. 104)

\upsilon   math Greek letter υ (p. 187)

\Upsilon   math Greek letter Υ (p. 187)

\v   check accent for text, as in ǒ (p. 100)

*\vadjust   produce vertical mode material after the current line (p. 120)

*\valign   align text in rows (p. 179)

\varepsilon   variant math Greek letter ε (p. 187)

\varphi   variant math Greek letter φ (p. 187)

\varpi   variant math Greek letter ϖ (p. 187)

\varrho   variant math Greek letter ϱ (p. 187)

\varsigma   variant Greek letter ς (p. 187)

\vartheta   variant math Greek letter ϑ (p. 187)

*\vbadness   badness threshold for reporting underfull or overfull vboxes, by default 1000 (p. 170)

*\vbox   produce a vbox whose baseline is that of the bottom box enclosed (p. 161)

*\vcenter   center the specified text on the math axis (p. 213)

\vdash   left turnstile symbol: ⊢ (p. 190)

\vdots   vertical dots for math: ⋮ (p. 203)

\vec   vector accent for math, as in $\vec{x}$ (p. 199)

\vee   logical "or" operator: ∨ (p. 189)

\vert   bar relation: | (p. 188)

\Vert   double bar relation: ‖ (p. 188)

*\vfil   produce infinitely stretchable vertical glue (p. 157)

*\vfill   produce even more infinitely stretchable vertical glue than that produced by \vfil (p. 157)

*\vfilneg   produce infinitely negative stretchable vertical glue (p. 159)

\vfootnote   produce a specified footnote with a specified reference mark, but don't produce the reference mark in the text (p. 145)

*\vfuzz   space threshold for reporting overfull vboxes, by default 0.1 pt (p. 171)

\vglue   produce specified vertical glue that doesn't disappear at page breaks (p. 156)

*\voffset   vertical offset relative to one inch from the paper's top edge (p. 140)

\vphantom   produce an invisible formula with zero width but natural height and depth (p. 169)

*\vrule   produce a vertical rule; legal only in horizontal modes (p. 172)

*\vsize   page height, by default 8.9 in (p. 140)

*\vskip   produce specified vertical glue (p. 155)

*\vsplit   break the contents of a specified box register to the specified height (p. 149)

*\vss   produce vertical glue that is infinitely stretchable and infinitely shrinkable (p. 158)

*\vtop   produce a vbox whose baseline is that of the top box enclosed (p. 161)

*\wd   the width of the box in a specified box register (p. 167)

\wedge   logical "and" operator: $\wedge$ (p. 189)

\widehat   math accent, as in $y + \widehat{z + a}$ (p. 199)

\widetilde   math accent $b + \widetilde{c + d}$ (p. 199)

*\widowpenalty   penalty for a single line beginning a page, by default 150 (p. 138)

\wlog   \write the specified token list in the log file (p. 261)

\wp   Weierstraß 'p' symbol: $\wp$ (p. 188)

\wr   wreath product operator: $\wr$ (p. 189)

*\write   write a line to a specified output stream (p. 249)

*\xdef   equivalent to \global\edef, i.e., globally define a macro, immediately expanding the replacement text (p. 231)

\xi   math Greek letter ξ (p. 187)

\Xi   math Greek letter Ξ (p. 187)

*\xleaders   produce leaders with leftover space distributed equally between the leader boxes (p. 174)

*\xspaceskip   if nonzero and \spacefactor $\geq$ 2000, overrides the normal interword glue (p. 107)

*\year   the current year, as a number (p. 225)

\zeta   math Greek letter ζ (p. 187)

Index

In the entries of this index, a page number in italics indicates a principal or defining entry.

About the authors

Paul W. Abrahams, Sc.D., CCP, is a consulting computer scientist and a past president of the Association for Computing Machinery. His specialties are programming languages, software systems design and implementation, and technical writing. He received his doctorate from the Massachusetts Institute of Technology in 1963 in mathematics, studying artificial intelligence under Marvin Minsky and John McCarthy. He is one of the designers of the first LISP system and the designer of the CIMS PL/I system, developed when he was a professor at New York University. More recently, he has designed SPLASH, a Systems Programming LAnguage for Software Hackers. Paul resides in Deerfield, Massachusetts,where he writes, hacks, hikes, hunts wild mushrooms, and listens to classical music.

Kathryn A. Hargreaves received her M.S. degree in computer science from the University of Massachusetts, Boston, in August 1989. Her specialities are digital typography and human vision. She is currently developing a set of programs to produce high-quality, freely distributable digital type for the Free Software Foundation and is working with Robert A. Morris as an Adjunct Research Associate. In 1986 she completed the Reentry Program in Computer Science for Women and Minorities at the University of California at Berkeley, where she also worked in the TEX research group under Michael Harrison. She has studied letterform design with Don Adleta, André Gürtler, and Christian Mengelt at the Rhode Island School of Design. A journeyman typographer, she has worked at Headliners/Identicolor, San Francisco, and Future Studio, Los Angeles, two leading typographical firms. She also holds an M.F.A. in Painting/Sculpture/Graphic Arts from the University of California at Los Angeles. Kathy paints watercolors, designs letterforms, plays piano, and reads feminist film criticism.

Like Kathy, Karl Berry received his M.S. degree in computer science from the University of Massachusetts, Boston, in August 1989. He is also working for the Free Software Foundation, doing research with Morris, and has studied with Adleta, Gürtler, and Mengelt. He has been working with TEX since 1983 and has installed and maintained the TEX system at a number of universities. Starting with the `web2c` system developed by Tim Morgan, he recently completed a port of the "new TEX" to Unix systems.

Colophon

This book was composed using TₑX (of course), developed by Donald E. Knuth. The main text is set in Computer Modern, also designed by Knuth, with some kerning pairs added by Karl and Kathy. The heads are set in Zapf Humanist (the Bitstream version of Optima), designed by Hermann Zapf.

The paper is Amherst Ultra Matte 45 lb. The printing and binding were done by Arcadia Graphics-Halliday. The phototypeset output was produced at Type 2000, Inc., in Mill Valley, California. Proofs were made on an Apple LaserWriter Plus and on a Hewlett Packard LaserJet II.

Cross-referencing, indexing, and the table of contents were done mechanically, using the macros of Section 12 together with additional macros custom-written for this book. The production of the index was supported by an additional program written in Icon.

Erratum

Because of an accident in the final typesetting of this book, three characters appearing in the headings of some command descriptions in Sections 5–9 have been printed erroneously:

Printed Character	Correct Character
–	{
˝	}
˙	–

Thus, for example, the command printed on p. 160:

\hbox – ⟨*horizontal mode material*⟩ ˝

should be read as:

\hbox { ⟨*horizontal mode material*⟩ }

Other command headings printed with the (–) and (˝) characters should be read similarly.

The underscore (_) has been printed as a raised dot (˙) in two places: the fourth command under "Special symbols" on p. 98, and the first command under "Superscripts and subscripts" on p. 197.

In all cases the usage of a command is correctly illustrated in the example that follows its description.

(This error resulted from the accidental substitution during final typesetting of an Optima font with the same graphics as the correct font but a different mapping of character codes to graphics.)